A Management Guide
to Leveraged Buyouts

WILEY PROFESSIONAL BANKING AND FINANCE SERIES
EDWARD I. ALTMAN. Editor

A Management Guide to Leveraged Buyouts

EDWARD K. CRAWFORD

JOHN WILEY & SONS
New York • Chichester • Brisbane • Toronto • Singapore

Copyright © 1987 by Edward K. Crawford.
Published by John Wiley & Sons, Inc.

Library of Congress Cataloging-in-Publication Data

Crawford, Edward K., 1933–
  A management guide to leveraged buyouts.

  (Wiley professional banking and finance series,
ISSN 0733-8945)
  Bibliography: p.
  Includes index.
  1. Leveraged buyouts. 2. Leveraged buyouts—Case
studies. I. Title. II. Series.
HD2746.5.C7 1987   658.1′6   86-32390
ISBN 0-471-83232-4

Printed in the United States of America

10 9 8 7 6 5 4 3 2 1

Series Preface

The worlds of banking and finance have changed dramatically during the past few years, and no doubt this turbulence will continue through the 1980s. We have established the Wiley Professional Banking and Finance Series to aid in characterizing this dynamic environment and to further the understanding of the emerging structures, issues, and content for the professional financial community.

We envision three types of book in this series. First, we are commissioning distinguished experts in a broad range of fields to assemble a number of authorities to write specific primers on related topics. For example, some of the early handbook-type volumes in the series concentrate on the Stock Market, Investment Banking, and Financial Depository Institution. A second type of book attempts to combine text material with appropriate empirical and case studies written by practitioners in relevant fields. An early example is a forthcoming volume on The Management of Cash and Other Short-Term Assets. Finally, we are encouraging definitive, authoritative works on specialized subjects for practitioners and theorists.

It is a distinct pleasure and honor for me to assist John Wiley & Sons, Inc. in this important endeavor. In addition to banking and financial practitioners, we think business students and faculty will benefit from this series. Most of all, though, we hope this series will become a primary source in the 1980s for the members of the professional financial community to refer to theories and data and to integrate important aspects of the central changes in our financial world.

EDWARD I. ALTMAN

Professor of Finance
New York University
Schools of Business

Preface

This book is for the management of companies who aspire to become owners, particularly smaller companies or divisions of larger companies. It is an attempt to enable management to understand better the risks and rewards of participation in a leveraged buyout and to gain an understanding of how the process works.

This book is also for owners of closely held companies who would like to get their cash out but keep their hand in management. It may enlighten owners as to the benefits of a sale to management and outside investors, as an alternative to selling out to another company or going public.

The use of actual cases permits the reader to gain insights into the reality of how the buyout procedure functions from beginning to end. It sheds light on how the key participants—investment bankers, lawyers, accountants, lenders and investors—interact to make the buyout happen. The dynamics of the process do not change although the techniques vary with changes in laws and regulations, particularly those which are tax related. The cases were selected to exemplify the most popular techniques employed in LBO transactions in the mid 80s. Examples include both large public companies and small privately held companies. Those who own closely held companies and those who manage companies or divisions of companies should gain a clearer understanding of the advantages and drawbacks of this important business acquisition technique.

Contents

1 What Management Should Know About Leveraged Buyouts

HISTORY AND BACKGROUND

In a leveraged buyout, a company is acquired in a transaction financed largely by borrowing. Ultimately, the debt is to be paid with money generated by the acquired company's operations or by sales of its assets.

This paragraph has appeared dozens of times in *Wall Street Journal* articles describing the financing technique that became popular in the early 1980s. The use of borrowed funds to buy businesses has long been practiced, however, because few companies or entrepreneurs had sufficient cash equity to finance the entire purchase price. Local banks made acquisition loans to enable the buyer to "bootstrap" the acquisition of a business and pay off the indebtedness with money earned in the acquired company's operations. The buyer succeeded by "pulling himself up by his bootstraps" or without the help of others. The entrepreneur often had to borrow his equity or was given "sweat" equity, a piece of the ownership in return for running the business. Lenders usually demanded adequate security based on the liquidation value of the assets.

The unsecured lender began to emerge in the late 1960s, leading to the evolution of the modern leveraged buyout (LBO). These lenders were usually aggressive insurance companies who agreed to take a subordinated debt position in return for a piece of the equity. This layer of debt in combination with senior debt and equity funds enabled the LBO structure to compete on a price basis with corporate buyers. This development coincided with the trend toward deconglomeration in the early 1970s (reversing the conglomeration trend of the 1960s) that was driven by the desire of conglomerates to increase their earnings per share by acquiring companies, usually for cash. This strategy overlooked the difficulty of managing a collection of disparate businesses, particularly after the entrepreneurs who had built these businesses had sold out and left the companies.

1

The desire to unload these unwanted subsidiaries provided the catalyst for many management buyouts. W.T. Grimm and Company reported 6107 acquisitions made in 1969, when growth through acquisition was still quite popular. By 1975, this activity dropped to 2297 acquisitions, but divestitures rose from only 828 in 1969 to no fewer than 1200 in each of the succeeding seven years.

Interest rates played a vital part in divestiture activity. The prime rate dropped from a high of 8.5 percent in late 1969 to a low of 4.75 percent in early 1972, reflecting the availability of funds. With money more available and the financial cost of borrowing down, investor groups were in a better position to meet the purchase price necessary for companies to make divestitures. In 1971 and 1972, divestitures hit a peak, averaging 1650 in those two years. However, the prime rate shot up to 12 percent in the last half of 1974, and the number of divestitures dropped to an average of 1220 in 1975 and 1976. Divestitures steadily declined from the peak of 1901 in 1971 to a low of 666 in 1980 according to W.T. Grimm. Coincident with the drop in divestiture activity from 1976 to 1980 was the rise in interest rates, which more than tripled from their lows. Leveraged buyout activity, however, was growing in popularity during this period, partly due to persistence of relatively high inflation.

Rising inflation is the friend of LBOs as real interest rates, adjusted for inflation on the acquisition debt, tends to be low and sometimes negative. In addition, the debt principal, fixed in dollar amount, is repaid with constantly inflated dollars. Replacement cost of the underlying assets also rises, comforting lenders about the safety of their loans. Moreover, high interest rates resulting from high inflation tend to depress the value of companies both in the public and private markets. Buyers capitalize earnings relative to yields on alternative investments, and as a result, price/earnings (P/E) ratios of publicly traded stocks tend to be the reciprocal of interest rates. Thus, high inflation increases asset values but decreases the multiple that investors are willing to pay for earnings.

As LBO activity gathered momentum in the 1970s, insurance companies became increasingly more comfortable in accepting higher risks in return for expected higher returns. The focus was on cash flow rather than collateral values. During this period, the banks' role was largely that of providing senior loans and working capital lines. In other words, banks were not making acquisition loans but, rather, relatively secure loans to companies being acquired. The unsecured funds to accommodate the acquisition were being supplied by investors, usually pension funds or venture capital funds, and insurance companies. Whereas the bank loan interest rates floated, interest on the subordinated debt was fixed, which provided vital interest cost stability as the prime rate soared to $21\frac{1}{2}$ percent in 1980. Not only were the high floating rates painful to highly leveraged companies, but high interest rates depressed business activity, causing cyclical companies to suffer a decline in operating earnings.

In the late 1970s, the banks expanded their lending into the higher risk portion of the deals in competition with the insurance companies. Since they were reluctant to take equity and limited by law to 5 percent of voting securities, promoters preferred bank money to insurance company money because insurance companies demanded a substantial equity participation in the deals. Whereas bank loans were shorter term than insurance company loans and their floating interest rates were less predictable, bank loans were still preferable in a high interest rate environment because locking in fixed interest rates ranging from 15 to 18 percent on insurance company loans was unappealing. Rates were expected to decline substantially in the next business downturn, thus benefiting the floating rate borrower. As a result, the banks became the principal lenders of the bigger deals that began in 1980.

In the mid-1970s, the middle market of corporate divestitures and private sellers started to expand. Deals involving companies with sales under $150 million have continued to make up the great majority of the transactions but are considerably less visible than the high profile large company deals. In the late 1970s, Prudential, the largest financer of buyouts in the 1970s, began to participate in deals exceeding $100 million in total financing. The breakthrough, though, on deal size was the Kohlberg, Kravis and Roberts (KKR) acquisition of Houdaille for $343 million in 1979. This was not only a breakthrough in terms of size, but the price of the deal and the low earnings coverage of interest expenses caused wonderment in financial circles. In addition, not only was the company highly dependent on cyclical businesses, it even sold bumpers to Chrysler, which at the time was near collapse.

Big deals became more commonplace following Houdaille. In 1980 First Boston acquired Congoleum for $448 million. In 1981, KKR made four more deals ranging in size from $354 million to $465 million: Fred Meyer, Norris Industries, American Forest Products, and Marley. Gibbons Green von Amerongen did the $390 million Purex Industries deal, and Merrill Lynch did the $430 million Signode deal. The top eight deals in 1981 totaled $2.3 billion. However, the jumbo deals did not occur until 1983–84. As measured by the total financing required for the deal, including refinancing of debt and the payment of expenses, there were 14 deals in 1984 that exceeded $400 million. The largest was Metromedia at $1.48 billion; although the City Investing buyout was proposed at $2.3 billion, it was eventually done in smaller pieces. KKR's $2.4 billion offer for Esmark was topped by Beatrice, which bid $2.8 billion. There were 60 LBOs of public companies in 1984, double the amount in 1983 according to *Mergers and Acquisitions* magazine. In 1985, the magazine reported 241 LBOs for a total value of $18.4 billion. Five deals in 1985 topped $1.0 billion, including KKR's acquisition of Storer Communications for $2.4 billion and 50 percent of Union Texas Petroleum (Allied-Signal Corporation subsidiary) for $2.1 billion. Farley Industries acquired Northwest Industries in a $1.3 billion LBO, and the Haas family acquired Levi Strauss for $1.1 billion. Other Fortune 500 companies that went private with LBOs in 1985 included Denny's, the restaurant chain; First National Supermarkets; Parsons, an engineering and construction company; and Uniroyal. In April 1986, KKR acquired Beatrice for $6.2 billion, the largest LBO transaction on record. The R.H. Macy buyout also closed in 1986 for $3.6 billion. Both the Beatrice and Macy deals had to be repriced down slightly because of the difficulty of financing the originally announced terms. Despite these huge deals, LBO activity in the first half of 1986 waned a bit due to rising stock prices and a tightening of bank credit. Activity quickened in the last quarter of 1986 due to the enactment of higher capital gains taxes in 1987.

Whereas the Houdaille LBO in 1979 was a watershed deal in size, the buyout of Gibson Greeting Cards in 1982 broke new ground on the financeability of a highly seasonal business. The $84.6 million financing required an education for lenders who were uncomfortable with a company that showed losses for the year from January through August. Gibson Greetings received tremendous publicity when it went public 18 months after the buyout, making former Treasury Secretary Bill Simon and his Wesray Corporation a fabulous profit in a short period of time. Although it looked in perfect hindsight as if RCA had sold Gibson Greetings too cheaply, the company had been on the market for over a year without any takers. The LBO produced an acceptable price for RCA, but it proved very difficult to finance because G.E. Credit Corporation (GECC) had to step in at the eleventh hour after Citicorp decided not to go ahead with the loan.

The hot new issue market in 1983 allowed recently consummated LBOs to go public and confirm excellent returns for both investors and lenders; it further encouraged more investment bankers to initiate LBOs with their clients. New LBO specialty houses began to spring up, and older ones raised large amounts of pension fund money for investment in LBOs, enabling buyers to commit more quickly to deals involving public companies. KKR obtained commitments for a $1.0 billion LBO fund and Forstmann Little for over $400 million in 1984. However, the popularity of LBO funds decreased in the last half of 1984 owing to generally bad press about LBOs being overleveraged and too risky. LBO activity regained its momentum in 1985, and investor interest in LBO funds returned. KKR marketed a $1.9 billion "1986 Fund." Some of the investors in the $1.0 billion "1984 Fund" were willing to double up on their commitments due to the consistent high returns produced by KKR buyouts. According to KKR, they provided a 47 percent compound annual return over a 9-year period. In 1985, other new LBO funds were marketed by firms including Forstmann Little, Butler Capital, Merrill Lynch, and Morgan Stanley. Wesray announced but then canceled the start-up of a fund in early 1986, in part reflecting Bill Simon's growing concern with the trend in buyouts. Simon and his partner, Raymond Chambers, believed that with the plethora of funds and participants bidding-up prices, it was unreasonable to expect the lofty returns of the recent past.

Bill Simon's concerns are similar to the concerns voiced in the press in late 1983 and 1984. Both periods followed strong stock market rallies and a surging new issue market. In both periods, the acquisition of large pools of capital to invest in LBOs affected the price buyers could and would pay for companies.

In addition, banks became more comfortable with the concept of making large, highly leveraged acquisition loans. This trend began in the early 1980s and grew as the banks experienced success and gained confidence with these loans. Banks were also aided by the greater availability of lendable funds as loans to the oil industry and less developed countries lost their appeal. LBOs created a great variety of new lending opportunities; in some cases, banks were offered an equity strip which helped compensate for the greater risks associated with LBO loans, but they were still limited by the Federal Reserve to 5 percent of voting securities.

All of these factors—more people attempting to do deals and more money available to do them—converged in 1983 and 1984 and resulted in a bidding-up of deals to a level many believed too high. But how excessive were these deals? The press cried the end was near, but was it?

HOW RISKY ARE LBOs?

The conventional wisdom among many business reporters and bankers is that LBOs in 1984 were recklessly hurtling down a fast track destined to crash if the economic road ahead did not continue upward. If a company's balance sheet becomes highly leveraged with debt, the risk of its failure is obviously increased. Also, a highly leveraged company facing rising interest rates could forego needed expenditures to remain fully competitive in its marketplace. This proved to be the undoing of the Thatcher Glass LBO: The company's financial inability to modernize led to its demise. As another example, imports began to erode the textile market environment in the early 1980s. Their impact accelerated dramatically during 1983–1984, and slowed only slightly in 1985 and 1986. The only way to significantly lower costs in the domestic textile industry is to increase productivity with new and expensive equipment. This imperative may not have been so obvious in 1983 and early 1984 when Dan River, Cone, Reaves Brothers, and TI-CARO were making projections for their LBO lenders and investors. Burlington Industries chairman Bill Klopman was quoted by *Textile World:* "Paying off such debts may consume seven or eight years' worth of cash flow—the equivalent of a whole generation of new plants and equipment."

It is doubtful that all the LBO loans made to textile companies will avoid default on some of their loan covenants, which could lead to a restructuring of these loans. This prospect is reminiscent of the real estate investment trusts (REITs) in the 1970s. Many REITs failed following a lending spree caused by too much pressure to put out too much capital in high yield, high risk real estate deals. The banks developed a workout posture, taking what interest the loans could bear but eventually getting most of their principal back. Many bankers have warned that LBOs are the REITs of the 1980s, but there are key differences. The major difference is that REITs involved only one industry, real estate, whereas LBOs cut across many industry lines. Also, REITs involved indirect lending by banks. The REITs took their borrowed funds and loaned them at higher rates to real estate developers, and the banks had no opportunity to approve or disapprove the credit. In LBO loans the lending is direct, which allows the banks to analyze the loans very carefully; LBO loans receive considerably greater attention and scrutiny than conventional bank loans.

Clearly, with some $9.4 billion in LBO financing executed in 1984 followed by $18.4 billion in 1985, the odds have increased that some of the deals will go sour, but lenders have become more flexible than in the past and most deals are structured to give recognition to a worst case scenario. If the worst happens, the lenders will likely work with the companies to restructure the debt. If there is a need to stretch out the principal payments or pass interest payments, then it will be done. Certainly no LBO lender dependent on cash flow and having no other way out will cause the company to stop operating unless business prospects are hopeless. The loans were originally made on the basis that the going-concern value of the companies was sufficient to reassure the lenders that their loans would be repaid. Thus, it would make no sense to trash the going-concern value by shutting it down. For example, Drexel Burnham has been very active in workout situations by using debt instruments tailored to a company's current ability to pay interest and principal. These so-called junk bonds are often structured to accommodate a company's lack of current cash flow in return for a very high long-term return to the bondholder for accepting higher risks.

The soundness of LBO loans relates to the soundness of the borrower's business. Lenders in leveraged deals are generally careful to target companies whose core businesses are sound and are likely to remain so. The lenders are willing to take a financial but not a business risk. In contrast, loans made to the oil industry had the uncontrollable risk of sharp commodity price changes. The gold rush created by sharply escalating oil prices, up over tenfold in 10 years, led to lending to participants in the oil business, which depended on a high price of oil or gas to be economically viable. In commodities, however, high prices depress demand and increase supply, which results in lower prices. The drop in oil and gas prices was the grim reaper of many exploration and oil service companies and resulted in markedly slowed activity in the oil patch. Suddenly, loans made to independent participants in the oil game soured in the face of declining prices and disappearing profits. Thus, the loan portfolio of banks heavily concentrated in the oil industry began to experience heavy losses, which ultimately led to the inability of Continental Illinois to survive without help from the Federal Reserve. Coincidentally, Continental Illinois was a high profile leading bank lender to many LBOs, and this fact, coupled with the disclosure that Continental Illinois had plenty of loan problems, led many to assume that the LBO portfolio was part of the problem. In fact, the LBO portfolio at Continental Illinois was reportedly relatively free of problem loans, but when Continental Illinois became a financial cripple, the press, the Securities and Exchange Commission (SEC), and the Fed all signaled a warning that the "overleveraging" of LBOs had to stop or disaster loomed down the road. John Shad, SEC chairman, commented, "The more leveraged buy-outs and takeovers today, the more bankruptcies tomorrow." Bank regulators, too, apparently began to focus on LBO loans and the Federal Reserve Board leaned on the banks to temper their LBO lending. It was rumored that the presidents of two money center banks even required their personal approval of large LBO loans, which would, if true, certainly signal to the crew downstairs to quit stretching on loans and get back to fundamentals.

But just how bad are these loans in the overleveraged deals? The two prime examples detailed in this book, Metromedia and Dr Pepper, are both instances where the vocal critics did not apparently appreciate the structure of the loans or the underlying values supporting them. The lead bank in the senior debt facilities in both Metromedia and Dr Pepper was Manufacturers Hanover, the largest, most experienced bank lender in the LBO business. Manufacturers Hanover was the first to set up a Special Financing Division to handle all its LBO financing. This removed from individual loan officers the temptation to approve potentially highly profitable loans in order to meet their budget. The Special Financing Division is not under any pressure to make loans to meet a budget; the only pressure is to make good loans. Working together, the Special Financing Division staff can achieve common standards of acceptability and pricing of loans. In the first year and a half after it was established in 1983, the Special Financing Division reviewed more than 750 LBO loan proposals and approved fewer than 10 percent. Loan losses on this portfolio have been comparatively small, according to bank officials. On balance, half of its LBO loan portfolio is paid off in the first year and a half. Virtually all LBO loans are repriced after the first year as repayments are made and competing banks are willing to step in and offer somewhat lower interest rates in view of lower risks.

In the Metromedia case, it certainly looked like folly to lend $1.3 billion to a company that had earned only $35 million in the latest 12 months, had a negative tangible net worth of $415 million, and would not have earned its interest payments had the deal taken place a year earlier. How could this possibly be? Had Manufacturers Hanover violated all sane lending practices? Hardly. The bank got an independent appraisal of the broadcasting properties which indicated that Metromedia's collective current value in the marketplace was sufficient to cover the loan. The structure of the loan was also important. The amortization schedule was so rapid that to meet it, Metromedia projected it would have to sell some of its assets. In fact, it promised to sell sufficient broadcasting properties to produce aftertax proceeds of $300 million in the first year following the buyout. Before that strategy was implemented, the company decided to completely refinance the bank debt with debt sold to the public. So, only five months after the deal closed, the banks were taken out of this incredible loan. The refinancing loan package offered to the public included zero coupon notes and debentures, which enabled the company to pay less current interest and keep the broadcasting properties it had committed to sell to service the bank loan. The banks did not want their loans repaid so quickly, but after pocketing $14.5 million in fees and five months of interest at $1\frac{1}{2}$ percent over prime, the loans proved to be nicely profitable. As final proof of the value of the assets backing the bank financing, Metromedia agreed to sell its seven television stations for $2.0 billion, nine radio stations for $285 million, and cellular radio and paging assets for $1.6 billion, less than two years after the LBO closed.

The Dr Pepper loan had similar characteristics. The senior loan of $490 million compared with trailing 12 month earnings of only $10 million and was over three times the company's net worth. Again, the amortization schedule was so rapid that only the sale of assets could meet its terms. Before the ink was dry on the deal, Dr Pepper sold off Canada Dry for over $180 million to provide the necessary funds to meet the first year's amortization schedule of $165 million. At the time of the deal, the company estimated that its bottling plants and real estate had market values of $250 million to $325 million. This estimate proved accurate in the first year. It agreed to sell its bottlers for $276 million, and had remaining real estate worth an estimated $50 million. A little over a year after the deal, the $490 million acquisition debt was down to $80 million.

Critics ask, what if interest rates return to 15 or 20 percent? The Houdaille experience answers that question. The deal was made in May 1979 when the prime was $11\frac{3}{4}$ percent and rising. Houdaille's debt service charges amounted to $35 million compared to pretax, pre-interest operating earnings of $41.6 million in 1978. The economy then headed into a recession and the prime rate soared to $21\frac{1}{2}$ percent in 1980. There were clearly some sweaty palms during this period by players on both sides of the loans. However, all but $60 million of the $305 million in debt was at fixed rates and Houdaille survived. Although the financials are not publicly disclosed, the company indicates it has repaid a substantial portion of its debt.

The LBO of Norris Industries, maker of products for the automotive, building, and defense industries, was structured with 79 percent of its debt floating. Another 15 percent of the debt bore rates ranging from 18 to $19\frac{1}{2}$ percent. The recession in 1982 hit Norris hard and interest expenses exceeded operating income by $20 million. By year-end 1983, Norris had regained profitability and was able to go public. With the proceeds, it reduced its acquisition debt from $349 million to $139 million and covered its interest charges 2.5 times.

The chairman of the First Chicago Corporation told a bankers' convention in the spring of 1984, "The first big accident could come next week or next year." It did not happen. Even in the biggest bankruptcy of LBOs, the $143 million Thatcher Glass deal, the banks emerged whole.

The LBO business is self-correcting. Clearly, in 1984 the deal makers were carried away. The bidding of many new LBO specialists with investor pools resulted in the higher pricing of deals. Jerome Kohlberg, of KKR, said in *The*

New York Times, "Sometimes the pendulum swings too far—too much money is chasing too few good deals." The higher price often meant more debt, higher risk, and a lower return to investors. The big established players all recognized this and refused to chase deals. The money center banks, along with the Prudential, Teachers Insurance, and G.E. Credit, all saw real risk in the market, and whereas they looked at more deals than ever before, they accepted a smaller percentage.

A First Chicago banker commented that an economic downturn or rising interest rates could prove the unknown that might rock the LBO boat. "Business plans of the company don't take all that into account and lenders don't build enough cushion for that." Whereas downside projections are always considered, it is true that few business plans build in a recession unless the business is highly cyclical. On the interest rate side, the risk is more manageable. Interest rates can be hedged in the futures market, capped, swapped for fixed rate loans, or insured. Cash cap facilities were part of the Cone financing whereby the company could borrow from the senior lenders up to $30 million to pay interest on the senior debt. That sounds strikingly like the games played with Argentina and Mexico, but at least it keeps the loan from defaulting during the trough of a recession. When the prime rate jumped two points in early 1984, Cone purchased some interest rate insurance from Citicorp.

All of the hue and cry about overpriced LBOs really refers to the highly publicized marketplace where large companies are being taken private in LBO transactions. The megadeals with fancy P/E ratios received all the press and perhaps resulted in a general misconception that all deals were being bid-up to their financeable limit and perhaps beyond prudent price points. This was not the case in the hundreds of middle market deals involving companies from $10 million to $150 million in sales. These companies are rarely caught up in an LBO bidding contest and often are divisions of publicly owned companies being quietly sold to management, financed by banks, pension funds, and venture capital investors. W.T. Grimm reported that from 1980 through 1984, there were approximately 4200 company divestitures, over three-quarters of which were sold for $50 million or less. In contrast, there were only 167 public companies taken private during this five-year period. Most conglomerate corporations discarded the questionable strategy of growth by acquisition of non-related businesses and have concentrated on more focused lines of business. They prefer to make a few large acquisitions to enhance their existing businesses. Thus, the principal market for the sale of middle market companies shifted from conglomerates to the leveraged buyer. The sale of divisions by corporations is usually done at reasonable price levels. Corporate executives know what these divisions are worth and usually do not demand any premium based on emotional factors. This is often not the case when a company's founder decides to sell his company. Whereas his asking price may be too high, he might aid the transaction by taking sellers' notes for part of the purchase price. If these notes are subordinated and carry below-market interest rates, the seller is actually getting less value than the nominal sale price. Corporate sellers will also aid the financing by taking a portion of the sale price in sellers' notes or preferred stock.

LBO FAILURES

Whereas there have not been any failures of very large LBOs, some smaller deals have fared poorly. As noted earlier, the largest LBO failure was Thatcher Glass, which was sold in 1981 by Dart & Kraft to the investment house of Dominick & Dominick for $143 million. The company was in a sharply eroding market for glass containers caused by a loss of market share to plastics and a switch by the beer and soda industries to lower priced aluminum containers. With a commodity product, the business was too competitive and too mature to service without costly modernization. The biggest producer, Owens-Illinois, spent over $600 million to modernize its plants, thereby reducing the labor content of the finished products by 20–40 percent.

Owens-Illinois' chairman Robert Lanigan was quoted by *Forbes:* "Back in the 1970s, Thatcher Glass was one of the most profitable glass container companies. It was milked down hard to pay the debt. Furnaces were not rebuilt, new technology was not installed, automation did not take place. And they are now bankrupt." The $110 million bank loan was down to $77 million at the time of the collapse, and with assets listed at $160 million in the bankruptcy filing, these loans were repaid in full. Those who were not so fortunate include Dart & Kraft with its $20 million sellers' note, and Dominick & Dominick's $13 million combination of notes and stock.

Three other LBOs in the glass container industry have succeeded despite poor industry conditions. An LBO formed out of the glass divisions of Dorsey and Norton Simon was unable to modernize and sold out to Diamond-Bathurst at a $17 million profit for its LBO owners. Two LBOs merged to form Anchor Glass Container and successfully slashed general and administrative costs by 60 percent in the first year. All excess cash has been reinvested in plant modernization. This most successful of LBOs in the glass container business has a greater percentage of ownership by management than any of the other LBOs in that industry.

Other failed LBOs include Eli Witt (formerly Havatampa), a tobacco distributor bought in a deal engineered by Oppenheimer and Company. Eli Witt management attributed its failure to poor homework on Oppenheimer's part, leading to the overleveraging of this inherently low margined business. Eli Witt was selling commodities and could only offer price and service to gain a competitive edge. After the LBO, it could no longer afford to remain price competitive, and the result was failure. Bristol Brass, AMC Corporation (not the carmaker), and Donkenny, a women's apparel maker, did not make it, along with Brentano's, a New York bookstore chain bought from Macmillan. Brentano's was unprofitable when it was purchased for $8 million in 1981 and filed for bankruptcy within a year. Cobblers, Inc., a shoe company bought for $20 million, ran into management misfortune and was sold without a loss to the lenders, but equity investors lost their $400,000 stake. Cape Craftsman, a $40 million buyout by Jordan Company, went under, defaulting on a $10 million loan by Manufacturers Hanover. Among larger deals experiencing problems, Imperial Clevite, a Gould division that went private in 1981 for $360 million, was hit hard by the 1982 recession. Imperial Clevite, which makes auto parts, was restructured with a decrease in investor ownership.

In 1979 KKR purchased F.B. Truck Line, which was sold for a loss of its $700,000 investment. KKR's $380 million buyout of the forest products division of Bendix Corporation resulted in some small equity loss. As part of the transaction Bendix took a sellers' note for $65 million secured by 27,000 acres of timberland. Timber prices plummeted, and Bendix traded back the timber for the note. Investors lost their $5 million cash investment but realized more than $12 million in tax deductions on the transactions.

The biggest potential problem deal for KKR is its purchase of 50 percent of Union Texas Petroleum from Allied-Signal Corporation for $2.1 billion, including assumed debt. The deal looked sound with oil at $30 per barrel, but when oil prices plummeted to around $10 per barrel, the deal looked substantially overpriced. KKR's investors are likely to be singed, if not burned, if oil prices stay below $20 per barrel for several years. Another oil company LBO, Delta Corporation, became a casualty of lower oil prices.

On balance, the number of failures has been few, mostly among small companies. Most of the companies in trouble were in commodity businesses which were severely affected by falling product prices. Oil, glass containers, timber, metals, and tobacco distribution are all commodity businesses which, when highly leveraged, have courted failure.

Both Citicorp and Prudential report that at any one time, 5–15 percent of their LBO portfolios are in trouble. This does not mean that the loans will be worthless, but it does indicate that these loans are not earning full interest and some principal could be lost. For its LBO loans, Prudential targets a 700 basis point higher return than single A credits. In other words, if the typical lending rate on a privately placed single A credit is 11 percent, Prudential would target an 18 percent total return on an LBO loan made to purchase the company. If Prudential achieved a 20 percent return on 85 percent of its portfolio, wrote off 5 percent, and only received principal back on 10 percent of the portfolio, the total return would be 15.3 percent compared to the conventional return of 11 percent on similar credit risks. Prudential's target LBO returns therefore substantially overcompensate for the higher risks.

WHY LEVERAGED BUYOUTS WILL REMAIN VIABLE

Acquiring a company in a transaction financed largely by borrowing is not a new phenomenon. The pace of activity has quickened, and the techniques have become more sophisticated. Lenders and investors alike are better able to assess the risks and rewards of LBOs.

As LBOs grew in size and success, they attracted more deal makers, lenders, pension fund money, and critics. In 1983 and 1984, the market for LBOs became subject to exaggerated swings, extravagant pricing, and excessive leveraging. The business, however, corrected itself as the lenders and mezzanine investors said no to the overpriced deals. Perhaps the critics hastened the sobering process as the press loudly predicted doom for LBOs during the excessive pricing period. In response to the critics, George Roberts of KKR perhaps put it best: "Ever since we started in the leveraged buyout business eighteen years ago, people have been telling us what we do doesn't work. Just wait until we have high interest rates and a bad economy, they kept warning us. Well, we've been through four business cycles—and we have yet to see their predictions come true."

Will LBO activity continue at a fast pace in the future? Very likely yes, depending on economic conditions and stock prices. Pricing may fluctuate widely, but deal activity will likely remain strong in a reasonably stable economic and interest rate environment. Carl Ferenbach, managing director of Thomas H. Lee Company said, "This is no passing fancy. Rather it is tangible evidence of John Naisbitt's decentralization megatrend—the need of American industry to focus its resources on what its managers in any given environment know best."

Jerry Kohlberg of KKR put it another way. "The whole emphasis on management involvement and motivation is at the heart of this, and it is not a fad."

2 Benefits to Owners and Management

WHY OWNERS SHOULD CONSIDER A LEVERAGED BUYOUT

In large, publicly owned companies, the directors, as representative of thousands of stockholders, decide whether or not an LBO should be undertaken. The shareholders benefit by the premium price offered in the buyout but rarely participate in the equity of the purchaser. Warrants for 10 percent ownership were offered to the Storer Broadcasting shareholders, and this offer apparently caused the board to remove its opposition to the proposal and recommend it to the shareholders. In the Multimedia deal, the LBO proposal backed by management and the founding family interests successfully fought off higher priced proposals by offering all stockholders equity participation in the new company. FMC and Colt Industries offered all shareholders equity ownership in their public LBOs. Whereas giving equity participation in the newly leveraged company to the public shareholders has application in certain special situations, its use is unlikely to become widespread because it substantially dilutes the equity of the new company.

For the closely held company, an LBO can provide the selling shareholders with benefits that are often not fully appreciated. There are the obvious benefits of providing liquidity for stock for which there is no active market and for which the prospects are poor for finding a taker to buy substantial minority stock holdings. Should a buyer be found, the price the buyer would be willing to pay would be substantially discounted to reflect its lack of both control and marketability. In instances where a thinly traded market exists, often the difficulty of buying and selling sizable positions without substantially affecting the stock price will discourage institutional investor interest. Stocks in this position often trade at a discount to comparable companies whose stocks are traded actively. Piece Goods Shops and Perfect Fit are two examples detailed in this book; undervaluation by the public market prompted the companies to go private. Thus, the benefit of turning illiquid stock into cash at a substantially higher price than could be obtained in private market transactions is reason enough to consider an LBO.

Another benefit is the diversification of a family's financial assets from a

13

concentration in a single company to a portfolio of blue chip investments. Putting all one's eggs in one basket and watching that basket very closely may be an excellent way to create wealth but is not the recommended way to preserve it.

A third benefit of an LBO which is rarely appreciated is the preservation of family wealth via estate tax savings through the transfer of at least half of one's ownership in a company to one's heirs. The case study of Glendale Fabrics, discussed later in this book, dramatically illustrates how this is possible.

The most unappreciated of all benefits of LBOs, however, is that value is often created that can substantially benefit the original owners if they participate in the ownership of the new entity. In every case narrated in this book, the value received on the LBO plus the value or projected value created in the new company equals or exceeds the projected value of the old company. In seven case studies where the LBO has been followed by a public offering, sale, or refinancing, the new value afforded the companies averaged 2.0 × their value on the LBO. The time interval between the two events averaged only 2.1 years.

Regardless of whether there is an increase in the value of the company, the former owners should improve their total financial profile as a result of the LBO. In the Pannill Knitting buyout, detailed in Chapters 4 and 5, the value of the company on its initial public offering (IPO) was 1.4 × higher than the value on the buyout. There was a 31 percent increase in operating earnings partly due to higher profit margins, but there was also a 72 percent increase in the multiple of operating earnings that investors were willing to pay. This provided a higher valuation of the equity even after substantial interest charges on the acquisition debt and amortization of written-up assets.

For family stockholders who did not participate in the equity on the new company, there are also important advantages from the buyout. First, the LBO gained complete cash liquidity for all of their shares in a very thinly traded stock. Second, the LBO enabled them to sell at a premium price, 24 percent above its all-time high and substantially higher than the alternatives of selling out to another company or going public. Third, it allowed the family to diversify its principal asset, with the premium price attained offsetting the cost of capital gains taxes. It also presented family members in active management an opportunity to invest substantial funds in the business they knew best, which resulted in a return of 21 × their investment in 2.2 years. Bill Pannill, CEO, received $23 million cash for his 10.1 percent ownership position and reinvested $3.1 million for 20.8 percent interest in the new Pannill Knitting. His stock in the new company was worth $64 million as a result of the company's IPO. This $84 million total value compares with the $25 million value his old stock would have attained in two years applying the actual P/E ratio at the time of the buyout to the company's earnings. If the company were sold, Bill Pannill would realize $67 million after capital gains taxes as a result of the LBO and IPO versus $19.2 million after taxes if no LBO or IPO had taken place. If it had been appropriate, he could have saved his family substantial estate taxes by letting his heirs invest in the new Pannill stock in his place. As it was, his son bought 8.3 percent of the new Pannill's stock in addition to Bill's 20.8 percent, and Bill gave his daughter 7 percent of his new stock.

In summary, as a result of the LBO, Bill Pannill gained a premium price, complete liquidity, portfolio diversification, and continued ownership worth 2.8 × his interests in the buyout. Lastly, he did the LBO when he had the opportunity and confirmed the first pay day. If the company's fortunes had subsequently declined in the future rather than grown, he only had $3 million out of his $23 million in LBO proceeds instead of all of his company stock at risk.

The higher value placed on earnings in the Pannill IPO is not an isolated case. There are many examples of a step-up in the valuation of earning on the refinancing of a buyout, suggesting that prospects for creating value are real. Raymond McGuire of First Boston Corporation postulates that value is created in LBOs in essentially two ways. The first results from management singularly focusing on operating the company with maximum efficiency. If the company had been publicly owned, there would be an immediate saving of the costs of being public—costs of reporting to the public and the SEC, stockholders' meetings, and so forth. More importantly, the higher risk financial structure and personal financial involvement are unequaled motivational factors for management. The imperative to pay down the high level of debt forces management to focus on cost savings and cash flow. The company becomes leaner and more efficient. Top management knows there will be no return on their equity position unless the company is successful, and failure could result in the ruination of both career reputations and personal finances. This attitude is in clear contrast to that of many companies where management's self-interest is often put before the interests of the corporation. This is likely to exist where management has little or no ownership in the company so that a meaningful increase in the value of the company results in little or no personal gain for management.

There are many examples of how companies became much more efficient after their buyout. In LADD Furniture's case, a division bought from Baldwin United, operating profit margins in 1979, the last boom year before the buyout, equaled 7.3 percent. In its second year following the buyout (1983), operating profit margins hit 16.6 percent. Charter-Crellin, a division bought by Charterhouse, increased its operating profit margins from 9.4 to 12.3 percent in the year following the buyout. Pretax margins jumped from 11.5 to 15.1 percent in the first year after the buyout of Piece Goods Shops. Operating profit margins leaped from 13.2 to 26.1 percent two years after the buyout of Guilford Industries. Operating margins dramatically increased 130 percent in the first full year after the first LBO of Leslie Fay. Pannill Knitting's operating margins were 26.3 percent before the buyout, almost unheard of in the apparel industry. They climbed to 29.1 percent in the 12 months prior to its IPO two years after the buyout. Much of the profit margin improvement in these deals came from a deliberate cutting of overhead expenses and strict management of working capital. In many cases, the new owners also made constructive contributions to the companies' business plans and strategies.

The second way that Raymond McGuire theorizes on how LBOs create value is more difficult to comprehend. It states that markets will value a leveraged company higher than in its unleveraged state. McGuire's second premise rests on the observation that the markets' judgment of risk and return is fundamentally wrong. The market grants high multiples of earnings to companies with high potential and high risk, and low multiples are afforded mundane, low risk companies. The theory holds that the way to obtain a high multiple on low risk companies is to acquire the financial profile of high risk growth companies. An LBO with acquisition debt results in a rapidly growing bottom line as deleveraging occurs. When the company is taken public, the high growth and high risk profile will command the multiple of a high growth and high risk stock and thus create value. To suggest that such financial engineering will result in meaningfully higher values in an efficient market stretches the bounds of rational thought. However, there is strong evidence that this modern day alchemy has some validity as shown in Table 2.1.

Perhaps these examples of higher values accorded companies after their LBO is largely due to the improvement in stock market values, a short-term market aberration. Perhaps a company's recent record of improving sales and profit margins portrays a growth company profile when, in fact, the improvement is largely attributable to a recovery from recession and lower interest expenses. In addition, the de-leveraging of an LBO accelerates bottom line growth.

Perhaps the high return on invested capital reinforces the growth stock image, but this is less the result of a high level of earnings than the mathematical

Table 2.1

Company	Value of Company (millions)		Years Later	Multiple Of Value
	On LBO	On Refinancing		
Pannill Knitting	$228.2	$315.0	2.2	1.4x
Gibson Greeting Cards	80.6	286.0	1.5	3.5x
LADD Furniture	70.2	90.7	2	1.3x
Leslie Fay I	54.5	178.5	3	3.3x
Leslie Fay II	178.6	300.0	2.1	1.7x
Shoe-Town	67.4	97.5	1.1	1.5x
Bench Craft	21.5	27.5	1.5	1.3x
Piece Goods Shops	20.0	60.0	2.7	3.0x
Kincaid Furniture	17.6	43.5	3.5	2.5x
Guilford Industries	13.0	25.0	0.8	1.9x
			2.0 years	2.1x

product of a small equity base. Perhaps it is the sponsorship of underwriters, focusing attention to a new investment opportunity. Perhaps it is the market itself, which is starved for new equity investments having experienced in this decade the removal of over $300 billion in equities net of new stock issued through mergers, acquisitions, stock repurchasing programs, and LBOs. Whatever the reasons, a number of LBOs went public or refinanced at multiples of earnings substantially exceeding the original buyout multiples of earnings.

For example, Gibson Greeting Cards was bought for $80.6 million or 6.9 × earnings. It went public 17 months later at approximately 20 × the prior year's earnings, valuing the company at $286 million. LADD Furniture was bought for $70.2 million and went public 22 months later at a pre-offering value of $90.7 million. Both of these companies were subsidiaries or divisions of larger companies and were debt free when acquired. Prior to the public offering, Gibson Greeting Cards had debt of $62.6 million, and LADD Furniture's debt was $25.1 million.

Shoe-Town, a shoe retailer, was bought for $67.4 million and went public a year later at a pre-offering value of $97.5 million. The effects of purchase accounting valuations, particularly related to inventories, resulted in a pro forma loss of $21.3 million in the year of the buyout. Although the pro forma loss coupled with a balance sheet showed $32.8 million in debt and only $219,000 in net worth, it did not deter investors on the public offering.

Leslie Fay, an apparel producer, went private for $54.5 million. Just over two years later, it considered going public but found it could maximize its value by undertaking a second LBO, valuing the company at $178.5 million. Two years following its second LBO, it went public at a pre-offering value of $300 million. Operating earnings rose 2.5 × over this four-year period, but the multiple of earnings before income and taxes (EBIT) in these three transactions increased from 2.8 to 5.1 to 8.6 ×, respectively. Bench Craft, a producer of upholstered furniture, was acquired for $21.5 million on an LBO. Approximately 19 months later, it went public at a pre-offering value of $27.5 million or 10.4 × earnings compared to the buyout price of 7.0 × earnings.

Piece Goods Shops, a specialty retailer, was priced at $20 million on its buyout and attempted unsuccessfully to go public at approximately $60 million a year and a half later. That deal missed the new issue window in 1983 but set the price for the company's eventual sale for an estimated $60 million a year and a half later.

Kincaid Furniture sold out for $17.6 million at 7.9 × earnings, a price that could not have been obtained at that time had the company elected to go public. Three years later, it went public in a favorable furniture stock environment for 17 × earnings, valuing the company at $43.5 million. Guilford Industries, a textile company, was valued on its LBO at $13 million and went public 10 months later at a pre-offering value of $25 million. Its P/E ratio rose from 5.3 × on the buyout to 10.7 × on the IPO. The stock more than doubled in the first six months after the offering, prompting a second one.

Continued good stock market performance resulted in a third offering 10 months after the second offering at 12.3 × earnings, valuing the company at $85.8 million.

Two other LBOs that went public in the hot 1983 new issue market did not exceed their buyout values on their IPO. NI Industries (formerly Norris Industries), a producer of products primarily for the automotive, building, and defense markets, was taken private by KKR for $420 million in December 1981. It went public in October 1983 at a pre-offering value of $368 million. The public offering price was 12.0 × earnings compared to the buyout multiple of 11.7 × earnings. It went private with only $23 million in debt, but was burdened with $232 million in debt when it went public. In the summer of 1985, the company was acquired by Masco Corporation for $533 million, which was $22 per share versus the IPO price of $20 per share.

Converse, Inc., a maker of athletic footwear, was sold by its parent, Allied Corporation, in March 1982 for approximately $100 million. Fourteen months later, it went public for approximately the same pre-offering value but at a P/E ratio of 11.8 × earnings versus the buyout multiple of 8.4 × earnings. Pannill Knitting went private at 9.5 × earnings and was valued on its public offering two years later at 17.8 × earnings.

In the examples where value was created, all the companies went deep into debt to finance the buyout. Logically, after an LBO, a company's value should be considerably less than its value on the buyout because it replaced substantially all of its equity with debt. The debt required for the buyout represents a claim on future earnings and cash flows necessary to service the acquisition debt, and the market should logically penalize the postbuyout values accordingly. However, in the cases illustrated above, the market clearly did not do so, at least in the short run. Certainly in a leveraged real estate transaction, which is somewhat comparable to the LBO of a stable company, the resale of a property with the mortgage assumed would not be likely to result in any creation of value. Real estate properties are typically valued on the basis of capitalizing operating earnings, and any debt assumed on its purchase is deducted to determine the value of the equity in the transaction. To create value, a higher capitalization of earnings would be required, which is precisely what has happened in public offerings or refinancing of many LBOs.

In the examples shown in Table 2.1, the prices of the LBOs represented the highest prices attainable either through a sale to another company or a public offering. Had the original controlling owners been able to acquire a 49 percent interest in the new company to obtain a noncontrolling position as required, this residual ownership would have been worth more on average than the entire original sale price. The average value of these 10 LBOs established either by a public offering or refinancing was 2.1 × the original LBO price. The average time from the refinancing was two years. Some of the higher values were due to gains in earnings but in all cases there was an increase in the multiple paid for earnings.

Certainly this arcane algebra is not applicable to every LBO. The examples above represent companies that refinanced, went public, or sold out at higher prices because their good record and, for some, a good stock market, presented them with a window of opportunity. The sample of companies in Table 2.1 is not representative of the universe of LBOs. There are hundreds of LBOs that have not yet matured or shown earnings growth that would prove attractive to the public market or corporate buyers. Of the 30 LBOs sponsored by KKR from 1977 through mid-1986, only five had gone public (one was a division) whereas Forstmann Little had taken only one of its 11 deals public. It is probable that the equity in virtually all of the successful LBOs could be refinanced after five years at a substantial profit to the equity investors. If the controlling owners acquired 49 percent of the new company, the second pay day within five years should be worth more than the original sale price if the company's earnings power remains strong.

WHY MANAGEMENT SHOULD CONSIDER A LEVERAGED BUYOUT

Management is the most critical element in judging the future success of a company. The ability to devise a good business plan or strategy and then see that it is executed efficiently will produce success in almost any business. A highly leveraged financial structure adds more elements of financial pressure and constraint which require management skill. Thus, LBO deal makers want to provide financial incentives to motivate management to remain and operate the company to the maximum of their abilities. Management, of course, recognizes the strength of its position and desires to obtain the largest percentage of the new company at the lowest possible cost. Whereas management may not be comfortable with the leveraged financial structure, they are confident of their knowledge of how to run their company, and they see the LBO as their one great opportunity to create substantial personal wealth. How much they actually can make may surprise them.

Certainly the top five executives of Gibson Greeting Cards would not have thought it possible that their $157,000 investment in the new company would be worth $30.3 million a year and a half later. Similarly, the 16 management investors in Pannill Knitting would not have believed that their $7.4 million investment would be worth $154.3 million in only two years. The top management of Converse was delighted that their $1.25 million investment rose to $20 million in only 14 months. NI Industries' management enjoyed an eight-fold increase in their stock in three and a half years. The three top executives of Leslie Fay were pleasantly surprised to see their $249,500 investment total $66 million in its second LBO, or 96 × their investment in a little over two years. When the company went public two years later, the managers again were the big winners with the public market valuing their $333,000 investment at $75 million. LADD Furniture management saw their $3.7 million investment leap to $52 million in value in less than two years. It took only three years for Perfect Fit's president's $10 investment to be worth $2.7 million. In three years, the management of Piece Goods Shops saw their $150,000 total investment increase a hundredfold to an estimated $15 million.

It is doubtful that any of the managements in these deals projected such a large gain in value in such a short time. To do so would have required blind acceptance that value would be created. Few, if any, could have guessed how high a value the public and private markets would place on a highly leveraged company, and few would have projected that companies would attain a multiple of earnings exceeding the buyout multiple.

In each of the remaining cases in this book, an analysis is made on the returns management might expect based on the company's projections of earnings. The capitalization of projected earnings was based on the same multiple of earnings realized in the LBO. No creation of value was factored into the equation. The two employee stock ownership plan (ESOP) deals, Dan River and Cone Mills, provide the smallest potential returns. Due to the equity dilution inherent in ESOPs and the two-stock structure of the deal, the Dan River management must look beyond its 5-year projections to see any meaningful return. Cone management's $8.2 million investment should be worth $63 million in five years if the company can somehow meet its projections. The management participants in the Levitz deal should see their $4.3 million investment soar to $76.3 million in five years. Of this amount, the CEO Bob Elliott's $1.1 million investment would be worth $20 million. Woodward & Lothrop's top three executives have options to buy 20 percent of the equity for $5.0 million, which could be worth $116 million in 10 years. This will trigger an enormous personal tax bill on the exercise of the options, but the company will provide the three executives with a bonus to accommodate this tax liability. If these values are reached, the 8 percent owned by Ed Hoffman, CEO, would be worth $46.4 million on a $2.0 million investment. In the sale of Dr Pepper, management saw their $4.3 million investment valued at $35.9 million, of which the CEO "Foots" Clements' share is $17 million. John Kluge, the CEO of Metromedia, however, wins first prize for the sheer size of his potential return on the sale of the company's various businesses. Whereas his top lieutenant saw his $3.0 million investment grow to over $40 million in two years, Kluge's $180 million investment is estimated to be worth over $1.5 billion. One can certainly conclude from these real and projected mindboggling returns that LBOs can be the quickest route to great personal wealth for corporate management.

Conflict of Interest

Leveraged buyouts have caused much debate on the conflict of interest between management and the stockholders of a public company. Management has a fiduciary responsibility to act in the best interest of the public shareholders. However, if management decides to pursue an LBO, they are no longer working strictly in the interest of the public shareholder, but in fact, move across the table in direct conflict. They become part of the buying group that desires to obtain the lowest feasible purchase price whereas the shareholders obviously desire the highest possible sale price. Moreover, critics claim that management has a distinct advantage because of its superior knowledge of the company compared to the less informed shareholders. The market, though, is itself a means of protecting public shareholders' interest. If the management offer is too low, the company is put into play and will attract high bids from other buyers. Also, the SEC has instituted procedures that limit the potential conflict of interest problems. These procedures include the requirement of full disclosure of the transaction and obtaining a fairness opinion rendered by an investment banker.

The SEC requirements, however, do not ensure that the public shareholders are adequately represented. It may be difficult for outside directors to take a tough negotiating stance against the management who appointed them directors in the first place. On the other hand, in these litigious days, outside directors are finding it increasingly in their own self-interest to see that the public shareholders are fairly treated.

Managers who are considering the acquisition of their company are not doing a disservice to the public shareholders or the parent company. There may be feelings of guilt or anxiety when managers who have spent most of their adult lives working for someone else now find themselves working to increase their personal net worth, but they should view the possible LBO pragmatically. All buyout transactions require a willing buyer and a willing seller. The initiation of the transaction will increase the market price of the company's stock or offer the parent corporation the opportunity to redeploy its investment in a division that no longer fits its long-term strategy or meets minimum return on investment criteria. Managers who contemplate a buyout should keep in mind that although they are acting in their own self-interest, the public shareholders or the parent corporation is properly motivated by corporate self-interest to agree to the sale.

WHAT BUYERS LOOK FOR IN LBO CANDIDATES

Many deal makers believe that only a small percentage of companies are good LBO candidates. Their selectivity makes it difficult for them to find the right business with the right management at the right price. Certainly in the public market, the need to pay a reasonable premium over the market price eliminates a large number of companies from serious consideration. If a company is a division of another company or is privately owned, then price and terms can be negotiated to fit the situation. There is a way to do every deal if the company is of reasonable size ($10 million plus in sales), profitable, reasonably priced, and the sellers are willing to help finance the transaction. Of course, management must be eager to remain and participate in the equity.

The types of companies that make good LBO candidates have traditionally been businesses in slow growing, mature industries with relatively predictable future performances. The financing concept is similar to obtaining a mortgage in the purchase of a home. The amount of the mortgage available bears a direct relationship to the individuals' ability to service the mortgage, and the equity build-up occurs steadily as the mortgage principal is repaid. If a home-owner borrows 80 percent of his home's purchase price, he will increase his equity investment fivefold when the mortgage is repaid before any consideration for the increase in the value of the home. Similarly, to obtain a high return on an investment in a company requires only that the initial equity investment be kept relatively small and that the company's cash flow is sufficient to repay the acquisition debt. This then creates a high return on the small equity investment. If the company's business shows moderate growth, all the better. But if growth is sufficiently high to absorb most of the internally generated cash flow, then repayment of the acquisition debt is more difficult.

This scenario is viable as long as the purchase price is reasonable and evaluation of the basic earning power is realistic. Clearly, there were many crazy prices put on basic industry deals in the go-go days of LBOs. Many were over-leveraged and could be in serious trouble if a recession hits their businesses harder than expected. Unfortunately, many mature, slow growth businesses are exceptionally competitive as a result of too many producers with excess capacity, who can increase their sales only at the expense of a competitor. This overly competitive environment restricts management's ability to maintain profits in weak economic periods. Many of the old-line companies also have high labor costs and are faced with product and equipment obsolescence. Low profits may not provide an adequate return on investment to justify the expense of new product development or plant modernization. Investors also recognize that divesting from these companies is difficult, as they are not attractive to new issue buyers and cannot be easily sold for a reasonable price to other companies. For these reasons, these basic businesses are being avoided by many deal makers.

Thus, the old-line basic company stereotype has somewhat given way to a greater appreciation for a growing company as an LBO candidate. Working capital lines to finance sales growth can be obtained, and capital expenditure budgets can be incorporated in the initial financing package. Everyone participating in the financing wants the going-concern value of the company to be enhanced. If a company can show good growth, it can seek the public markets to raise equity, and these proceeds can be used to reduce the acquisition debt. An excellent example of this is the case of Guilford Industries (see Chapter 5). The need to finance the company's rapid growth resulted in structuring the buyout with equity amounting to 50 percent of the cash portion of the purchase price. By financing the company's rapid growth, earnings almost tripled in two years, enabling the company to go public at twice the LBO multiple of earnings and providing the investors with an excellent 12 × return on their relatively low leveraged investment.

The most desirable candidates for LBOs are companies operating in a stable competitive market, defined by the Boston Consulting Group as a market that never has more than three significant competitors, the largest of which has no more than four times the market share of the smallest. Furthermore, the market share of the number two company is half that of the number one company, and the number three company is half the market share of the number two company. This market share distribution produces a state of maturity and equilibrium. All three of the significant competitors would qualify for an LBO, with the higher the market share, the stronger the candidate. Any company that has a proprietary product or has found a niche in the marketplace and dominates that niche is an ideal candidate. Good growth potential is also sought after because it enables the company to go public when the market is receptive. Also desirable are large current assets in relation to total assets, low debt, and stable, high margined earnings. Perhaps the most important criterion is that the management team must be competent and eager to be equity participants.

Still considered risky as LBO candidates are high technology companies that have either high technical or high market risks. If these companies are truly successful, they will require substantial outside capital to sustain their growth and will obtain this capital at very high multiples of earnings in the public markets. To finance both large capital requirements needed for growth and large amounts of acquisition debt required to buy high multiple companies is not feasible. Leveraged buyouts of high technology companies tend to require substantial equity investments to compensate for the lack of sufficient cash flow to support both debt service and corporate growth. Other relatively undesirable LBO candidates are commodity businesses whose product prices are uncontrollable and can drop below production costs for extended periods of time. Agricultural products, timber, metals, oil, and building materials are examples. Many fungible manufactured products fall into this category such as certain chemicals, plastic and paper products, glass, aluminum, and steel products. Some textile products are commodities and are proving troublesome for LBO lenders and investors.

Companies with labor problems are poor candidates because a work stoppage stops cash flow. Unions are considered undesirable for this reason and because they could result in higher labor costs than nonunion competitors. Companies with a poor competitive position, as reflected in a small market share or low profit margins, are also poor candidates. In contrast to companies with large market shares of their businesses, these companies cannot adequately protect themselves in a difficult economic environment. In addition, companies highly dependent on a few large customers are considered risky, although deals can be structured to compensate for this risk, as in the case of Glendale Fabrics (see Chapter 5). Companies whose business is becoming technologically obsolete are also undesirable. Service companies were at one time considered poor candidates, but in some recently selective instances, service companies have done LBOs. Steel service centers have done LBOs, and two business and equipment appraisal companies were bought by employees. Seller financing is the most likely source of acquisition debt for service company deals because banks are reluctant to lend to companies whose assets go home every night. The owners of privately owned service companies are likely to be the key management people so that having them take sellers' notes provides them with the incentive to make the company sufficiently successful to pay off these notes.

Whatever the business, the single most important factor in the LBO candidate selection process is management, followed by the type and strength of the business, and then the price of the deal. Truly impressive management attracts lenders and investors in a company with only average business prospects, whereas unimpressive management might cause a relatively good business prospect to go unfunded. Management might also be able to run the business effectively under secure financial conditions but could be very uncomfortable with the prospect of operating under the financial constraints of a highly leveraged balance sheet.

The test of management's entrepreneurial character could be its willingness to risk its own money in the deal. Deal makers and lenders alike need alert management during the first two years following an LBO—the high risk phase of the deal. To assure that management will devote almost every waking hour to paying down the acquisition debt, investors and lenders insist that management take considerable financial risks in return for potentially great financial rewards. Some deal makers demand that management invest half of its liquid net worth in the deal. If the management group nets large sums in the buyout, it is usually asked to reinvest a meaningful part of the proceeds or accept sellers' notes as part of the purchase price. These notes will be subordinate to the senior debt and rank equal to or below any other subordinated debt. There is little enthusiasm for deals where management retires from an active role in management or retains all the money from the buyout. Bringing in totally new management from the outside has been successfully accomplished in the purchase of a corporate division where the outside management had direct experience in that business, but promoting second line management in the company is usually a more suitable alternative.

The acquisition price is also a critical element in the LBO equation. Most deals are priced on the basis of what debt load the projected cash flow can comfortably service plus an amount of equity on which an acceptable return is projected. Asset sales are generally viewed by lenders as a second way out of the loan if cash flow fails to service the debt. However, if salable assets are large in relation to capitalized cash flows, the purchase price can be increased substantially. If these loans are larger than the company can service out of cash flows, the loans are likely to contain rapid amortization schedules to force asset sales early in the life of the loan. Three cases detailed in this book (see Chapter 5) are examples of large acquisition debt backed by large asset values but not supported by cash flows. To meet its debt requirements, Dr Pepper sold its Canada Dry division and bottling plants in a major restructuring. Woodward & Lothrop refinanced its bank debt with junk bonds, and Metromedia refinanced its bank debt and broke up the company with the sale of almost all of its operating companies. All of these restructuring moves were undertaken in the first year following the buyout.

The definition of a reasonable price would generally be a 4–6 multiple of EBIT, plus free cash and minus existing debt. Chapter 3 shows a statistical breakdown of the price paid in 30 LBOs, generally occurring from 1982 to 1984. The multiple of projected EBIT paid in the 26 deals not dependent on asset sales averaged 5.6 ×. The seven largest deals (excluding break-up deals) averaged 6.9 × projected EBIT compared to 4.0 × for the 10 smallest deals.

The reasonableness of the price also relates to the stability and growth of earnings in the past. If earnings have fluctuated widely, a lower multiple of EBIT is necessary. If the company has substantial excess inventories or other assets that can be a meaningful source of funds for debt reduction, a higher multiple of EBIT can be obtained. If the company has a need for substantial capital expenditures, the deal structure and purchase price must reflect these needs.

In summary, competent management, a secure business, and a reasonable price are the necessary ingredients to qualify a company for an LBO. The better these three elements are, the better the prospects are for the creation of value. If the seller is able to participate in the equity of the new company, the total value received in the two deals combined will likely exceed the value that can be obtained for the company by any other financial alternative. If the seller is an individual, the sale gives him liquidity and diversification of his principal asset. It also provides him with the chance to pass ownership to the next generation outside of his estate and gives him an opportunity to share more of the company's ownership with management. Finally, the LBO gives management a once-in-a-lifetime chance to obtain substantial wealth by risking capital and working hard to make the buyout successful.

3 Statistical Comparison of 30 Leveraged Buyouts

Thirty LBOs have been compared as to price, management participation, bankers and fees, debt terms, coverage, and financial structure. These deals were grouped according to size of the financing, with the 10 largest deals averaging $801 million, the second 10 averaging $241 million, and the smallest 10 averaging $38 million. Five deals were $22 million or less whereas three deals exceeded $1.0 billion.

The following is a thumbnail sketch of the 30 companies, ranked by size of financing.

Metromedia, Inc.—$1,483 Million.   Deal closed in June 1984. Headquartered in New York City, the company operated 7 television and 13 radio stations, and produced television programs. It was one of the largest radio paging and two-way mobile radio companies and had substantial interests in cellular radio. It managed the largest outdoor advertising business and owned the Ice Capades and Harlem Globetrotters.

Wometco Enterprises, Inc.—$1,075 Million.   Deal closed in March 1984. Headquartered in Miami, Florida, the company operated four network-affiliated television stations and two UHF stations used to broadcast subscription television programs. It owned one radio station and had 47 cable television systems. It was one of the nation's largest Coca-Cola bottlers and operated 45 movie theaters. It ran vending machines, ice cream shops, and video game machines.

ARA Services, Inc.—$1,032 Million.   Deal closed in December 1984. Headquartered in Philadelphia, the company was engaged principally in the management of food and refreshment services furnished to business, government, educational, and health care institutions. The company also was a wholesale distributor of magazines and books, and provided health and family care services. It operated textile rental, maintenance, and laundry services and owned two trucking lines.

Harte-Hanks Communications, Inc.—$997 Million. Deal closed in September 1984. Headquartered in San Antonio, Texas, the company published 23 daily and 20 nondaily newspapers. It provided commercial printing and published printed advertising materials for shoppers and direct mail. It operated four television and nine radio stations, and had established cable television operations.

Denny's, Inc.—$752 Million. Deal closed in January 1985. Headquartered in La Mirada, California, the company operated over 1000 Denny's restaurants and more than 800 Winchell's Donut Houses. It also owned a small chain of Mexican restaurants called El Pollo Taco.

Malone & Hyde, Inc.—$685 Million. Deal closed in August 1984. Headquartered in Memphis, Tennessee, the company's principal business was wholesale food distribution. It also operated a system of over 900 Piggly Wiggly franchised retail grocery stores. Operations included drug, sporting goods, and automobile parts stores.

Dr Pepper Company—$648 Million. Deal closed in March 1984. Headquartered in Dallas, Texas, the company sold soft drink concentrates and syrups to bottlers, and bottled and distributed Dr Pepper and Welch's brand soft drinks. At the time of the deal, the company also owned the Canada Dry soft drink business.

Blue Bell, Inc.—$611 Million. Deal closed in November 1984. Headquartered in Greensboro, North Carolina, the company manufactured apparel products, principally Wrangler jeans, Jantzen swimwear, and Red Cap work clothes.

Cone Mills Corporation—$465 Million. Deal closed in March 1984. Headquartered in Greensboro, North Carolina, the company's principal business was the production of denims and corduroys used in making jeans and casual sportswear. It also finished decorative fabrics and provided commission dying and printing services. It provided polyurethane foam and hardware accessories to the furniture industry and developed commercial and residential real estate.

Levitz Furniture Corporation—$461 Million. Deal closed in June 1985. Headquartered in Miami, Florida, the company operated a chain of over 80 retail furniture stores located in 25 states.

National Medical Care—$411 Million. Deal closed in November 1984. Headquartered in Waltham, Massachusetts, the company's principal business was operating outpatient artificial kidney treatment centers. It also ran health risk obesity centers and managed hypertension treatment programs. The company manufactured and distributed kidney dialysis supplies, and sold and distributed respiratory therapy equipment.

Cole National Corporation—$330 Million. Deal closed in September 1984. Headquartered in Cleveland, Ohio, the company was a specialty retailer, operating approximately 90 toy supermarkets and 500 optical departments, primarily in Sears and Montgomery Ward stores. It also managed approximately 380 personalized products gift stores, 590 key shops, 120 cookie stores, and 10 bakery shops, all located in enclosed mall shopping centers.

Woodward & Lothrop Inc.—$314 Million. Deal closed in September 1984. Headquartered in Washington, DC, the company was one of the leading fashion department stores, not only in that metropolitan area but also in Baltimore, Columbia, and Annapolis, Maryland. The chain consisted of 15 stores, two-thirds of which were owned.

American Sterilizer Company—$263 Million. Deal closed in February 1985. Headquartered in Erie, Pennsylvania, the company made and distributed a wide range of equipment, systems, instruments, and disposable products for use in the health care industry. Equipment included sterilizers, operating room tables, surgical lights, and washing products. The company also distributed a wide variety of medical, surgical and laboratory supplies, instruments, and equipment to the Canadian health market.

Pannill Knitting Company, Inc.—$232 Million. Deal closed in April 1984. Headquartered in Martinsville, Virginia, the company manufactured knitted and fleeced sportswear, including sweatshirts, sweatpants, jogging suits, and warm-up outfits. It also manufactured swimwear.

TI-CARO, Inc.—$220 Million. Deal closed in May 1984. Headquartered in Gastonia, North Carolina, the company manufactured yarns, sewing threads, and knit fabrics made from cotton and synthetic fibers, all sold to other manufacturers for further processing.

Raymond International, Inc.—$219 Million. Deal closed in October 1983. Headquartered in Houston, Texas, the company was a leader in specialized foundations and heavy, industrial, and marine construction. The company also fabricated and installed permanent oil and gas drilling and production platforms, and provided engineering, design, and construction management services for a wide variety of companies.

Amerace Corporation—$200 Million. Deal closed in September 1984. Headquartered in New York City, the company manufactured a variety of fluid power and metal components products, including hose and tubing, metal couplings, and metal fastener products. It also made a variety of molded rubber connectors used primarily by electrical power companies. The company fabricated plastic molded products, such as reflective lenses used in tail light assemblies and molded key buttons for typewriters and telephones.

Dan River—$154 Million.   Deal closed in May 1983. Headquartered in Danville, Virginia, the company manufactured woven and knitted fabrics for apparel and fabricated finished products for the home. Home products included sheets, bedspreads, draperies, towels, and carpeting.

Atlas Van Lines, Inc.—$72 Million.   Deal closed in October 1984. Headquartered in Evansville, Indiana, the company maintained a network of independent agents to move household goods throughout the United States. It also had international freight forwarding operations and shipped new furniture and fixtures through owner-operators.

LADD Furniture, Inc.—$70 Million.   Deal closed in September 1981. Headquartered in High Point, North Carolina, the company manufactured upholstered, wood, and metal furniture for the home.

Shoe-Town, Inc.—$69 Million.   Deal closed in July 1982. Headquartered in Totowa, New Jersey, the company was the largest off-price retailer of brand name shoes in the country. The company's self-service stores sold women's shoes and handbags, and men's and children's shoes. The company was also the largest wholesaler of brand name women's shoes.

Genicom Corporation—$63 Million.   Deal closed in October 1983. Headquartered in Waynesboro, Virginia, the company was formerly a part of General Electric Company. It was one of the largest independent computer printer companies, producing teleprinters and serial dot matrix printers. It was also a leader in the crystal can relay market.

Leslie Fay, Inc.—$55 Million.   Deal closed in April 1982. Headquartered in New York City, the company designed and manufactured a diversified line of women's dresses, sportswear, and suits. The company's women's apparel was sold under various trade names and covered a broad retail price range.

Perfect Fit, Inc.—$31 Million.   Deal closed in May 1981. Headquartered in Monroe, North Carolina, the company made a complete line of fashion bedroom furnishings, including mattress covers, bedspreads and comforters, draperies, sheets, and pillowcases.

Bench Craft, Inc.—$22 Million.   Deal closed in May 1982. Headquartered in Blue Mountain, Mississippi, the company manufactured moderately priced upholstered furniture.

Piece Goods Shops—$21 Million. Deal closed in August 1982. Headquartered in Winston-Salem, North Carolina, the company operated over 100 retail stores that sold fabrics, patterns, and sewing notions for the home sewing market.

Kincaid Furniture Company, Inc.—$19 Million. Deal closed in February 1980. Headquartered in Hudson, North Carolina, the company manufactured solid wood American traditional bedroom and dining room furniture.

Guilford Industries, Inc.—$18 Million. Deal closed in March 1982. Headquartered in Guilford, Maine, the company was an integrated manufacturer of specialty fabrics for open-plan office furniture systems and office interiors.

Glendale Fabrics, Inc.—$11 Million. Deal closed in December 1983. Headquartered in Greenville, South Carolina, the company processed synthetic yarns to give elastic qualities, for sale to makers of stretch garments.

PURCHASE PRICE

The purchase price of LBOs as measured by a multiple of earnings tends to increase proportionately with the size of the deal. The purchase price × net income, or P/E ratio, averaged 20.7 × for the largest 10 deals, dropped to 12.7 × for the next 10, and fell to 11.1 × for the smallest 10. At least three deals were break-up deals that were priced and structured to service debt partially with the sale of assets. If these three deals are eliminated, namely Metromedia, Wometco, and Dr Pepper, the P/E ratio for the largest deals drops to 15.3 ×. In the small deal grouping, the P/E ratio comparisons were distorted by the fact that the earnings of both LADD Furniture and Genicom at the time of the buyout were cyclicly depressed. Dropping these two deals from the comparisons puts the average P/E ratio at a reasonable 7.2 ×.

Purchase price compared to net worth averaged 195 percent for all 30 deals. Again, the 10 largest deals were the highest priced at 250 percent of book value. Dropping the break-up deals brings the average purchase price for the largest 10 deals to 203 percent and drops the average for all deals to 179 percent of book value.

The best measurement of the price of an LBO from a financial standpoint is comparing the total financing package with the company's cash flow or EBIT. Table 3.1 shows a comparison of the latest years' EBIT or actual EBIT to the total financing and compares the first year's projected EBIT as a multiple of the total financing. The table shows that the larger the deal, the higher the price as a multiple of EBIT. Based on the first year's projected EBIT, the 10 largest deals were done at almost twice the multiple of EBIT of the smallest 10 deals. Dropping the break-up deals, the remaining seven largest deals were done at 7.0 × the projected first year's EBIT compared to 4.0 × for the 10

Table 3.1 Purchase Price

Size of Financing[1] (000)		Purchase Price To		Multiple of Earning	
		Net Income	Net Worth	Pro Forma EBIT	Projected EBIT
$1,287	Metromedia	20.6x	366%	18.7x	13.3x
1,075	Wometco	26.7	371	13.9	11.2
1,032	ARA	14.0	154	8.1	7.4
997	Harte-Hanks	25.1	337	10.5	9.3
752	Denny's	17.1	221	10.0	7.8
685	Malone & Hyde	13.1	271	8.0	6.7
648	Dr Pepper	52.5	341	13.2	5.0
611	Blue Bell	9.8	146	6.4	5.7
465	Cone Mills	18.7	121	12.0	6.5
461	Levitz	9.3	173	6.1	5.5
Average 7 companies[1]		15.3x	203%	10.7x	7.8x
411	National Medical Care	14.2x	249%	7.0x	4.7x
330	Cole National	16.1	314	8.8	6.1
314	Woodward & Lothrop	15.4	193	8.1	7.0
263	American Sterilizer	15.1	160	5.9	5.2
232	Pannill Knitting	9.3	267	4.5	4.4
220	TI-CARO	13.0	152	7.1	6.9
219	Raymond International	11.9	114	6.3	5.2
200	Amerace	11.2	136	6.9	6.9[3]
154	Dan River	10.5	72	8.2[2]	6.7
72	Atlas Van Lines	10.6	205	9.8	9.8[3]
Average 10 companies[1]		12.7x	189%	7.3x	6.3x

(cont.)

Table 3.1 Purchase Price *(continued)*

Size of Financing[1] (000)		Purchase Price To		Multiple of Earning	
		Net Income	Net Worth	Pro Forma EBIT	Projected EBIT
70	LADD Furniture	24.2x	68%	8.4x	7.1x
69	Shoetown	8.1	156	4.6	3.6
63	Genicom	19.5	132	10.2	3.6
55	Leslie Fay II	9.0	363	5.2	5.2[3]
31	Perfect Fit II	8.0	130	3.8	3.8[3]
22	Bench Craft	7.2	111	3.5	3.8
21	Piece Goods Shops	7.0	203	3.5	3.1
19	Kincaid Furniture	7.9	154	3.6	3.2
18	Guilford Industries	5.3	152	3.3	2.3
11	Glendale Fabrics	8.7	149	4.1	4.1[3]
Average 10 companies[1]		10.5x	162%	5.0x	4.0x
Average all companies Except Break-Up Deals[2]		12.8x	179%	6.8x	5.6x

[1]Excludes Metromedia, Wometco, Dr. Pepper.
[2]Three-year average EBIT.
[3]No projections made; assumed EBIT unchanged.

32

smallest deals. The overall average, dropping the four break-up deals, was 5.6 × the projected first year's EBIT.

To put the total financing as a multiple of cash flow into focus, if a deal were financed at 5.6 × the first year's EBIT, assuming 5 percent growth in earnings, 84 percent debt in the financial structure, and a 13 percent interest rate, the debt would be fully repaid in the tenth year. If this same analysis is applied to the average actual EBIT (4.0 ×), financial structure (80.9 percent debt), and actual average interest rate (15 percent) for the 10 smallest deals, the debt would be totally repaid in the sixth year compared to the average term of the senior debt of 8.7 years for these deals. This indicates that the smaller deals, even assuming a high interest rate, are reasonably priced.

MANAGEMENT PARTICIPATION

Table 3.2 compares how much money management received from the deals by cashing in their stock and options with how much they reinvested in the new company. It also indicates how their percentage of ownership changed from the old to the new company. In the average deal, management cashed in their common shares and stock options for $21.4 million and reinvested $13.6 million in the new company. The average of all 30 deals shows that management's percentage of ownership rose from 12.8 to 29.6 percent. Eliminating the five deals where management included the scion of the controlling families, management's average ownership of 5.1 percent rose to 28.6 percent. Surprisingly, management actually invested more money in the new company than it received in the buyout in 11 instances. In three of these instances, management did not own any stock because the company was a division of a larger one. In the 11 deals where management invested more than it received, its average percentage of ownership increased from 2.1 to 27.8 percent.

It is clear from this analysis that management showed its enthusiastic support for the LBO by its willingness to make a substantial investment in the new company. Management received financial assistance to buy the new stock in one-third of the buyouts. The reason management was willing to put back such a large percentage of what it got out (in many cases a large percentage of its personal net worth) is the investment potential it saw in the structure. Table 3.2 shows that the investment leverage for management investors averaged 23 × in these 30 deals. This is defined as the value management received for its stock at the buyout price compared to the value of the stock bought in the new company to maintain the same percentage of ownership. In other words, management could buy the same percentage of ownership in the new company as it had in the old company for one twenty-third of the price paid for the stock in the buyout. By private market measurement, however, the new company is not worth as much as the old company until it substantially reduces its debt. although there are many examples of increased public market value after leveraging. Interestingly, the investment leverage rose

Table 3.2 Management Participation in Ownership

Size of Financing (Millions)		Management		Percentage Ownership by Management		Company Loans to Management	New Ownership Multiple of Old Ownership[4]
		Received from Buyout[1] (Millions)	Invested in Buyout[1] (Millions)	Before Buyout	After Buyout		
$1,287	Metromedia	$322.2	$200.3	29.2%	81.5%	Yes	5x
1,075	Wometco	13.9	10.8	2.2	10.2	No	11
1,032	ARA	22.2	18.0	4.2	31.3	No[2]	11
997	Harte-Hanks	62.6	35.9	9.0	42.6	Yes	10
752	Denny's	15.2	8.1	8.7	18.2	No	17
685	Malone & Hyde	25.9	36.5	5.7	23.2	Yes	4
648	Dr Pepper	4.4	4.3	1.2	15.5	Yes	17
611	Blue Bell	4.5	7.7	1.4	24.7	Yes	14
465	Cone Mills	20.2	8.3	5.0	40.7	No	20
461	Levitz	6.6	4.3	3.6	15.0	No	11
	Average 10 companies	$49.8	$33.4	7.0%	30.3%		12x
411	National Medical Care	$9.7	$2.0	7.2%	37.0%	No	66x
330	Cole National	21.9	22.3	6.8	20.0[E]	Yes	3
314	Woodward & Lothrop	6.4	5.0	3.3	20.0	No	10
263	American Sterilizer	4.6	10.0	1.6	66.7	No	15
232	Pannill Knitting	32.6	7.4	16.2	49.0	No	15
220	TI-CARO	5.5	8.0	3.1	40.0	No	10

						No/Yes	
219	Raymond International	8.1	6.9	4.3	15.3[E]	No	4
200	Amerace	1.9	2.5	2.0	22.8	Yes	52
154	Dan River	2.8	3.6	2.0	25.0	Yes	9
72	Atlas Van Lines	9.3	0.8[E]	13.8	27.3	No	27
	Average 10 companies	$10.3	$6.9[3]	6.0%	32.3%		21x
70	LADD Furniture	$0	$1.0	0%	25.0%	No	18x
69	Shoetown	0	0.258	0	6.1	No	16
63	Genicom	0	0.195	0	20.4	No	77
55	Leslie Fay	3.9	0.249	9.9	44.9	No	55
31	Perfect Fit	1.1	(3)	3.8	10.0	Yes	(3)
22	Bench Craft	9.8	0.544	45.7	48.0	No	28
21	Piece Goods Shops	0	0.150	0	25.0	No	34
19	Kincaid Furniture	9.1	0.600	51.2	15.0	No	4
18	Guilford Industries	5.5	0.278	42.5	18.5	No	3
11	Glendale Fabrics	11.1	0.245	100.0	49.0	No	22
	Average 10 companies	$ 4.1	$0.352	25.3%	26.2%		36x
	Average 30 companies	$21.4	$13.6	12.8%	29.6%		23x

[1] Includes options.

[2] Guaranteed 10% of bank loan.

[3] Management purchased 10% of the common stock for $10. Actual investment leverage is 30,500x. Used 100x in calculation.

[E] Estimated.

[4] The degree of equity leverage in the new ownership structure. For example, Metromedia management received for their stock on the buyout five times the amount of investment needed to maintain the same percentage ownership in the new company.

Table 3.3 Bankers and Fees

Size of Financing (Millions)	Fees and Expenses as Percentage of Financing	Investment Banker	Investment Banker Fees (000)	Leading Senior Lender	Commercial Bank Fees (000)
$1,287 Metromedia	2.3%	Lehman Bros./ Boston Ventures Bear, Stearns/	$ 4,685 4,000 2,500	Manufacturers Hanover	$14,525
1,075 Wometco	1.9	KKR Drexel/ Merrill Lynch/	10,000 4,000 300	Continental Illinois	2,000
1,032 ARA	1.9	Goldman Sachs Salomon Bros./	11,000 1,250	Chemical Bank Morgan Guaranty	4,325
997 Harte-Hanks	1.4	Goldman Sachs Salomon Bros./	9,000 1,000	Manufacturers Hanover	2,000
752 Denny's	2.8	Merrill Lynch Dean Witter/ Goldman Sachs/	10,000 500 350	Morgan Guaranty Wells Fargo	6,000
685 Malone & Hyde	2.6	KKR Lehman Bros. Kidder, Peabody/	6,750 3,500 750		N.A.
648 Dr Pepper	2.5	Forstmann Little Lazard/ Blythe/	5,000 2,500 250	Manufacturers Hanover	5,600
611 Blue Bell	4.1	Drexel Kelso First Boston/	4,900 4,500 3,275	Bankers Trust	6,975

465	Cone Mills	2.0	Saloman Bros.[f]	4,000	Morgan Guaranty	1,775
461	Levitz	3.2	Drexel Citicorp Venture	7,800 1,600	Manufacturers Hanover	1,300
	Average	2.5%		$10,361		$4,943
$411	National Medical Care	1.3%	Dillon Read[f]	$200	Manufacturers Hanover	$4,000
330	Cole National	2.6	KKR Kidder Peabody[f]	4,000 390	Bankers Trust	2,375
314	Woodward & Lothrop	4.5	Oppenheimer Goldman, Sachs[f]	2,200 1,500	Manufacturers Hanover	5,750
263	American Sterilizer	5.8	First Boston Kelso Lazard[f]	2,100 2,100 750	Morgan Guaranty	2,000
232	Pannill Knitting	1.0	Wheat, First Securities[f]	200	Manufacturers Hanover	1,000
220	TI-CARO	2.0	Lazard Interstate Securities[f]	2,270 125	Citibank	250
219	Raymond International	3.9	Kelso Kidder Peabody Merrill Lynch	1,650 1,262 375	Manufacturers Hanover Bank of America	2,300
200	Amerace	3.9	First Boston Kidder Peabody	2,000 1,300	Bank of Boston	1,700
154	Dan River	2.8	Kidder Peabody Kelso	1,296 900	Chemical Bank	375

(continued)

Table 3.3 **Bankers and Fees** *(continued)*

Size of Financing (Millions)		Fees as Percentage of Financing	Investment Banker	Investment Banker Fees (000)	Leading Senior Lender	Commercial Bank Fees (000)
72	Atlas Van Lines	3.3	Alex Brown[f] Wesray	1,000 500	General Electric Credit	750
	Average	3.1%		$2,613		$2,050
$70	LADD Furniture	0.3%[E]	None	$0	Manufacturers Hanover	N.A.[2]
69	Shoetown	2.9	AEA Investors	1,475		N.A.
63	Genicom	0.3[E]	None	0		N.A.
55	Leslie Fay	1.3	Bear, Stearns[f]	350	Chemical Bank	N.A.
31	Perfect Fit	1.0	Charterhouse	0	Electra	N.A.
22	Bench Craft	2.7[E]	Jordan Company	400	Manufacturers Hanover	N.A.
21	Piece Goods Shops	3.1	Jordan Company	400	N.A.	N.A.
19	Kincaid Furniture	3.5	Wheat, First Securities	276	Manufacturers Hanover	N.A.
18	Guilford Industries	1.1	Thomas H. Lee	0	Prudential Capital	N.A.
11	Glendale Fabrics	1.5	Wheat, First Securities	130	First Union	None
	Average 10 companies	1.8%		N.A.		
	Average 30 companies	2.5%				

[f] Includes Fairness Opinion.
N.A. = Not available.
[E] Estimated.

on average as the average deal size declined. The largest 10 deals averaged 12 × investment leverage compared to 36 × for the smallest 10 deals. The higher leverage in the smaller deals was made possible by seller financing in 8 of the 10 small deals. When sellers take company securities as part of the selling price, these securities are typically long-term subordinated debentures bearing below market interest rates. Senior lenders view subordinated debenture as quasiequity and thus often permit the capital structure to contain less true equity.

BANKERS AND FEES

The fees and expenses for the 30 deals averaged 2.5 percent of the total financing. All of the deals employed investment banking services except two which were divisions of large companies. In three deals, investment bankers were used only to render a fairness opinion. In the 21 deals in which investment bankers structured the deals and secured the financing, their fees averaged 1.5 percent. Only Gil Butler in the Pannill Knitting deal and Tom Lee in the Guilford Industries deal did not compensate themselves for their structuring and financing services. The largest fee to a single investment banker as a percentage of the financing was Drexel Burnham's 1.7 percent fee in the Levitz deal. Drexel Burnham truly earned this fee, however, as they may have been the only investment bankers at that time who could put together the junk bond financing required in that deal. (See Table 3.3.)

Commercial bank fees varied greatly as a percentage of the bank financing. In the 19 deals that disclosed commercial bank fees, these fees averaged 1.0 percent of the senior financing.

DEBT TERMS AND COVERAGE

Table 3.4 shows the average length of the senior debt financing to be 8.2 years. The longest term was the 15 years provided by insurance companies, but seven deals received bank financing for 10 years. In every case, interest rates on the senior debt floated, except in the instance with the 15-year insurance company loan. The average price was prime plus $1\frac{1}{2}$ percent, but five of the smaller deals were priced at prime plus 2–3 percent. Interest rates on the subordinated debt were fixed in all but five cases. In the 12 deals that did not involve seller financing, the fixed interest rate on the subordinated debt averaged 15.8 percent. In the seven deals where the subordinated debt was held by the sellers, the fixed rate averaged 13.6 percent (five deals) and the floating rate was approximately prime (two deals). The disparity in interest rates on sellers' debt compared with subordinated debt sold institutionally indicates that the market value of the sellers' debt was probably substantially lower than the principal value. Also, sellers' debt was not sold in a mezzanine unit or generally with

Table 3.4 Debt Terms and Coverage

Size of Financing (Millions)		Length of Term—Years	Percent Repaid After		Interest on		Coverage	
			3 Years	5 Years	Senior	Subordinated	Senior	Total
$1,287	Metromedia	8.5	35%	58%	P + 1.5%	(1)	1.26x	1.26x
1,075	Wometco	10.0	17	30	P + 1.36	N.A.	.82	.82
1,032	ARA	9.0	20	40	P + 1.5	16.5%	1.49	1.30
997	Harte-Hanks	10.0	17	35	P + 1.5	16	1.37	1.20
752	Denny's	10.0	N.D.	N.D.	P + 1	P + 2.5	2.07	1.60
685	Malone & Hyde	10.0	0	N.D.	P + 1.3	N.A.	1.35	1.35
648	Dr Pepper	4.0	82	100	P + 1.5	14.375	1.05	.74
611	Blue Bell	9.0	31	55	P + 1.5	17	1.97	1.69
465	Cone Mills	7.5	46	73	P + 1.5	P + 3	1.48	1.24
461	Levitz	7.0	19	49	P + 1.5	15%–16%	2.65	2.08
	Average 10 companies	8.5	29%	55%	P + 1.4%	N.A.	1.55x	1.33x
411	National Medical Care	7.0	16%	51%	P + 1.5[s]	N.A.	1.68x	1.68x
330	Cole National	9.5	7	19	P + 1.375[s]	N.A.	2.34	1.99
314	Woodward & Lothrop	5.5	46	63	P + 1.5	N.A.	1.38	1.38
263	American Sterilizer	N.D.	N.D.	N.D.	P + 1.75–1.25	15%	1.47	1.24
232	Pannill Knitting	10.0	22	42	P + 1.5	14.3	2.28	1.77
220	TI-CARO	10.0	16	33	P + 1	16	1.42	1.15
219	Raymond International	8.0	30	58	P + 1.5	N.A.	1.58	1.58

200	Amerace	7.0	N.D.	N.D.	P + 1.5	17	1.50	1.08
154	Dan River	5.0	35	100	P + 1	N.A.	1.33	1.33
72	Atlas Van Lines	Secured	N.A.	N.A.	P + 2	P + 3	1.73	1.01
	Average 10 companies	7.7	24%	51%	P + 1.4%	N.A.	1.67x	1.42x
70	LADD Furniture	N.A.	N.A.	N.A.	P + 2%	14%	1.39x	1.20x
69	Shoetown	10.0	0	16	P + 3	FDR + 3[2]	2.33	2.20
63	Genicom	N.D.	N.D.	N.D.	P + 1	P	3.62	2.50
55	Leslie Fay	5.0	60	100	P	19–20	5.26	4.21
31	Perfect Fit	Secured	45	N.D.	P + 2	15	2.16	2.00
22	Bench Craft	7.0	26	56	P + 2.5	12	1.86	1.47
21	Piece Goods Shops	7.0	31	62	P + 2.5	12.5	5.66	3.60
19	Kincaid Furniture	5.0	70	100	P + 1.5	11.25–12.75	3.01	2.48
18	Guilford Industries	9.0	N.A.	N.A.	P × 110.5 + .5	18	3.91	2.32
11	Glendale Fabrics	N.D.	N.D.	N.D.	P	12	N.A.	1.61
	Average 10 companies	7.5	39%	67%	P + 1.6%	N.A.	3.24x	2.36x
	Average 30 companies	7.9	31%	58%	P + 1.5%	N.A.	2.12x	1.70x

[1] No interest for five years, 16% thereafter.

[2] Federal discount rate.

P = Prime.

s = Sliding.

N.A. = Not applicable.

N.D. = Not disclosed.

Table 3.5 Financial Structure Breakdown

Size of Financing (Millions)		Senior Debt	Subordinated Debt	Total Debt	Preferred Stock	Common Stock	Total Equity	Cash In Company
$1,287	Metromedia	88.6%	(1)	88.6%	9.7%	1.7%	10.4%	
1,075	Wometco	75.9	1.5%	77.4		22.6	22.6	
1,032	ARA	74.8	15.5	90.3	1.9	7.8	9.7	0.5%
997	Harte-Hanks	61.0	29.9	90.9		8.6	8.6	
752	Denny's	57.6	18.0	75.6	4.7	5.9	10.6	13.8
685	Malone & Hyde	82.5		82.5		17.5	17.5	
648	Dr Pepper	75.4	18.5	93.9		4.6	4.6	1.5
611	Blue Bell	76.4	8.2	84.6	9.0	5.3	14.3	1.1
465	Cone Mills	79.6	10.7	90.3	7.6	2.1	9.7	
461	Levitz	49.5	35.6	85.1	10.4	4.5	14.9	
	Average 10 companies	72.1%	13.8%	85.9%	4.3%	8.1%	12.4%	1.7%
411	National Medical Care	76.6%		76.6%	14.6%	3.3%	17.9	5.6%
330	Cole National	65.2		65.2		31.8	31.8	3.0
314	Woodward & Lothrop	87.6		87.6		6.4	6.4	6.0
263	American Sterilizer	58.6	23.2%	81.8		5.7	5.7	12.4
232	Pannill Knitting	63.5	20.5	84.0	4.1	6.1	10.2	5.9

220	TI-CARO	70.4	13.6	84.0		9.1	9.1	6.9
219	Raymond International	82.1		82.1		17.9	17.9	
200	Amerace	71.8	21.5	93.3	3.6	3.0	6.6	
154	Dan River	96.7		96.7		3.3	3.3	
72	Atlas Van Lines	58.3	38.2	96.5		3.5	3.5	
	Average 10 companies	73.1%	11.7%	84.8%	2.2%	9.0%	11.2%	4.0%
70	LADD Furniture	85.8%	11.4%	97.2%		2.8%	2.8%	
69	Shoetown	19.5	51.0	70.5		15.1	15.1	14.4%
63	Genicom	66.9	26.7	93.6		6.4	6.4	
55	Leslie Fay	55.0	11.1	66.1		20.1	20.1	13.8
31	Perfect Fit	49.2	3.3	52.5	6.5%	23.0	29.5	18.0
22	Bench Craft	66.8	31.2	98.0		2.0	2.0	
21	Piece Goods Shops	63.6	33.5	97.1		2.9	2.9	
19	Kincaid Furniture	65.0	18.5	83.5		16.5	16.5	
18	Guilford Industries	40.6	32.4	73.0		27.0	27.0	
11	Glendale Fabrics	9.0	69.3	78.3		4.5	4.5	17.2
	Average 10 companies	52.1%	28.8%	80.9%	6%	12.1%	12.7%	6.4%
	Average 30 companies	65.8%	18.1%	83.9%	2.4%	9.7%	12.1%	4.0%

[1] Discount debentures given as part of the purchase price not considered part of the financing.

an equity kicker as was the case in some of the subordinated debt sold institutionally.

Interest coverage is computed by dividing the projected first year EBIT by
projected interest expenses. The bigger deals generally can support lower interest coverage, as the table indicates. The 10 largest deals had senior debt
coverage of 1.55 × versus 3.24 × for the 10 smallest deals. The 10 largest
deals, however, included three break-up deals in which initial coverage was
less important because assets were to be sold to repay debt. Eliminating these
deals produced an average coverage for the remaining seven large deals of 1.77
×. If the three break-up deals were dropped from the calculation, the average
interest coverage would rise to 2.28 × on the senior debt. Total interest coverage amounts to 1.49 × for the largest seven deals when the three large break-
up deals are dropped, and the average of all deals except the break-up deals
shows total interest coverage of 1.88 ×.

FINANCIAL STRUCTURE BREAKDOWN

Table 3.5 shows that the larger deals tend to support more senior debt than
smaller deals, and also more total debt as a percentage of the total financing.
The smaller deals had substantially greater subordinated debt than the larger
deals, mostly due to the existence of sellers' notes in 6 of the 10 smaller
deals. The larger 10 deals were structured with 85.9 percent total debt versus 80.9
percent for the smaller 10 deals, but the percentage of equity was closely comparable at 12.4 percent versus 12.7 percent. The smaller deals used more cash
in the company to complete the financing than did the larger deals. Whereas
the equity in all of the deals averaged 12.1 percent, almost one-half of the
deals were structured with less than 10 percent equity. The inclusion of sellers'
debt in the financial structure enabled three of the smaller deals to be structured with less than 3 percent equity.

4 Anatomy of a Leveraged Buyout

The cases in this book encompass a variety of reasons for undertaking an LBO. In some cases, the catalyst putting the company in play came from the outside. Carl Icahn pushed Dan River into action, and Ron Baron caused Woodward & Lothrop to consider an LBO. The Levitz deal was initiated by Jay Pritaker, its largest shareholder. In most cases, however, the forces causing a company to consider an LBO came from management seeking a solution to a problem. The desire to give the family stockholders liquidity and diversification motivated Pannill Knitting, Kincaid Furniture, Guilford Industries, Glendale Fabrics, Reliable Stores, and Leslie Fay. In all of these examples, the controlling family was willing to sell out their interests where no market existed, or the market was too thinly traded to enable the family interest to realize the true value of their holdings. In the case of Piece Goods Shops, Perfect Fit, and Reliable Stores, the controlling families correctly believed the public market was substantially discounting the real worth of their companies. In many instances, a sellout to another company was explored but usually abandoned due to price. Where the controlling shareholders also managed the business, selling out to another company was emotionally unappealing as well. Dr Pepper put itself in play by asking its investment banker to review its alternatives. Metromedia's management owned 29 percent of the company; they wanted to own it all. LADD Furniture's parent responded favorably to management's overtures because of the parent's self-interest in recovering taxes and raising cash.

The 16 cases detailed in this book are illustrative of different financing techniques, each tailored to suit the particular company. Two cases used ESOPs. In the Dan River case, the ESOP was the principal financing vehicle, and in the case of Cone Mills, the ESOP was used to create losses in order to recover past taxes paid and to shelter future taxable income. Leslie Fay used the technique of pairing the purchasing company with a company with large tax losses in order to shelter income from taxes in the early years. Both Dr Pepper and Metromedia were structured as break-up deals where some of their assets would have to be sold to meet financing obligations. Woodward & Lothrop chose to issue junk bonds to pay off the initial bank debt, and Levitz used junk bond financing to fund its tender offer. Multimedia was structured as a recapitalization merger, which enabled all shareholders to participate in the equity of the LBO.

Seller financing figured importantly in seven deals as a means of increasing the sale price without greatly increasing the risk occasioned by the additional leverage. In all three of the cases involving the sale of divisions, the selling corporations took back paper. In the case of General Electric's sale of Genicom and Heck's sale of Shoe-Town, the willingness to take sellers' notes could have been a way for them to maximize the financial reporting of the sale. General Electric supplied 27 percent and Heck 51 percent of the total financing of their division's sales. In Sperry and Hutchinson's sale of LADD Furniture, the parent retained a debenture convertible into 75 percent of LADD. In the cases of Guilford Industries, Piece Goods Shops, and Bench Craft, the seller financing amounted to 23, 34, and 31 percent of the total financing respectively, whereas in the case of Glendale Fabrics, the sellers provided 69 percent of the initial financing. Sellers' debt is an excellent way to increase the price without greatly increasing the risk since it is held in friendly hands and thus does not threaten the long-term financial viability of the company.

The principal lenders in all but a few cases were commercial banks. Both Kincaid and Guilford Industries used insurance companies as principal lenders, but the Kincaid deal was done in 1980 when the banks were less aggressive in making LBO loans. Perfect Fit's principal lender was a British mutual fund, and LADD's lender was the asset-based lending arm of a bank.

The 16 cases represent a variety of businesses that exhibit only one common thread to qualify them as LBO candidates. Several companies share the same industry, namely textile, broadcasting, and furniture, and 4 of the 15 companies are retailers, but in almost no instance do any of these companies directly compete with one another. The only thing they seem to have in common in considerable history in their respective businesses. Seven of the 16 companies date back 75 years or more whereas the youngest company at 15 years old, Glendale Fabrics, was an old established participant in a young business. In all cases, the companies had established themselves in niches in their industry and enjoyed a strong competitive position in those business segments. There was little similarity in the condition of the companies' balance sheets. A few had substantial cash and no debt, but Dr Pepper and Metromedia had debt to equity ratios exceeding one to one. Dan River, Cone Mills, and Dr Pepper had shown lower earnings in the year prior to the buyout, and LADD Furniture was caught in a cyclical downturn in its business.

In all cases, management stayed on to operate the business and with the exception of Reliable Stores, invested in the new company. In Reliable's case, management received attractive incentives through a profit sharing arrangement. In instances where management owned either none or a small percentage of the company before the buyout, they quickly saw the LBO as perhaps their once-in-a-lifetime opportunity to build their net worth. In the 11 cases where management owned a relatively small amount of the company, the LBO provided them with the opportunity to increase their ownership by an average of sixfold. In these instances, management went from an average of 4.2 percent ownership to an average of 25.3 percent ownership. In the Piece Goods Shops and LADD Furniture deals, management went from no ownership of the old company to 25 percent ownership of the new company. In the cases of LADD, Leslie Fay, Piece Goods Shops, Perfect Fit, Kincaid, and Pannill Knitting, a second financing has taken place, providing evidence of the success of the LBO from management's perspective. These are companies lacking high growth characteristics and high stock market capitalization of earnings. These are basic companies making furniture, apparel, bedspreads, and selling fabrics at retail. Yet, these deals provided the right management incentives and the right amount of leverage to produce these large returns in very short time frames.

Among all the case studies in this book, Pannill Knitting stands out as the most ideal LBO candidate as measured by conventional criteria. Pannill had almost no debt, substantial excess cash, strong cash flow, an excellent record, high profit margins, and a number two market share. However, it had no significant salable assets and was dependent on its cash flow to service its debt. The outside funds required to finance the buyout amounted to a reasonable $4.9 \times$ trailing 12-month EBIT. The buyout was done by Gil Butler of Butler Capital, an old hand at LBO financing. The source and application of funds statement is as follows:

Sources of Funds

Senior borrowings	$155,000	63.5%
Subordinated notes	50,000	20.4
Preferred stock	10,000	4.1
Common stock	14,570	6.0
	$229,965	94.0%
Utilization of company's cash	14,395	6.0
	$243,965	100.0%

Application of Funds

Payment for common stock	$228,191
Payment for preferred stock	300
Repayment of debt	974
Fees and expenses	2,500
Tax recapture liability	12,000
	$243,965

Senior Bank Debt

Bank term loan	$108,000
Revolving credit agreement	62,000
	170,000
Acquisition requirements	155,000
Unused availability under revolving credit facility	$ 15,000

The term loan bore a 10-year maturity and interest at Manufacturers Hanover's prime rate plus $1\frac{1}{2}$ percent payable quarterly. An optional rate of $2\frac{1}{2}$ percent above the two, three, or six-month London Interbank Offered Rate (LIBOR) could be elected by the borrower, and fixed rate pricing options were also a possibility.

Amortization Schedule (000)

Year 1	$ 5,000
Year 2	7,500
Year 3	11,000
Year 4	11,000
Year 5	11,000
Year 6	11,000
Year 7	11,000
Year 8	13,500
Year 9	13,500
Year 10	13,500
	$108,000

A requirement of mandatory prepayments of the term loan out of excess cash flow was made. The senior loan facility was secured by a lien on substantially all of the assets of the company.

The $62 million revolving credit facility had a five-year maturity and also bore an interest rate of prime plus $1\frac{1}{2}$ percent. In addition, a fee of one-half of 1 percent was charged annually on the unused portion of the revolver. Manufacturers Hanover received a commitment fee on the amount of the term loan other than its portion of one-half of 1 percent from the date the loan was made, a period of about 40 days. Manufacturers Hanover also received a fee of $1.0 million for arranging the senior borrowings and an annual agent's fee of $50,000.

MEZZANINE FINANCING

Mezzanine financing is usually in the form of debt in combination with equity and generally targeted at pension funds or insurance companies. The use of subordinated debt sold to an equity investor enables the company to deduct the interest for tax purposes and provides the investor with stronger rights than any equity position. Sometimes, preferred stock is the principal mezzanine investment vehicle, particularly when the newly formed company is highly leveraged and expected to generate tax losses with the write-off of assets written-up in the acquisition. In this case, the preferred stock affords a better balance to the financing that senior lenders prefer. The loss of the tax-deductible feature of this preferred dividend only affects the loss carryforward and not actual taxes paid during the period when earnings are sheltered from taxes by write-up deductions. The Pannill preferred stock was converted into or exchanged for subordinated debt with similar maturity and interest rate, at the option of the company, subject to an acceptable legal opinion. The deductibility of interest payments on the debenture versus the aftertax dividends on the preferred stock was the principal motivating factor to trigger the debt for the preferred exchange; the IRS frowns upon transactions solely driven by the desire to save taxes. However, the election was made two years after the buyout.

Often, the mezzanine investment consists of two or more securities and is sold as a unit or strip. That is, each investor would get the same percentage of all of the securities in the mezzanine unit. In the Pannill case, the mezzanine unit consisted of $50.0 million in subordinated debt, $10.0 million in preferred stock, and $4.5 million in common stock. Thus, the total value of the units was $64.5 million and was sold in a strip. For example, a 10 percent investor would purchase $5.0 million in subordinated debt, $1.0 million in preferred stock, and typically, $450,000 in common stock. Butler's stated reason for including the preferred stock was to have the equity portion of the total financing exceed 10 percent. At one time, the IRS proposed rules that would disallow the deductibility of interest on debt that exceeded 90 percent of the total capital structure. The rationale of the IRS was that any greater leverage was actually equity but appeared in debt form simply to enable the company to make a pretax deduction on interest payments to investors rather than pay aftertax dividends. These rules never went into effect, and many LBOs contain less than 10 percent equity. The average equity percentage of the total financing of the 30 cases compared in Chapter 3 was 12.1 percent, but in half of the cases, total equity was less than 10 percent of total financing.

In the Pannill case, Gil Butler employed original discount debentures which gave the investor a higher actual return than the nominal interest rate. The principal amount of the subordinated debentures was $55.0 million, but the purchase price of these debentures was only $50.0 million. They are redeemed for the principal amount, increasing their yield to maturity, and interest is paid on the principal amount. The Pannill subordinated debentures pay interest of 12 percent in the first three years and 15 percent until maturity in 12 years. Because interest is computed on the principal amount, the debentures actually pay 13.2 percent in the first three years and $16\frac{1}{2}$ percent thereafter based on the purchase price of the debentures. The $5.0 original issue discount is amortized over the life of the debentures, but a substantial percentage of this amortization is allocated to the first three years prior to the 12 percent interest rate being stepped-up to 15 percent and thus becomes a more useful write-off for tax purposes.

The Pannill preferred stock portion of the mezzanine unit had a 12-year maturity and a dividend rate of 12 percent for the first three years, and 15 percent beyond. The mandatory redemption scheduled called for a $1.0 million redemption per year in years 7–11, and $5.0 million in year 12.

The mezzanine units were allocated 30 percent ownership of the common stock, or $4.5 million out of a total of $15.0 million. The amount of this allocation relates to a targeted total rate of return on the mezzanine unit. Other securities are often used in mezzanine investing, such as convertible debentures, debentures with warrants, and convertible preferred stock, but they all amount to different means of providing the investors with an acceptable internal rate of return commensurate with the risk.

The targeted compound rate of return for the mezzanine investors in the Pannill case was 25–27 percent in five years, depending on the estimate of the value of the equity portion of the unit. The yield to maturity on the units, excluding any consideration of gain on the common equity, was 14.3 percent. The value of the common stock is computed by capitalizing the sixth year of estimated earnings by a multiple approximating the multiple of the original buyout. In the Pannill case, the buyout multiple based on trailing 12 months was 9.3 ×. Using an exit multiple of 8–10 × produces an internal rate of return of 25–27 percent. To calculate this return, it is assumed that both the subordinated notes and preferred stock have a present value at the end of five years of their face, or par value. Discounting the future stream of interest, dividends, principal payments, and stock redemptions at a 12 percent rate produces a value approximating face value of the debentures and preferred stock in the Pannill mezzanine unit.

The common stock is the mother lode of any LBO. A return on investment of 10–15 × in five years is not uncommon in an reasonably priced LBO. If the purchase price is a stretch, a greater percentage of the common equity will have to be allocated to the mezzanine investors in order to maximize the amount of funds raised at this level. Thus, the higher the percentage of the common equity sold to management, the lower the amount of mezzanine money available because the high return on the common stock is needed to pull the internal rate of return up into the mid-20 percent range. All LBOs depend on management's investment participation at some level. For tax reasons, the purchase price of the common stock should be the same for all purchasers.

Management, however, is usually not required to purchase preferred stock or subordinated debentures and thus buys only the highest prospective return security. Management, though, was required to buy securities other than common stock in some instances. On the bigger deals, the amount of management's investment can be tens of millions. Chapter 3 shows that in 20 out of 30 cases, management invested over $1.0 million, and in seven instances, they invested over $10 million. Because of size of this investment can be so large in comparison to the net worth of the key management people, the company will often lend the management group purchase money at no interest or low interest rates. Loans were made to management in 9 of the 30 cases analyzed in Chapter 3. In 19 of the 30 cases analyzed in Chapter 3, management investors received more money in the buyout than they invested in the new company. In some instances, management was able to exchange their stock and options in the old company for stock in the new company free of taxes.

If management or family attributed to management owns more than 50 percent of the stock in the target company, it cannot own a controlling interest in the new company, or more than 49.9 percent, and still get capital gain treatment on the sale.

The benefit of obtaining capital gain treatment is now largely moot due to the elimination of preferential capital gains rates under the Tax Reform Act of 1986. Consequently, there is no tax penalty to maintaining a controlling interest in the new company on the part of the seller.

In the Pannill case, Bill Pannill, his son, and sisters owned over 60 percent of the stock, so they could not own more than 49 percent of the new company. Bill Pannill's primary objective was to sell the company at a fair price but not necessarily a full price. He believed that 10 × earnings was fair and could be financed without overleveraging the company. He insisted on a structure that provided substantial outside investor capital, thereby reducing the amount of bank debt in the total capitalization. His desire to keep the purchase price and leverage at reasonable levels reflected his sense of responsibility to his new management investors, his employees, and to the community. In short, he wanted a deal that did not endanger the survival of the company and was fair to both his shareholders and employees. Since the purchase price was a reasonable 4.9 × EBIT, there was sufficient cash flow to service the debt and satisfy the rate of return requirements of the mezzanine investors and still have enough common stock remaining to offer management 49 percent. The purchase price of the new stock was approximately one-fifteenth the sale price of the old stock. Bill Pannill sold his 10.1 percent ownership position for approximately $23 million and could have acquired a 10.1 percent interest in the new company for approximately $1.5 million. In fact, he doubled his ownership in the new company to 20.8 percent for an investment of approximately $3.1 million. His chief operating officer increased his ownership from 1.1 to 8.3 percent, and all of the remaining officers either substantially increased their ownership or were granted incentive stock options. No loans were provided by the company to purchase the stock, but Bill Pannill personally loaned his chief financial officer $200,000 for this purpose.

PROJECTING A PROFIT AND LOSS STATEMENT, A CASH FLOW STATEMENT, AND A BALANCE SHEET

The heart of any LBO that intends to service its debt out of the future operations of the company is the projected cash flow statement. Unless assets are to be sold to meet debt repayment schedules or new funds are to be raised with a public offering of equity, the cash flow generated by the company's operations is the means by which the company pays back its debt.

This exercise is based on estimates made at the time of the buyout. Estimates of the value of assets on appraisal differed from the actual appraisal value that was made public in the company's IPO prospectus. Whereas the estimated amount of write-up deduction, tax deductions, and goodwill are at substantial variance with recorded amounts, the principals and methodology are valid and instructive.

Sales and Earnings Projections

The cash flow statement begins with and is critically dependent on the company's earnings projections. Thus, the construction of a projected cash flow statement must begin with a realistic projection of future profits. Management is in the best position to project future performance but usually is reluctant to do so beyond a year or two. It is best to first assume an economic background and analyze the industry's relative performance compared to the economy. Within this framework, management is asked to estimate unit volume growth measured in today's dollars. A reasonable projection of inflation is then added to the unit volume projection to provide the long-term projection of sales. If the industry is clearly cyclical, a sales projection assuming a recession might also be prepared. This may be done by analyzing the company's actual performance in the last recession. However, the timing and severity of any future recession tends to produce projections that vary substantially from a steady growth projection and are thus rarely used. The use of a steady growth projection can be viewed as the long-term trend around which cycles occur. Whereas recession years will fall below the trendline, the recovery years will exceed the trendline and therefore balance out over the longer term. Awareness of the inevitability of down years should be recognized in the structuring of the deal, and a cushion ought to be provided to enable the company to service its debt commitments out of reserve funds apart from cash flow. This was done in the Pannill structuring by obtaining a commitment for $15 million in excess of acquisition requirements. Some lenders prefer tight covenants which almost assure default in poor performance years, thereby strengthening the lenders' ability to control the company's resources.

In the Pannill case, Butler management projected sales to grow 8 percent annually, a decidedly conservative projection when viewed from the company's record. Sales had grown over the past five years at an average annual rate of 23.7 percent and cash flow (net income plus depreciation) at a 26 percent average annual rate. Over a 20-year period, sales growth had averaged 16.6 percent and net income 28.1 percent per year. This rapid growth in sales and earnings reflected the fitness boom which dramatically increased the demand for sweat clothes and jogging suits. Butler Management prepared the projections for Pannill after obtaining management's opinion and after analyzing the domestic and foreign competitive situation. Butler assumed a generally improving economic trend, with real GNP growing at 2–3 percent per annum and an overall inflation rate growing at 5–6 percent per year. Butler assumed sales growth for Pannill of 2–3 percent in constant dollars, which when adjusted for inflation, produced a constant 8 percent dollar sales growth projection. In view of the company's extraordinarily high pretax profit margins of 27.8 percent for the trailing 12 months prior to the buyout, Butler projected a gradual decline in gross profit margins of five percentage points over five years. Although there was no evidence that margins were going to decline, Butler believed that the high profit margins would attract sufficient competition to force margins down. Thus, with the sales trend and profit margin projections, a long-term projection of EBIT was generated.

Interest Rate Assumptions

Interest expenses are a major cost item in any LBO, and thus the interest rate assumption can importantly influence the projected cash flows. Most senior debt facilities float with prime, generally at $1\frac{1}{2}$ percent over prime, and many offer LIBOR options.

Fixed Rate Options and Interest Caps

In recent years, banks have encouraged the use of interest rate swaps, caps, or fixed rate options for the first 2–3 years of the buyout when runaway interest rates could be devastating. Interest rate caps can be obtained for a fee that varies with the level and length of the cap. The lower and longer the cap, the higher the fee. A typical cap at 120 percent of the current interest rate might cost 1 percent per year, paid in advance. If, for example, prime was 13 percent and the floating rate at $1\frac{1}{2}$ percent over prime put the effective rate at $14\frac{1}{2}$ percent, a cap at $15\frac{1}{2}$ percent for a year might cost around 1 percent. The company would benefit from this option if the prime exceeded 15 percent because prime plus $1\frac{1}{2}$ percent would produce a $16\frac{1}{2}$ percent rate that equates to the fixed rate of $15\frac{1}{2}$ percent plus the 1 percent fee. However, if the prime dropped, the company's effective rate would also drop. A fixed rate, on the other hand, would not enable the company to benefit from any drop in rates. Fixed rates can be obtained for three years at 50–100 basis points above the current prime plus $1\frac{1}{2}$ percent. In the example above where the company would be paying $14\frac{1}{2}$ percent with the prime rate at 13 percent, it could probably fix the rate at $15\frac{1}{4}$ percent for three years. The pricing on both caps and fixed rate options become less favorable in periods of rapidly rising rates. In addition to the fixed rate and interest cap options, Citicorp offers floating rate insurance. This caps the effective rate at two points over the current rate for a year at the cost of $\frac{1}{2}$ percent. Cone Mills entered into such an arrangement with Citicorp in mid-1984 when the prime rate rose from 11 percent in March 1984 to 13 percent in July 1984. As it happened, prime dropped to 10 percent during the insured year, and Cone's interest expenses floated down with the lower prime. Had Cone chosen to exercise its fixed rate options, it would have locked in a rate of approximately $15\frac{1}{2}$ percent for a year (with prime at 13 percent) and not benefited from the subsequent drop in prime.

Generally, the assumed interest rate in LBO projections reflect the current rate and the trend in rates at the time the projections are made. In the Pannill case, Butler Management assumed an interest rate of 14 percent for the bank term loan and the revolver. The projections were made when the prime was 11 percent but was under upward pressure because rising rates on other debt instruments had pushed up the bank's cost of money. The three point premium over the prime looked conservative at the time, but four months later when the prime stood at 13 percent, the estimated 14 percent rate was actually lower than the company's effective floating rate of $14\frac{1}{2}$ percent. A year after the deal closed, prime dropped to 10 percent, lowering Pannill's floating rate to $11\frac{1}{2}$ percent and making the projected rate of 14 percent look very conservative. The computations in this chapter assume an average prime of 11 percent.

Working Capital Ratios

Other important aspects of the projected cash flow statement include the development of a working capital ratio. This estimates the amount of investment in inventories and accounts receivables, net of accounts payables, that are required with any increase in sales level. The company's actual past experience can be an important guide to the establishment of this ratio, but often a conservative company can learn to live with lower inventories, higher accounts payables, and work their accounts receivables harder to speed collections. LADD Furniture was able to reduce its inventories from $30.8 million to $15.1 million and reduce its accounts receivables from $18.4 million to $16.2 million in the first 16 months following its buyout. As a result, despite a poor economic environment and weak earnings, the company's revolver was reduced from $30.3 million to $3.2 million in the first 16 months.

Capital Additions

As sales are projected to increase, allowances must be made for investment in plant and equipment to provide the needed production capacity. There is an ongoing need to replace certain equipment annually, such as machinery and rolling stock. However, the need for bricks and mortar expansion usually involves significant cash outlays although equipment can be leased and buildings can be leased or mortgaged. Management must provide estimates as to how much and when plant capacity is needed. These expenditures along with the usual year-to-year capital needs are factored into the projected cash flow. In the Pannill case, the need for a new dyehouse was factored into the first two years' cash flow projections.

Accounting for Purchase Price Premium

The purchase price of most LBOs done in recent years has exceeded book values, often by a substantial amount. Of all the cases discussed in this book, only Dan River, LADD Furniture, and Reliable Stores were sold below book value. All of the remaining cases sold at a premium to book value, and in the case of Metromedia, the purchase price was approximately 366 percent of book value. The average purchase price of the 16 cases was 186 percent of book value. Where a premium exists, the new company can elect to write up the assets under Section 338. Under Section 338, the purchaser can make an "asset election" within 75 days of acquiring 80 percent of the outstanding stock. Asset elections allow for the write-up of assets, or "step-up" the tax basis, but require the immediate payment of tax on the full amount of the appreciation in the value of the property as a result of the Tax Reform Act of 1986.

In one of its most far-reaching changes, the Tax Reform Act of 1986 repealed the *General Utilities* doctrine relating to the nonrecognition of gain by a corporation on the distribution or sale of appreciated property in complete liquidation. Under the new law, property distributed by a corporation is treated as if it were sold at fair market value. The corporation must pay tax on the full amount of the appreciation in the value of the property. Under the prior law, a liquidating corporation recognized gain only to the extent of any tax recapture. Thus only the shareholders recognized capital gain to the extent the value of the property received exceeded their cost basis in the stock of the liquidating corporation. Under the 1986 Act, both the liquidating corporation and its shareholders must recognize full gain or loss in such transactions.

The significance of this change is that it materially alters the after-tax price realized in the sale of corporate businesses. Two taxes must now be paid before the purchaser obtains a fair market basis in the acquired property. This is true whether or not there has been an actual sale or deemed sale in which a Section 338 election was made. The result is that taxable takeovers made with a view to stepping up the basis of the purchased assets to fair market value are now unattractive. Taxable purchases of stock without a Section 338 election or tax-free acquisitions are now encouraged because the corporate level tax is deferred. The impact of this on cash flow, however, is mitigated by the lower corporate tax rates. The additional cash flow afforded by Section 338 election resulting in sheltering future taxes as the written-up assets are depreciated and amortized is substantially offset in many instances by the drop in corporate tax rates from 46% to 34% after 1987. If a company chooses not to make an asset election, the old tax basis is "carried over," and no tax recapture is triggered. If the company elects to write up assets, these assets are then depreciated or amortized over their estimated useful lives and serve to reduce taxable earnings.

Calculation of the Purchase Price

The allocation of purchase price over the assets acquired begins with the calculation of the purchase price. This consists of adding the amount paid for the common stock, the existing debt repaid, the current liabilities assumed, and the recapture taxes. The sum of these items represents the total purchase price to be allocated to the assets required. The total purchase price also includes the transaction costs, but these costs cannot be allocated to the assets acquired.

Calculation of Purchase Price—Pannill Knitting

Calculation of Purchase Price

Common stock	$228,191
Existing debt repaid	974
Liabilities assumed	17,044
Recapture taxes—LIFO, ITC, etc.	12,200
Total purchase price to be allocated	258,409
Transaction costs	2,600
Total purchase price	$261,009

Allocation of the Purchase Price

There are two ways to allocate the purchase price over the relative fair market value of the assets and each entails an appraisal of the assets. In the so-called residual method, all of the assets, both tangible and intangible except goodwill, are appraised, and any residual amount is assigned to goodwill. The second method is the excess earnings method and is similar to the residual method except that goodwill is appraised along with the other assets. The standard method for establishing a value for goodwill is to determine the extent to which earnings exceed a reasonable rate of return on the tangible assets of the company. These excess earnings are then capitalized to produce a value for the goodwill. The capitalization rate used for goodwill should be substantially higher than the capitalization rate applied to tangible assets because goodwill is an intangible and a somewhat unstable asset, compared with tangible assets, which usually have an independent market value. In 1986, the IRS issued regulations under Section 338 requiring the use of the residual method of allocation to determine the basis of the assets deemed purchased.

Justification for Purchase Test

A justification for purchase test can be applied to determine if the expected future return (tax savings) provides an acceptable return on the investment (tax on gain). If the tax on gain expense is too large in relation to the future taxes saved, then the company may take the "stock election" under

Section 338, thereby carrying over the old basis of the assets and avoiding both the write-up deduction and tax recapture.

The calculation consists of estimating the amount of write-up deduction available as determined by an asset appraisal. The write-up deductions are then used to determine how much lower income taxes would be over the early years of the buyout. These tax savings represent the return on the investment, represented by tax on gain which results from the asset write-up. If the return is high enough, the purchase test justifies the election to write up the assets.

In the Pannill case, the asset election under Section 338 was chosen because of the favorable justification for purchase test. However, under the 1986 tax law, the justification for purchase test would have been unfavorable.

Tangible Asset Valuation

The appraisal process must be carried out by an independent qualified appraiser and preferably one who has had experience in valuing intangible assets. Appraisals of land, buildings, machinery, and equipment (including vehicles) are fairly straightforward.

Inventories provide a fertile area of write-up and rapid write-off of the written-up value. Since the written-up inventories will be sold in the first year, this write-up deduction is also written off in the first year. In the Pannill case, the finished goods of $14.0 million were stated at cost and would be valued at their sale price less cost to sell them. In that case, cost of goods sold was approximately 67 percent of sales. Thus, their sale price would be $20.9 million, less 5 percent or $1.0 million cost to sell them. Therefore, the appraised value of the finished goods inventories would be $19.9 million. Work-in-process inventories are assumed to be halfway through their manufacturing process, and an estimate must be made on the cost to complete them. If labor and overhead amount to 40 percent of the cost of goods and raw material the balance, approximately two-thirds of the cost to finish has been accounted for. Thus, the $3.7 million work-in-process would be valued at $5.5 million when finished and sold for $8.2 million. Adding to the stated value of $3.7 million, the cost to finish the work-in-process of $1.8 million, and the cost to sell these goods of $400,000, these inventories had a cost of $5.9 million. Raw materials are valued at their current cost, which was $3.0 million in the Pannill case. Therefore, the total fair market value of Pannill's inventories was $29.5 million versus their book value of $21.3 million.

Intangible Assets Valuation

Goodwill In the Pannill case, the purchase price to be allocated was approximately $258 million compared to tangible assets of approximately $105 million. Cash and receivables accounted for $56 million of the $105 million and must be recorded at their face value. Thus, the remaining $202 million of the purchase price had to be allocated to the remaining $49 million tangible and intangible assets, including goodwill. Under the residual method, the goodwill would be $55 million if all the remaining tangible assets were appraised for $134 million and other intangible assets were valued at $13 million.

Under the excess earnings method of valuing goodwill, however, the appraiser could value the goodwill separately and allocate the residual over all the tangible (except cash receivables and prepaids) and intangible assets pro rata. If an assumed fair market value of the tangible assets was $134 million and a reasonable rate of return on these assets was 15 percent, $20 million of earnings could be attributed to tangible assets. This would leave $4.7 million in excess earnings, which if capitalized at 20 percent, would value goodwill at $24 million. This amount was increased by the pro rata allocation of the premium over fair market value of both the tangible and intangible assets. It produced a value of goodwill of $41.9 million, some $13 million lower than the goodwill would be if valued under the residual method.

Other Intangible Asset Valuation

Customer lists are an intangible asset that can be valued on an estimate of the cost to acquire the customers. Customer turnover can be calculated to provide the basis for the amortization period. In Pannill's case, the customer lists were estimated to be worth $10 million and could be written off over five years.

Sales backlog is an asset representing the embedded profit in the backlog of orders. Some or all of the backlog can be satisfied by the shipment of inventories to fill these orders. Any backlog in excess of inventories would contain a gross profit which could be valued based on the company's gross profit margins and written off in the first year when the backlogged orders were shipped. Pannill's excess sales backlog was valued at $2.9 million.

Computer software can be valued and written off over the period of its estimated life. Pannill's software was valued at $500,000 and written off over five years.

Other assets that can be valued include employment contracts, which are written off over the life of the contracts, and patents, licenses, and favorable leases, which are written off over their remaining lives. Trade secrets, contracts, negative covenants, favorable financing, franchises, and distributorships are all intangible assets that can be valued.

Table 4.1 shows that the appraised value of all assets, both tangible and intangible, amounts to $172.3 million. The total purchase price is $258.4 million, which leaves $76.1 million in excess purchase price to be allocated to the appraised value of all the assets except cash and accounts receivable. This pro rata allocation of the excess purchase price results in an inventory value rising from an appraised value of $29.5 to $51.5 million. This produces a step-up in

Allocation of Purchase Price—Pannill Knitting

	3/3/84 Balance Sheet	Appraised Value	Allocation of Excess Purchase Price	Depreciation/ Amortization Period
Cash	$27,129	$27,129	$27,129	1
Accounts receivable	29,314	29,314	29,314	1
Inventories	21,288	29,500	51,521	1
Land	2,488	4,000	6,986	1
Buildings	17,400	28,300	49,425	18
Machinery and equipment	6,400	15,200	26,546	5
Furniture and fixtures	381	600	1,048	5
Vehicles	100	300	524	3
Leasehold improvements	0	0	0	1
Goodwill	0	24,000	41,915	1
Customer lists	0	10,000	17,465	5
Sales backlog	0	2,900	5,065	1
Software	0	500	873	5
Other assets	598	598	598	0
Total	$105,098	$172,341	$258,409	

value of $30.2 million over the actual carrying value of $21.3 million. Adding the LIFO reserve of $6.4 million to the LIFO value of the inventories and deducting this amount from the $51.5 stepped-up value, a write-up deduction from inventory alone of $23.8 million is produced.

A total of all the write-ups that can be written off in the first five years is as follows:

Year	Estimated Old Depreciation (Millions)	Write-Up Deductions (Millions)	Net Write-Up Deductions	Taxes Saved
1	$3.2	$40.8	$37.6	$ 5.9
2	4.4	14.9	10.5	6.6
3	5.4	15.7	10.3	7.4
4	6.4	16.5	10.1	7.9
5	7.4	17.5	10.1	8.4
	$26.8	$105.4	$78.6 × 46% =	$36.2

The tax savings in the first five years from the write-up deduction is $36.2 million. The cost to get these tax savings is the recapture taxes, totaling $12.2 million. Thus, the justification for purchase test shows that for an investment of $12.2 million (recapture taxes), the internal rate of return is 48 percent (taxes saved), which well justifies the election to write up the assets.

Pannill Knitting Company, Inc. Leveraged Buyout Projected Balance Sheets (Consolidated tax basis)
($000)

	Years						
	1	2	3	4	5	6	7
Sales	$172,800	$186,624	$201,554	$217,678	$235,092	$253,900	$274,212
Interest income	1,146	1,146	1,146	1,146	1,146	1,146	1,146
Operating costs	125,134	139,382	152,640	167,119	182,932	197,657	231,562
Earnings before interest and taxes	44,410	46,096	47,768	49,413	51,014	55,097	59,504
Adjustments:							
Interest expense	28,300	27,193	26,009	25,776	23,767	21,373	19,789
Depreciation—purchased assets	7,068	8,995	8,724	8,530	8,530	2,955	2,955
Depreciation—capital additions	683	1,766	2,780	3,767	4,813	5,082	5,367
Excess inventory valuation	23,830	0	0	0	0	0	0
Amortization—intangible assets	9,252	4,188	4,188	4,188	4,188	0	0
Adjusted taxable income	(24,724)	3,955	6,067	7,152	9,717	25,687	31,393
Net operating loss generated	24,724	0	0	0	0	0	0
NOL carryover (prior years)	0	24,724	20,769	14,702	7,550	0	0
NOL utilized	0	3,955	6,067	7,152	7,550	0	0
NOL available for future years	24,724	20,769	14,702	7,550	0	0	0
Taxable income before taxes	(24,724)	0	0	0	0	25,687	31,393
Income taxes	0	0	0	0	1,040	12,330	15,069
Investment tax credit generated	400	424	449	476	505	535	567
ITC carryover (prior years)	0	400	824	1,273	1,749	709	0
ITC utilized	0	0	0	0	1,040	1,233	568
ITC available for future years	400	824	1,273	1,749	709	0	(0)
Total income taxes	0	0	0	0	0	11,097	14,501
Book net income	($24,724)	$3,955	$6,067	$7,152	$9,717	$14,590	$16,892

Pannill Knitting Company, Inc. Leveraged Buyout Projected Cash Flow Statements
($000)

	Years						
	1	2	3	4	5	6	7
Book net income	($24,724)	$3,955	$6,067	$7,152	$9,717	$14,590	$16,855
Adjustments:							
Add:							
Depreciation	7,752	10,761	11,504	12,297	13,343	8,037	8,322
Excess inventory valuation	23,830	0	0	0	0	0	0
Amortization	9,252	4,188	4,188	4,188	4,188	0	0
Subtract:							
Increase in working capital	0	2,765	2,986	3,225	3,483	3,762	4,062
Capital expenditures	7,000	7,240	4,494	4,764	5,050	5,353	5,674
Scheduled payments:							
Term loan	5,000	7,500	11,000	11,000	11,000	11,000	11,000
Subordinated debt	0	0	0	0	0	0	6,000
Redemption of preferred stock	0	0	0	0	0	0	1,000
Preferred stock dividends	1,200	1,200	1,200	1,500	1,500	1,500	1,500
Net cash flow	2,910	198	2,079	3,148	6,215	1,013	(4,059)
Opening cash balance	12,734	12,734	12,734	12,734	12,734	12,734	12,734
Total cash	15,644	12,932	14,813	15,882	18,949	13,747	8,675
less: Minimum cash balance	(12,734)	(12,734)	(12,734)	(12,734)	(12,734)	(12,734)	(12,734)
Available for prepayment of debt	2,910	198	2,079	3,148	6,215	1,013	(4,059)
Prepayment of:							
Revolving credit line	2,910	198	2,079	3,148	6,215	1,013	(4,059)
Term loan							
Subordinated debt							
Excess cash	0	0	0	0	0	0	0
add: Minimum cash balance	12,734	12,734	12,734	12,734	12,734	12,734	12,734
Ending cash	$12,734	$12,734	$12,734	$12,734	$12,734	$12,734	$12,734

Pannill Knitting Company, Inc. Leveraged Buyout Projected Balance Sheets (consolidated tax basis)
($000)

Assets				End of Years			
	1	2	3	4	5	6	7
Cash	$12,734	$12,734	$12,734	$12,734	$12,734	$12,734	$12,734
Accounts receivable	30,240	32,659	35,272	38,094	41,141	44,433	47,987
Inventory	28,512	30,793	33,256	35,917	38,790	41,894	45,245
Other	0	0	0	0	0	0	0
Current assets	71,486	76,186	81,262	86,745	92,665	99,060	105,966
Land	6,986	6,986	6,986	6,986	6,986	6,986	6,986
Buildings	52,425	55,425	55,425	55,425	55,425	55,425	55,425
Machinery and equipment	30,546	34,786	39,280	44,044	49,094	54,447	60,121
Furniture and fixtures	1,048	1,048	1,048	1,048	1,048	1,048	1,048
Vehicles	524	524	524	524	524	524	524
Leasehold improvements	0	0	0	0	0	0	0
Total PP&E	91,529	98,769	103,263	108,027	113,077	118,430	124,104
less: accumulated depreciation	7,752	18,512	30,017	42,314	55,657	63,694	72,016
Total PP&E, net	83,777	80,257	73,247	65,713	57,420	54,736	52,088
Intangible assets (excludes goodwill)	16,750	12,563	8,375	4,188	0	0	0
Goodwill	41,915	41,915	41,915	41,915	41,915	41,915	41,915
Other	5,598	5,598	5,598	5,598	5,598	5,598	5,598
Total assets	$219,527	$216,519	$210,397	$204,159	$197,599	$201,309	$205,567

Pannill Knitting Company, Inc. Leveraged Buyout Projected Balance Sheets (consolidated tax basis) *(continued)*
($000)

Liabilities and Stockholders' Equity	End of Years						
	1	2	3	4	5	6	7
Payables and Accruals	$18,791	$20,726	$22,817	$25,074	$27,512	$30,145	$32,989
Current portion of debt:							
Revolving credit line	44,090	43,892	41,813	38,665	32,450	31,437	35,497
Term loan	7,500	11,000	11,000	11,000	11,000	11,000	13,500
Subordinated debt	0	0	0	0	0	6,000	6,000
Current liabilities	70,381	75,618	75,629	74,739	70,962	78,582	87,985
Term loan	95,500	84,500	73,500	62,500	51,500	40,500	27,000
Subordinated debt	55,000	55,000	55,000	55,000	55,000	49,000	43,000
Total long-term debt	150,500	139,500	128,500	117,500	106,500	89,500	70,000
Other liabilities	0	0	0	0	0	0	0
Total liabilities	220,881	215,118	204,129	192,239	177,462	168,082	157,985
Preferred stock	10,000	10,000	10,000	10,000	10,000	10,000	9,000
Common stock	14,570	14,570	14,570	14,570	14,570	14,570	14,570
Retained earnings	(25,924)	(23,169)	(18,302)	(12,650)	(4,433)	8,657	24,012
Total stockholders' equity	(1,354)	1,401	6,268	11,920	20,137	33,227	47,582
Total liabilities and stockholders' equity	$219,527	$216,519	$210,397	$204,159	$197,599	$201,309	$205,567

Pannill Knitting Company, Inc. Projected Mezzanine Investors' Five-Year Rate of Return
($000)

	Multiple of Net Income		
	8	9	10
Projected net income in year 6[1]	$11,796	$11,796	$11,796
Aggregate market value of common stock	$94,365	$106,161	$117,956

Proforma Cash Flows for Years						
	0	1	2	3	4	5
Initial investment	($64,500)					
Interest and dividend income		7800	7800	7800	9450	37,760
Capital repayment[2]						65,000

	Multiple of Net Income		
	8	9	10
Share of proceeds from sale of equity	28,310	31,848	35,387
Internal rate of return on investment[3]	18.48%	19.06%	19.63%

[1] On a financial reporting basis.
[2] Assumes mezzanine debt and preferred stock repaid at face value.
[3] Compounded quarterly.

With the calculation of the write-up deduction, the income statement can now be projected. (See page 60.)

The projected income statement shows that no taxes are paid in the first five years. This saving of $36.5 million was needed to meet the cash flow requirements in the first five years. The cash flow statement begins with the book net income and adds back the noncash write-offs from net income. Year 1 shows a book net income deficit of $24.7 million, but when the deductions for depreciation, excess inventory valuation, and the amortization of the tax deductible intangibles are added back, the company actually projects a positive cash generation of $16.2 million. Needed cash is deducted from this to increase working capital, capital expenditures, term loan principal repayment, and preferred dividends. The remaining $1.9 million is available to prepay debt and is used to reduce the revolving line of credit. Each of the first six years shows that excess cash is generated to prepay debt while keeping a minimum cash balance of $12.7 million. In the seventh year, however, the repayment of the subordinated debt and redemption of the preferred stock begins, and the projections show a cash flow deficit of $4.1 million. This necessitates borrowing from the revolving line of credit. The revolver is needed again in year 8 to make up the projected cash flow deficit, and amounts to $36.2 million at the end of year 10 when the term loan is completely repaid. At the end of year 12, all debt is repaid, and the preferred stock is redeemed. At that time, cash equals $22.1 million, and net worth amounts to $192.5 million.

These projections, based on conservative cash flow assumptions, show the debt can be repaid comfortably out of cash flow. Based on conservative projections, the estimated return for the mezzanine investors ranged from 18.5–19.6 percent, depending on the value of the common stock. Butler Capital projected an internal rate of return of 25–27 percent for the mezzanine units by using different write-up and interest rate assumptions. In fact, when Gil Butler took the company public two years after the LBO, the mezzanine investors' actual return ranged from 65% to 108%. The market for the stock on the IPO was sufficiently strong that the underwriters did not require the company to sell any new stock to reduce the acquisition debt, which at that time amounted to $150 million.

A complete computer printout of all of the financial projections is included in Appendix I.

5 Leveraged Buyout Cases

PANNILL KNITTING

The Pannill Knitting LBO resulted from efforts to provide liquidity for the controlling family interests. The family investigated the company's worth if it sold out and its value on a public offering. They found the LBO offered the highest value by a substantial margin. Furthermore, the LBO offered complete liquidity for all shareholders and allowed the company to go private and remain independent. It also provided management with the opportunity to increase its ownership of the company from 16.2 percent to 49.0 percent. A little over two years later, the company had a public offering, providing management with a 21 times increase in their investment. Even the IRS benefited, by collecting more taxes as a result of the two transactions.

Pannill Knitting was an ideal candidate for an LBO. It had a consistent record of strong cash flow, was virtually debt free, and had cash of more than $27 million. Pretax profit margins and returns on investment were unusually high for an apparel producer.

The company was founded in 1925 by Will Pannill in Martinsville, Virginia. Pannill worked in a Mayoden, North Carolina cotton-spinning mill until he decided to enter the profitable business of knitted underwear, which was made exclusively in northern textile mills. In order to learn the business, he worked as a janitor in Utica, New York in the largest underwear mill in town. He eventually returned South to establish Pannill Knitting and in 1928 helped a friend start Bassett-Walker, now Pannill Knitting's largest competitor. Will Pannill also set up his son-in-law in business, starting Tultex in 1937. These three firms now have approximately 65 percent of the $750 million knitted fleece business and have made Martinsville, Virginia the "sweatshirt capital of the world."

In the early days, underwear was often fleeced, a process in which a knitted fabric is run through a napping machine, tearing the knitted threads on one side of the fabric and making it fuzzy. In the early 1930s, as fleeced sweatshirts became popular, Pannill's product line moved away from underwear. Today, the company produces knitted fleece sportswear, including sweatshirts, sweat pants, jogging suits, warm-up outfits, and hooded jackets.

The fitness and jogging fad and the energy crises of the 1970s caused the demand for fleece apparel to soar and enabled Pannill Knitting's sales and earnings to grow from 1973 to 1983 at a compound rate of 37.8 percent and 43.8 percent respectively. Sales rose from $16.9 million in 1973 to $160 million in 1983 and net income from $1.3 million to $22.7 million. This growth occurred under the leadership of Will Pannill's son Bill, who became president in 1966 at the age of 39. Bill was friendly and popular with the mill workers and was able to assemble a management team that produced faster growth, higher profit margins, and a greater return on investment than its major competitors.

Bill and his six sisters, who ranged in age from 53 to 73 and owned approximately 50 percent of the common stock, watched the price rise from a low of $68 in 1982 to $420 in early 1984. The only market for the stock was the Martinsville branch of Wheat, First Securities, and trading was sporadic.

The Pannill family had seen its across-town competitor Bassett-Walker go public in 1983. The public market's recognition of the strong earning power of Bassett-Walker was contagious and helped push up Pannill Knitting's stock price. Considering the age of the major stockholders and their need for liquidity, Bill Pannill asked his board's approval to explore three alternatives: a public offering of common stock, sale to another company, or an LBO. Pannill met with Wheat, First Securities and Goldman, Sachs, and both indicated that an IPO price of about eight times earnings was the highest the public market would support.

Pannill also solicited interest in the acquisition of the company. Several large acquisition-minded companies, such as Interco, Beatrice Foods, Consolidated Foods, and General Mills looked seriously at the company, but the highest price any of them considered was approximately 6 × earnings.

Both Wheat, First Securities and Goldman, Sachs advised Pannill that an LBO would result in the highest price to the stockholders and would provide complete liquidity for all shareholders. Although Pannill recognized that the new investors in an LBO could eventually take the company public, he preferred to remain private as long as possible. He also figured that 10 × earnings was a minimum price that would be acceptable to the family and the board. A look at Pannill Knitting's financial statements shows that the company was an ideal candidate for an LBO from a financial point of view. It had $26 million in cash net of debt, excellent profit margins, and had earned an average of 40.8 percent on equity for the last five years. The table on Selected Financial Data shows this record and financial condition.

The company's pretax profit margins and return on equity are particularly worth noting. Pretax margins were 27.1 percent in 1983, and the company earned an average of 42.3 percent on equity in each of the prior four years. Margins and returns on investment this high for an apparel producer are almost unheard of although an obvious mark of the strength of the company in the marketplace also represented a potential vulnerability. It is illogical to assume that competition, either domestic or foreign, will allow this high rate of return to go unchallenged over the longer term.

In the fall of 1983, Bill Pannill discussed the possibility of an LBO with

Selected Financial Data

		For the Fiscal Year[1]			
	1983	1982	1981	1980	1979
Operating results:					
Net sales	$160,053	$144,754	$112,342	$91,962	$58,576
Cost of goods sold	106,334	96,809	75,136	63,552	41,801
Gross profit	53,719	47,945	37,206	28,410	16,775
Expenses:					
Selling and administrative	11,622	10,978	8,910	6,371	4,466
Interest expense	225	246	459	161	121
Interest and other income, net	(1,429)	(1,109)	(1,564)	(656)	(217)
Total	10,418	10,115	7,805	5,876	4,370
Income before income taxes	43,301	37,830	29,401	22,534	12,405
Income taxes	20,549	17,975	14,160	11,081	6,088
Net income	$22,752	$19,855	$15,241	$11,453	$6,317
Pretax profit margins	27.1%	26.1%	26.2%	24.5%	21.2%
Per share data:					
Net income per common share	$36.3	$42.6	$44.4	$46.4	$34.4
Book value per common share	$183.12	$142.79	$106.15	$77.80	$55.45
Period-end financial condition:					
Working capital	$55,936	$44,753	$31,512	$23,943	$15,085
Total assets	$103,568	$84,400	$66,789	$51,092	$36,178
Long-term debt (including current maturities)	$ 1,469	$ 2,290	$ 3,122	$ 2,179	$ 2,737
Stockholders' investment	$80,409	$62,708	$46,632	$34,382	$24,796

[1]The company's fiscal year closes on the Saturday nearest November 30 of each year.

Forstmann Little and Ira Hechler. Forstmann Little expressed interest at 10 × 1982 earnings of $45.23 per share. Hechler discussed a possible structure at 10 times 1983 earnings estimated at $48 per share. Hechler proposed a structure using a partnership as the purchaser, with one partner having large tax loss carryforwards to shelter future earnings. Under this proposal, management would be offered 49.9 percent of the company. The loss partner, usually a large savings bank such as Goldome with more than $1 billion in losses, is allocated 90 percent of the income and losses for the first four or five years, thereby avoiding taxes on 90 percent of the earnings. These funds are used to repay loans from the banks. After the first four or five years, the allocation flip-flops, granting the investment partner 90 percent of income and losses.

However, Pannill's tax advisors could not completely assure the company that the IRS would not challenge the Hechler proposal on the allocation of gains and losses. It was known that the IRS was attempting to challenge these types of transactions administratively or through proposed legislation affecting future deals. In any case, these deals were somewhat difficult to refinance, either with a public offering or another LBO. In Pannill's case, it was clear that the potential write-up of assets could shelter taxable income for two years, thereby mitigating the need to shelter income from taxes by use of a loss partner.

Gil Butler entered the bidding in late January 1984. His company, Butler Capital, had considerable experience in financing LBOs, although the Pannill deal would be the biggest ever attempted by the company. Butler Capital had recently raised $130 million in capital from banks and pension funds to commit to LBO financings, giving him credibility with Bill Pannill. As it appeared that the company's 1983 earnings would approximate $50 per share, the asking price was $500 per share. Butler proposed a transaction in which common shareholders would receive $500 per share, and management of the company could buy up to 49 percent of the newly formed acquiring company. Actual audited earnings for the year came to $51.84 per share, exceeding the $50 per share estimate in part because the accounting year contained 53 weeks. This represented by all accounts a record year for the company. However, Bill Pannill is a modest man as illustrated by the entire message to shareholders in the 1984 annual report other than financial statements reproduced below.

To consider buyout proposals, the board appointed a special committee of four board members who would not have any interest in the proposed acquiring company. Gil Butler presented his proposal to the committee and its financial and legal advisers on February 8, 1984.

Five days later, the company received a letter from the First Chicago Investment Corporation, a bank holding company whose principal asset is the First National Bank of Chicago. The letter contained a proposal to purchase all the common stock at $518.50, or 10 times the reported 1983 earnings. The proposal was structured so that management other than Bill Pannill would obtain 10 percent of the acquiring company for $280,000. Bill Pannill could purchase as little as 10 percent for $280,000 or as much as 65 percent for an

KNITTING COMPANY
INC
MANUFACTURERS OF KNITTED GOODS
MARTINSVILLE, VIRGINIA 24115 • AREA CODE 703 638-8841

January 24, 1984

To Our Stockholders:

1983 was another good year. Our sales were up 10.6% and our income increased 14.6%.

During the year we doubled the size of our new knitting facility and completed an addition to our Distribution Center.

Our order backlog going into 1984 is good.

I want to thank the management and employees of all of our plants for their continuing hard work and loyalty.

Sincerely,

Wm. G. Pannill
President

investment of $1.8 million in common stock and $20 million in preferred stock. The balance of the equity would be purchased by First Chicago in amounts ranging from $20 million for an 80 percent interest down to $6.7 million for a 25 percent interest. The proposal also indicated that an attempt would be made to structure the transaction so that Bill Pannill would be able to reinvest the proceeds of the sale of his stock on a pretax basis. Thus, he could exchange his 10.1 percent ownership position worth $22.9 million at $518.50 per share for up to 65 percent ownership in the acquiring company with an investment of $21.8 million, and keep the change.

In response to the First Chicago proposal, Butler increased his offer to $520 per common share, conditioned upon an agreement by the company not to seek or negotiate with others for 45 days. A further condition was that management would not be prepared to invest in another LBO unless the offer had conditions no more burdensome than Butler's proposal, was fully backed by commitment letters from banks, and provided at least as much financial stability as the Butler proposal. First Chicago's proposal called for at least $35 million more senior debt than Butler's proposal. Butler was offered a break fee in excess of $1 million to be paid if the company broke off the deal, but he refused. Butler Capital prides itself in not taking any fees in LBO transactions except a percentage of the profits on the invested funds provided by his capital backers. (Butler Capital did, however, have the company commit to pay it up to $1.8 million for investment banking services and the reimbursement of expenses in the 1984–86 period.)

Since the Butler proposal contained more favorable terms than those proposed by First Chicago, the special committee voted to recommend the Butler proposal, subject to receipt of a fairness opinion from Wheat, First Securities. The board received the fairness opinion at its meeting on March 20, 1984 and unanimously agreed to the merger. The following source and application of funds statement for the deal are given. Note that the senior borrowings reflect $15 million unused availability under the revolving credit facility.

Source of Funds

Senior borrowings	$155,000
Subordinated notes	50,000
Preferred stock	10,000
Common stock	$ 14,570
Total funds from financing	229,570
Utilization of the company's available cash (estimated)	14,395
Total	$243,965

Application of Funds

Payment for company common stock	$228,191
Payment for company 10% preferred stock	300
Repayment of existing company debt	974
Payment of fees and expenses (estimated)	2,500
Tax recapture liability (estimated)	12,000
Total	$243,965

The bank financing was led by Manufacturers Hanover and included four major banks, two smaller Virginia banks, and Merrill Lynch Interfunding. Manufacturers Hanover received a $1 million fee for arranging the senior borrowings.

The senior debt consisted of a $108 million term loan and a $62 million revolving credit facility. The term loan matured in 10 years and carried an interest rate that floated 1.5 percent above prime. Interest rates tied to the short-term Eurodollar rate were also available, as was a fixed rate option. Principal repayments rose gradually from $5 million and $7.5 million in years one and two, to $11 million for the next four years, and finally, $13.5 million for the final three years. The $62 million revolving credit facility matured in five years and also carried interest rates similar to the term loan except that there is an annual fee of one-half of 1 percent on the unused portion of the commitment. Only approximately $43.2 million of the revolver was used in financing the acquisition, leaving $19 million as a cushion against future cash needs.

Institutional investors and management subscribing to the remaining financing included Venture Lending Associates, sponsored by Butler Capital; Merrill Lynch Interfunding; General Electric Pension Trust; Morgan Guaranty as a Trustee of a Commingled Pension Trust; and BancBoston Capital, Inc. of Boston, an affiliate of the Bank of Boston. These investors purchased subordinated debt, preferred stock, and common stock in a strip or mezzanine unit. The debt portion of the unit consisted of $55 million principal amount of subordinated debentures, due in 1996 and sold at a discount of $5 million. Interest rates were 12 percent for the first three years and 15 percent thereafter, producing a yield to maturity of 14.3 percent. Amortization of the debentures was $6 million in years 7–11, and balloon payment of $25 million is due in year 12. The $10 million in preferred stock matured in 12 years and had a 12 percent dividend for the first three years, rising to 15 percent in year four and thereafter. The mezzanine unit was allocated 30 percent of the common stock for $4.5 million. (The preferred stock was exchanged in May 1986 for $10 million in subordinated notes due in 1996. The subordinated notes paid tax-deductible interest in amounts equal to the aftertax dividend on the preferred stock.)

Whereas the mezzanine units were purchased in a strip, the amount of common stock allocated to each purchaser was far from pro rata, as Table 5.1 indicates.

Butler Capital allocated its Venture Lending Associates proportionately more common stock than the other investors and favored Merrill Lynch Interfunding over the remaining investors. Butler's Venture Lending Associates invested 1.9 × the amount invested by Merrill Lynch Interfunding but received 2.8 × the amount of common stock. It invested 2.4 × the amount invested by General Electric Pension Trust but received 5.1 × the amount of common stock.

Sixteen members of management and family purchased 47.5 percent of the

Table 5.1   Mezzanine Units

Purchaser	Total Investment (Millions)	Percent of Total Investment	Percent of Common Allocated To Mezzanine Units
Venture Lending Associates	$30.0	14.4%	59.0%
Merrill Lynch Interfunding	15.5	22.9	20.7
General Electric Pension Trust	12.6	18.6	11.5
Others	9.5	14.1	8.8
	$67.6	100.0%	100.0%

common stock issued at the same price per share but without the requirement to purchase any of the subordinated debentures or preferred stock. Bill Pannill sold his 10.1 percent interest in the selling company for $23 million and bought a 20.8 percent interest in the acquiring company for $3.1 million. From his share, he also established a foundation and gave his daughter stock totaling 1.8 percent. His son, Will, vice-president, received $6.9 million on the buyout and bought 8.3 percent of the new company for $1.2 million. He gave his children 1.7 percent of his stock to be held in trust. John Decker, President and CEO, bought 8.3 percent for $1.2 million, and Bryce Middleton, executive vice president and chief financial officer, bought 1.7 percent for $250,005, of which $200,000 was lent to him by Bill Pannill.

Despite compounded growth in sales of 25.2 percent experienced over the past decade, the projections used in the financing estimate growth in sales of only 8 percent per year and unit growth of only 2–3 percent per year. Furthermore, whereas profit margins have steadily increased over the past 10 years, future projections allowed for a slow decline in pretax margin down to 21.7 percent in year five. Since the purchase prices represented a premium over book value of about 2.8 ×, the tangible and intangible assets were appraised and written up to allocate the purchase price premium. Tangible items such as inventory, land, buildings, and equipment were written up to their appraisal value, and intangibles such as customer lists and goodwill were also assigned values. With the aid of the faster write-offs provided by the Tax Act of 1981, depreciation was substantially increased, sheltering pretax earnings from taxes.

Inventories were written up to approximately $21.2 million, and plant and equipment increased on appraisal by $43.0 million. Intangibles were appraised at $5.3 million and goodwill at $58.1 million. In the first eight months following the buyout, amortization of the excess of assigned value of acquired inventory reduced income by $11.1 million, and the amortization of acquired order backlog reduced income by $3.4 million. In addition, depreciation charges rose to $5.6 million in 1985 from $2.6 million in 1983, largely as a result of the write-up of those assets. Other deductions from pretax income resulting from the buyout included the amortization of deferred financing costs and the original issue discount on the subordinated debentures. These write-downs coupled with heavy interest charges caused the company to report a loss of $7.2 million for the first eight months following the buyout. Without these write-downs and interest charges, the company would have reported pre-tax income of $31.2 million for this eight-month period. The $7.2 million loss was carried forward, helped shelter income from taxes in 1985, and reduced that year's effective tax rate to 30.2 percent.

In June 1985, some 26 months after the buyout, the company had a public offering of common stock. The company did not sell any new stock, despite having $150.0 million in debt and stockholders' equity of only $7.2 million. All shareholders participated in the sale, selling approximately 40 percent of their holdings each.

The IPO price was $21 per share. The trailing 12 months' earnings on a fully taxed basis were only $1.18 per share, putting the P/E ratio at 17.8 ×. This was a discount to the P/E ratio of two of its principal competitors, Tultex and Russell Mills, which sold at an average of 20.5 × at that time. However, VFC Corporation, a leading apparel company, which owns Bassett-Walker, traded at only 12.9 × earnings at the time Pannill went public. Pannill's earnings per share, though, were showing very rapid growth, in part due to the leveraged financial structure, lower interest rates on steadily declining debt, and declining amortization charges.

Table 5.2 below demonstrates how earnings per share gains are exaggerated by the deleveraging of a highly leveraged financial structure.

Earnings before interest and taxes gained 67 percent in 1985 over 1984, but earnings per share jumped 409 percent. The table shows that the $21.0 million increase in EBIT was accompanied by only a $1.6 million increase in interest expense and amortization. A similar pattern followed for the first quarter of 1986 compared to the same quarter in 1985. EBIT showed a sharp 93 percent gain, but earnings per share (EPS) rocketed up by 557 percent. The EBIT gain

Table 5.2

	Year Ended		Quarter Ended	
	December 31, 1984	December 31, 1985	March 31, 1985	March 31, 1986
EBIT	$30,950	$51,949	$8,896	$17,141
Less Interest Expense and Amortization	23,308	24,938	6,352	5,110
Pretax income	7,642	27,011	2,645	12,031
Net income available for common	3,109	12,758	1,068	5,784
Earnings per share (EPS)	0.21	0.86	0.07	0.39
EBIT gain over prior period		+67%		+93%
EPS gain over prior period		+409%		+557%

of $8.2 million was accompanied by a decline in interest expenses and amortization charges of $1.2 million. The combination of rising operating earnings and the deleveraging of the financial structure produced earnings estimates of $1.65 per share for 1986, putting the IPO price at a reasonable 12.7 ×. The market agreed with the reasonableness of the IPO price, and the stock traded as high as $28 in the first month following the offering. The company believed it could show operating earnings growth of 13 percent per year over the 1986–90 period, which would enable it to completely repay its debt. This rate of growth would propel EBIT from $51.9 million in 1985 to $95.6 million in 1990. The repayment of debt and the slowdown of amortization charges would enable pretax earnings after interest and amortization to rise from $27.0 million to approximately $95.0 million. Thus, reported earnings per share (assuming similar tax rates) would rise 3.5 × on a 1.8 × gain in EBIT. This earnings leverage in part accounts for the creation of wealth, which often occurs when LBOs are refinanced or go public.

Table 5.3 shows the value of the company's earnings and equity on the LBO and the IPO.

The value of the equity on the IPO was $315.0 million versus $228.5 on the LBO. When free cash and debt are factored into the equation, however, the value placed on earnings for the IPO was $461.3 million versus $204.5 million in the LBO. The multiple of EBIT on the LBO was a modest 4.5 × and rose to 7.8 × on the IPO, an increase of 72 percent. The creation of value is the increase in the multiple of EBIT. Much of this increase is undoubtedly attributable to the increased values in the stock market. It is most unlikely, however, that had Pannill not undergone the LBO followed two years later by the IPO, the stock would have traded at 17.8 × earnings. The stock was too thinly traded to attract much institutional interest, but this might have been remedied by a large secondary stock offering. The price of such an offering would still be tied to its historical price, which was 8.0 times earnings at the time the LBO was announced. It would appear unlikely that the market would find reason to give over twice the value of the company's earnings in 1986 than in 1984, especially because earnings had dropped 26 percent in 1984 only to rebound by 67 percent in 1985. By going private and re-emerging as a public company

Table 5.3

	12 Months Ended		Percentage Change
	March 31, 1984	March 31, 1986	
Value of earnings	$204,465	$461,334	
plus free cash	25,000	13,700	
less debt	974	160,034	
Value of equity	$228,491	$315,000	+38%
EBIT	45,432	59,436	+31%
Earnings multiple of EBIT	4.50x	7.76x	+72%

showing substantially more rapid growth in earnings per share than it would have in its unleveraged state, and with the sponsorship of Merrill Lynch and Bear, Stearns, the stock would hit the street running at 2.2 times its old P/E ratio.

Everybody Wins.   The LBO and subsequent IPO of Pannill Knitting presents the opportunity to access how the public, the new investors, and the IRS fared as a result of these transactions. Whereas all stockholders received a premium for their stock on the LBO, the large profits realized by the LBO investors are often believed to come at the expense of the IRS. Although in this case the IRS will show a significant overall revenue gain as a result of the two transactions. The company saved about $19.5 million in taxes from asset write-ups and interest expense deductions in the first 20 months. The future savings from higher depreciation and amortization charges is estimated at $14.0 million, putting the total IRS "subsidy" at $33.0 million. However, the write-up of assets triggered recapture taxes of an estimated $12.0 million, which was paid within months of the close of the transaction.

Interest expenses over the estimated life of the loans are estimated at $82 million, of which approximately $49.0 million becomes taxable income to the lending banks. It is assumed the IRS will obtain $15 million of this income in taxes.

Since all shareholders had to sell their stock, including family holdings amounting to over 65 percent of the stock for which there was no intention to sell, the taxable gain on the $228 million in proceeds is estimated to exceed $175 million. At this level, taxes due the IRS would amount to $35.0 million. The new majority owners initiated yet another tax event for the IRS by effecting a public offering of stock and recording another taxable gain for shareholders of $129 million. The tax bill is another $25.8 million. The IRS scoreboard is as follows:

Capital gain taxes—initial transaction	$35.0
Taxes lost due to asset write-ups	(29.7)
Recapture taxes associated with asset write-ups	12.0
Taxes lost due to interest expenditures	(37.8)
Taxes collected on interest income	15.0
Capital gain taxes on stock sold on the public offering	25.8
Net taxes collected	$20.3

The IRS will also potentially collect at least another $20 million in capital gains taxes when management sells its remaining shares. Thus, the IRS benefited by the two transactions despite the substantial tax savings the company alone realized.

Table 5.4 details the returns realized by the management and mezzanine investors in the buyout.

Table 5.4 Investor Returns

	Common Stock	Subordinated Debenture and Preferred Stock	Total Investment	Value on IPO
Investors				
Venture Lending Associates I and II	$4,520,940	$25,479,060	$30,000,000	$120,418,800
Merrill Lynch Interfunding	1,587,210	13,950,000	15,537,210	47,281,410
General Electric Pension Trust	879,855	11,732,440	12,612,295	30,209,395
Others	661,995	8,838,500	9,500,495	22,740,395
Mezzanine investors				
Total	$7,650,000	$60,000,000	$67,650,000	$220,650,000
Management				
William G. Pannill	3,120,000		3,120,000	65,520,000
John G. Decker	1,249,995		1,249,995	26,249,895
William L. Pannill	1,249,995		1,249,995	26,249,895
Frank M. Lacy, Jr.	799,995		799,995	16,799,895
Bryce N. Middleton	250,005		250,005	5,250,105
Norman H. Philips	250,005		250,005	5,250,105
Management investors total	$6,919,995		$6,919,995	$145,319,895
Significant Employees				
10 people[1]	473,072			9,030,015
Grand total	$15,043,067	$60,000,000	$75,043,067	$374,880,000

[1]Purchased stock on May 30, 1985 for $1.10 per share.

Venture Lending Associates, Butler Capital's pool of pension fund capital, fared the best of the mezzanine investors because their mezzanine units contained the greatest allocation of common stock. Venture Lending Associates' internal rate of return was approximately 108.6 percent, followed by Merrill Lynch Interfunding at 83.9 percent. The remaining mezzanine investors, receiving the lowest allocation of common stock, realized an internal rate of return of 64.7 percent.

Management enjoyed the highest return by virtue of not being required to purchase either subordinated debentures or preferred stock. The top six members of management saw their $1.00 per share stock appreciate 21 × based on the IPO price of $21 per share. Ten significant employees were sold stock at $1.10 per share 13 months prior to the offering, which valued their investment up 19 times. John Decker, President, received $2.6 million on the LBO and reinvested $1.2 million worth $26.2 million at the IPO price. Will Pannill received $6.9 million on the LBO and reinvested $1.2 million worth $26.2 million at the IPO. Bryce Middleton, chief financial officer, invested $250,005 in the LBO worth $5.3 million at the IPO price of $21.

Bill Pannill's total return confirmed the wisdom of his choosing an LBO over a large public offering or selling out to another company. Bill received $23.1 million on the LBO and reinvested $3.1 million in the LBO, approximately doubling his percentage of ownership in the company. He gave approximately 7 percent of his new stock to his daughter, and they together netted approximately $27.9 million on the IPO and retained $36.1 million worth of stock. Thus, Bill has received $45.9 million in cash, net of his $3.1 million reinvestment, and his daughter has obtained another $2.0 million from his share of the stock. Adding the $36.1 million in stock they retain brings the total value to $84.0 million. Had Bill elected to sell his stock on a secondary offering or sell completely to another company, his highest expectation would have netted him approximately $17.5 million and no residual ownership in the company. Had he done nothing and sold his stock at 8 × the trailing 12 months earnings as of March 31, 1986, he would have received approximately $24.9 million. In the highly unlikely event the old Pannill stock would have shed its trading range of 7–8 × earnings and traded at 17.8 × earnings as it did on the IPO, Bill's original ownership would have been worth $58.2 million or only 63 percent of the actual value of $84.0 million. Earnings would have been higher without the LBO interest expense and amortization—approximately $32.4 million versus an actual $18.7 statement fully taxed for the 12 months ended March 31, 1986. The difference is that Bill cashed in a 10.1 percent share of the $228 million LBO and was able to acquire a 20.8 percent ownership share of the new company valued at $315 million on the IPO. Of the $59.1 million difference in his $84.0 actual worth versus the $24.9 worth of his old ownership valued at 8 × current earnings, $33.3 million is attributable to the higher valuation of earnings, and $25.8 million is attributable to the opportunity to increase his percentage of ownership for a relatively small investment. The LBO provided Bill the opportunity to double his ownership position. Thus, the LBO, in addition to providing total liquidity for all shareholders at the highest price attainable, also contributed to a leveraging of the multiple of earnings on the IPO and provided management the ability to leverage their percentage of ownership in the newly capitalized company. This is an example of financial engineering at its best.

Bill Pannill deserves special kudos for a job well done. First, he increased sales 13 × and net income 36 × in his first 18 years of running the company through 1983. He achieved this without the benefit of outside capital and with only one small acquisition. His profit margins are believed to be the highest in the apparel industry and more than double in all industries. Removing the influence of cash on earnings and net worth, in 1983 the company earned pretax 92.1 percent on net worth. Bill also kept a watchful eye on the value of other producers of fleeced sportswear, and when the time was right, he launched a plan to gain stockholder liquidity. He carefully sought out professional advice for each alternative—to sell out, go public, or do an LBO. Recognizing that an LBO produced the highest and most liquid return, he found a buyout partner he felt comfortable with. He resisted proposals that treated him differently from other stockholders and insisted on a fair deal for everyone. He also insisted that the deal be done at a reasonable price rather than the highest price possible. He believed he was responsible for getting his stockholders a fair if not full price, and he felt an obligation to his employees and community not to overleverage the company and court financial disaster. Then, he ensured that his key management people were able to obtain meaningful equity participation in the new company, even to the extent of making a personal loan.

Bill Pannill and his management team greatly exceeded earnings projections in the second year following the LBO, enabling the company to have a successful public offering. At the offering price, the six members of top management and 10 significant employees saw their $7.4 million investment skyrocket in value to $154.3 million only 26 months after the LBO. Nice deal, nice company, nice man.

DR PEPPER

The Dr Pepper LBO resulted from the company assessing its alternatives occasioned by the first earnings decline in 25 years. The company's investment bankers advised them of their alternatives, which included selling assets, restructuring its debt, seeking a merger partner, or continuing to do business as before. When the press learned the company was considering selling out, the company was effectively put into play. It took persuasion by the investment bankers even to consider the LBO alternative as it appeared illogical to add large amounts of debt to its already leveraged balance sheet.

The agreement to sell the company to Forstmann Little on an LBO attracted another serious LBO competitor. The ensuing fight points up the difficulties of attempting to finance an LBO when management is on the opposing team. The case also illustrates how a lower firm offer can defeat a higher offer, subject to financing.

The Dr Pepper soft drink was formulated in 1885 and first served in a corner drug store in Waco, Texas. The company moved to Dallas in 1923, then headed by J. B. O'Hara, the son-in-law of the founder. In 1927, O'Hara used the findings of a Columbia University Ph.D. proving that sugar provided energy and demonstrating that the average person experienced a letdown during the normal day at 10:30 A.M., 2:30 P.M., and 4:30 P.M. O'Hara concluded that Dr Pepper, because of its sugar content, would supply energy that would overcome these periods of fatigue. Thus, the slogan, "Drink a Bite to Eat at 10, 2, and 4 o'clock" became one of the most famous and significant soft drink slogans ever.

O'Hara's claim that Dr Pepper provided energy proved to be a lifesaver during World War II when sugar rationing threatened to curtail operations of the soft drink industry. His theory, along with other evidence supplied by in-

Pannill Knitting Company, Inc.—Selected Financial Data

	Predecessor Company[1]				The Company[1]			
	(In thousands, except per share data)							
	Year ended			January 1, 1984 to April 18, 1984[2]	April 19, 1984 to December 31, 1984[2]	Year ended December 31, 1985	Three Months Ended	
	November 28, 1981	November 27, 1982	December 3, 1983				March 31, 1985	March 31, 1986
Statement of Operations Data								
Net sales	$112,342	$144,754	$160,052	$50,609	$117,865	$191,522	$39,918	$55,184
Cost of sales:								
Amortization of purchase price in excess of Predecessor Company book value of inventory and other current assets[3]	—	—	—	—	14,506	—	—	—
Manufacturing costs	75,136	96,809	106,333	32,668	78,345	126,562	28,227	34,257
	75,136	96,809	106,333	32,668	92,851	126,562	28,227	34,257
Gross profit	37,206	47,945	53,719	17,941	25,014	64,960	11,691	20,927
Selling, general and administrative expenses	8,910	10,978	11,622	3,554	8,451	13,011	2,694	3,760
Income from operations	28,296	36,967	42,097	14,387	16,563	51,949	8,997	17,167
Other (income) expense:								
Interest expense	459	246	225	112	18,935	20,369	5,298	4,436
Amortization	—	—	—	—	5,018	3,990	1,012	942
Interest income	(1,318)	(950)	(1,279)	(765)	(292)	(179)	(59)	(268)
Other, net	(246)	(159)	(150)	195	105	758	101	26
	(1,105)	(863)	(1,024)	(458)	23,766	24,938	6,352	5,136
Income (loss) before income taxes and extraordinary credit	29,401	37,830	43,301	14,845	(7,203)	27,011	2,645	12,031
Provision for income taxes	14,160	17,975	20,549	6,888	—	13,053	1,277	5,947
Income (loss) before extraordinary credit	15,241	19,855	22,752	7,957	(7,203)	13,958	1,368	6,084
Extraordinary credit[4]	—	—	—	—	—	4,872	1,277	—
Net income (loss)	$ 15,241	$ 19,855	$ 22,752	$ 7,957	(7,203)	18,830	2,645	6,084
Cumulative preferred stock dividend[5]					840	1,200	300	300
Net income (loss) available for common stock					$ (8,043)	$ 17,630	$ 2,345	$5,784
Per Share Data								
Income (loss) before extraordinary credit					$ (0.55)	$ 0.86	$ 0.07	$ 0.39
Extraordinary credit[4]					—	0.33	0.09	—
Net income (loss)					$ (0.55)	$ 1.19	$ .16	$ 0.39
Weighted average common shares outstanding					14,570	14,821	14,570	15,000

	Predecessor Company[1]			The Company[1]		
	(In thousands)					
	November 28, 1981	November 27, 1982	December 3, 1983	December 31, 1984	December 31, 1985	March 31, 1986
Balance Sheet Data						
Current assets[6]	$ 48,455	$ 63,742	$ 76,831	$ 55,064	$ 64,857	$ 70,226
Plant and equipment, net	18,334	20,658	26,737	68,126	65,336	65,279
Goodwill and other assets				61,367	58,722	58,161
Total assets	66,789	84,400	103,568	184,557	188,915	193,666
Current liabilities	16,943	18,989	20,895	13,030	22,514	22,462
Long-term debt, less current portion[5]	2,291	1,580	827	178,247	146,837	139,909
Cumulative preferred stock[5]	50	50	50	10,000	10,000	10,000
Common stockholders' equity	46,582	62,659	80,359	(16,720)	1,383	7,167

[1] The Company acquired the Predecessor Company on April 18, 1984. The data with respect to the Predecessor Company are based upon the historical costs of the Predecessor Company, and the data with respect to the Company are based upon the application of the purchase method of accounting to the acquisition.

[2] After the Acquisition, the Company elected the calendar year as its fiscal year. Statement of operations data for the period form December 4, 1983 through December 31, 1983 are not included.

[3] Represents nonrecurring charges to cost of sales as a result of the application of the purchase method of accounting to the Acquisition.

[4] The extraordinary credit represents utilization of a tax-loss carryforward generated in 1984.

[5] Subsequent to March 31, 1986, the cumulative preferred stock issued in the Acquisition was repurchased in exchange for $10,000,000 aggregate principal amount of Subordinated Notes due 1996.

[6] In connection with the Acquisition, the method of accounting for the cost of the Predecessor Company's fleeced knitwear inventory was changed from the last-in, first-out method to the first-in, first-out method.

Pannill Knitting Company, Inc.—Balance Sheets

ASSETS

	December 31,		March 31, 1986
	1984	1985	(Unau-
		(In thousands)	dited)
Current Assets			
Cash and temporary investments	$ 3,551	$ 4,591	$ 15,801
Accounts receivable, net of allowances for doubtful accounts of $375,000, $625,000 and $550,000, respectively	26,896	42,622	36,387
Inventories:			
Finished goods	16,835	8,556	10,805
Work in process	3,866	4,384	3,687
Raw materials and supplies	3,524	4,307	3,211
	24,225	17,247	17,703
Prepaid expenses	392	397	335
Total current assets	55,064	64,857	70,226
Plant and Equipment			
Land and improvements	1,802	1,934	2,029
Buildings and improvements	33,763	34,593	34,616
Machinery and equipment	33,981	35,337	36,451
Furniture, fixtures and other	1,769	2,004	2,161
Construction in progress	498	741	666
	71,813	74,609	75,923
Less—Accumulated depreciation	3,687	9,273	10,644
	68,126	65,336	65,279
Other Assets:			
Excess of purchase price over fair value of assets acquired (goodwill)	57,053	55,602	55,239
Deferred financing costs	1,842	1,595	1,532
Other intangible assets	2,472	1,525	1,390
	61,367	58,722	58,161
	$184,557	$188,915	$193,666

LIABILITIES AND STOCKHOLDERS' EQUITY

	December 31,		March 31, 1986
	1984	1985	(Unaudited)
Current Liabilities:			
Current maturities of long-term debt	$ 6,250	$ 9,250	$ 10,125
Accounts payable	3,348	8,461	7,234
Accrued payroll and related benefits	2,700	4,051	4,158
Other accrued liabilities	732	752	945
Total current liabilities	13,030	22,514	22,462
Long-term debt, net of current maturities	178,247	146,837	139,909
Deferred income taxes		8,181	14,128
Cumulative Preferred Stock—1,000,000 shares authorized and outstanding, subject to mandatory redemption requirements from 1991–1996	10,000	10,000	10,000
Stockholders' Equity:			
Common stock, $.01 par value—40,000,000 shares authorized; 14,569,995 shares outstanding in 1984 and 15,000,000 shares outstanding in 1985 and 1986	145	150	150
Capital in excess of par value	14,425	14,893	14,893
Retained earnings (deficit)	(8,043)	9,587	15,371
Excess of purchase price over book value of net assets of Predecessor Company applicable to management interest therein	(23,247)	(23,247)	(23,247)
	(16,720)	1,383	7,167
	$184,557	$188,915	$193,666

The accompanying notes are an integral part of these balance sheets.

dustry leaders, persuaded the War Rationing Board to rescind an earlier ruling that eliminated any sugar quotas for the manufacture of soft drinks.

Dr Pepper's distribution gradually expanded in the 1950s, and by 1960, the drink was available in 75 percent of the nation. In 1963, a major roadblock to domestic franchise expansion was removed when a U.S. District Court ruled that Dr Pepper was not a cola. Bottlers were formerly restricted by agreements with cola franchisors, principally Coke and Pepsi, from producing and selling two cola brands. These other bottlers were now able to join the network of Dr Pepper franchise operations, and by 1973, less than 1 percent of the nation remained unfranchised.

By 1981, the company had recorded 24 consecutive years of increased sales and earnings. Sales reached $364 million and net income $29.4 million. Dr Pepper was now the number three selling soft drink in the United States. 1981 also saw Dr Pepper implement a strategy of broadening its soft drink base to include top brands outside the cola segment. It invested heavily in expansion of plants and new equipment, including production facilities, vending machines, and trucks. Capital expenditures for 1980 and 1981 totaled $47.7 million, exceeding depreciation by $27.7 million.

Capital outlays included the purchase of Welch's carbonated soft drink in 1981. Despite these expenditures, total debt rose only moderately and totaled $9.8 million at year-end 1981 compared to net worth of $123.7 million. In early February 1982, the company purchased Canada Dry from Norton Simon, Inc. for $131.8 million, plus $10 million for a 5-year covenant not to compete and $2.0 million for technical assistance. The acquisition was financed with a $105 million bank loan and $38.8 million in subordinated debentures. The bank loan was at prime and the subordinated debentures at prime less $3\frac{1}{2}$ percent, but collared to fall no lower than 14 percent and to rise no higher than 20 percent. Canada Dry had shown sales growth over the three years ended June 1981, but net earnings had declined markedly. Sales grew from $136.8 million to $156.7 million over those three years, but net earnings declined from $14.8 million to $5.8 million, largely due to heavy price discounting.

The acquisition of Canada Dry, accounted for as a purchase, resulted in booking goodwill of $62.9 million. Pro forma results for 1981, as if Canada Dry had been acquired on January 1, 1981, showed net income of $22.3 million, down from $29.9 million actually earned without Canada Dry. The additional interest payments, depreciation, and amortization of goodwill exceeded Canada Dry's earnings contribution by $7.6 million after taxes. Canada Dry further depressed earnings in 1982. Dr Pepper recorded the first earnings decline in 25 years as net earnings declined to $12.5 million, down 58 percent from reported 1981 earnings. Management attributed the decline to heavy price discounting in the industry and particularly in the Southwest where Dr Pepper is the strongest. Management also blamed poor results on too much overhead in several divisions and too broad promotional efforts, resulting in a dilution of marketing support in key areas. As a result of this poor performance, Charles Jarvie, president, was fired.

In 1980, the Board had urged Woodrow Wilson "Foots" Clements, who had been CEO since 1970 and had turned 65, to select a successor. Jarvie had had a successful career in Proctor and Gamble and was thus hired as president. Jarvie's successor was Dick Armstrong, head of the recently acquired Canada Dry. Armstrong had spent many years in advertising in New York City before his appointment at Canada Dry.

Clements and Armstrong decided to access the alternatives. In July 1983, the company hired Lazard Freres & Co. to act as financial advisor to consider possible business and financial alternatives. The alternatives seriously considered were 1) to sell certain assets (including Canada Dry) to reduce the outstanding debt, 2) to restructure Dr Pepper's debt, 3) to seek a merger partner, or 4) to continue to do business as before. Lazard was authorized to develop a list of major United States and international companies that might be interested in acquiring all or part of Dr Pepper. Lazard prepared a confidential memorandum and distributed it to a number of such companies.

The *Wall Street Journal* announced in September that Dr Pepper had retained Lazard and was considering selling out. Dr Pepper confirmed that it had retained Lazard and was considering its alternatives. Clements was asked in an interview what his personal reaction would be to a $24 per share offer for Dr Pepper, and he replied, "I'd tell them to get lost." The stock had traded in a range of 19\frac{1}{4}$–$9$\frac{1}{2}$ during the previous five years. Because of the publicity, Lazard and Dr Pepper received a number of inquiries from a number of companies, including Forstmann Little, which indicated to Lazard its interest in studying an LBO transaction for Dr Pepper.

Dr Pepper's management was initially reluctant to consider an LBO, not fully understanding how such a transaction made sense. Lazard, however, convinced management that Forstmann Little's background, substantial available capital, and its prior business experience with LBOs and the soft drink business qualified it to receive the confidential memorandum. For example, Forstmann Little in 1983 purchased Beverage Management from Beatrice Foods for $106 million. Beverage Management has the only franchise that bottles 7 Up in Ohio. As far as capital resources were concerned, Forstmann Little in 1983 obtained commitments of $302 million from pension funds for investment in LBOs. The availability of this capital proved to be of prime importance in the quest for Dr Pepper.

At the regular board meeting in October, Lazard reported that it had furnished the confidential memorandum to over 20 companies and that no offer to acquire all of Dr Pepper's business had been received. The only ongoing discussions were with Forstmann Little concerning an LBO. Clements reported at that meeting that he had received a phone call from Ian Wilson, president and CEO of Castle and Cooke, Inc. (C&C), stating that C&C wished to make an offer to acquire Dr Pepper. Wilson was a former Coca-Cola executive, and C&C was part owner of the A&W Root Beer brand. Wilson shared with Clements his concept of establishing a soft drink entity that would include Dr Pepper, Canada Dry, Welch's, A&W Root Beer, and another national brand. Clements told Wilson to contact Lazard to obtain the confidential memorandum, and in early November, Drexel Burnham discussed with Lazard the way in which Drexel Burnham, C&C, and Citicorp Venture Capital might arrange the financing for the acquisition of Dr Pepper through their acquisition entity DPCC.

The next day, following further negotiations, Forstmann Little indicated to Lazard that its entering into an agreement in principal was contingent upon Forstmann Little's obtaining two binding agreements from Dr Pepper: that Dr Pepper would not solicit or encourage other acquisition proposals, and that Dr Pepper would grant Forstmann Little an option on 4,150,000 shares at the subsequent offer price.

On November 17, 1983 at a special board meeting, Forstmann Little presented a formal written offer for all of Dr Pepper's stock at $22 per share. The offer indicated that Forstmann Little and its affiliate, the MBO Partnership (consisting of $250 million in pension fund money), were committed to invest $150 million with the balance to be supplied by banks, led by Manufacturers Hanover. The board unanimously approved the agreement in principal with Forstmann Little. Three weeks later, Forstmann Little obtained a definitive bank loan agreement for all of the bank financing. Thus, the Forstmann Little offer of $22 cash was fully financed and on the table awaiting acceptance. The board, however, felt obligated to consider DPCC's proposal of $560 million, which came to $23.28 per share. The written proposal consisted of $550 million bank financing subject to extensive due diligence, $131 million in subordinated debt to be raised on a "best efforts" basis by Drexel Burnham's high yield bond department, and $50 million in equity, only $5 million of which was from Citicorp Venture Capital.

Dr Pepper's board held a special meeting to consider the DPCC proposal and decided it was unreasonable to abandon a $22 firm offer in order to pursue a higher proposal that contained a series of conditions. Three days later, DPCC announced it was increasing its proposal to $24 per share. Clements told the press they could make a cash tender offer for Dr Pepper. This, of course, would be impossible for DPCC to finance without obtaining sufficient information on the company to satisfy the banks and investors, and Dr Pepper was prohibited by the agreement from encouraging other acquisition proposals and furnishing information to third parties except upon advice of counsel. Dr Pepper requested and obtained consent from Forstmann Little to furnish only information that had been given to Forstmann Little prior to signing the merger agreement. This led to an unusual and rather comic meeting between DPCC and its lenders with members of Dr Pepper management. DPCC would ask if Forstmann Little had asked a certain question, and management would huddle to decide whether or not the answer to the question had been supplied to Forstmann Little prior to signing the merger agreement.

Lazard had advised the Dr Pepper board to furnish information to DPCC only on a basis that did not jeopardize the Forstmann Little offer. Lazard noted that the present value of the difference between $24 and $22 per share would decrease quickly if the DPCC proposal took substantially longer to close. Lazard advised that the limited additional information that Forstmann Little received prior to signing the merger agreement was not DPCC's problem, but rather the problem might be a lack of confidence by lenders in DPCC's ability to put together a deal of this size.

Further damage to DPCC's efforts to put the financing together was the adoption of a resolution by the Dr Pepper Bottlers Association urging Dr Pepper to reject the DPCC proposal. Some 380 of the Dr Pepper bottlers were Coke and Pepsi bottlers, many of whom did not want the Dr Pepper brand falling in the hands of Ian Wilson. One of the largest Dr Pepper bottlers threatened to terminate its franchise if Dr Pepper were acquired by C&C. Clements also informed DPCC that it was very likely that many of Dr Pepper's key executives would leave if Dr Pepper were acquired by DPCC. Obtaining commitments from banks and investors in the face of opposition from both management and bottlers proved impossible. DPCC announced on January 26, 1984 that they had withdrawn their proposal. The press release blamed the lack of information that Dr Pepper supplied on its inability to finance the proposal. Since DPCC was given the same information that Forstmann Little was given when it successfully obtained bank loan commitments, the true reason for DPCC's failure lies elsewhere.

Was the $22 price fair to the stockholders? Both Lazard and Blythe Eastman Paine Webber, Inc. said yes, but the inevitable lawsuits said otherwise. The issue did not seem to be that the purchase price was 23.6 × 1983 earnings and 3.3 × book value, and that the stock closed on the New York Stock Exchange (NYSE) at $13\frac{5}{8}$ before the announcement that Dr Pepper had retained Lazard. The fact was that a deal was proposed and then opposed, raising the opportunity to earn legal fees. Ted Forstmann, himself an attorney and a person with a high sense of fairness, fought these lawsuits as a matter of principal. There were six shareholder lawsuits started with the public announcement of the deal. One was actually settled, benefiting the plaintiff's attorneys only when it became apparent that a jury trial was possible, but the other five were successfully defended.

The source and application of the funds financing the deal were as follows (footnotes are on page 86):

Sources of Funds

Borrowings from the banks	$490,000,000
Issuance of subordinated debentures	120,000,000
Issuance of equity interests in Parentco	27,837,500[1]
Dr Pepper surplus cash	10,000,000
	$647,837,500

Application of Funds

Payment of Dr Pepper common stock	$521,300,000
Payment in respect of Dr Pepper options	3,302,000
Payment of fees and estimated expenses	16,435,000[2]
Repayment of Dr Pepper long-term debt	105,000,000
Available for additional working capital	1,800,000
	$647,837,500

[1]Does not include $2,162,500 principal of notes from management used to finance their equity interest in Parentco.
[2]Fees included $5.6 million to Banks, $5.0 million to Forstmann Little, $2.5 million to Lazard, and $250,000 to Blythe. Another $3.1 million went for expenses related to the merger, most of which were legal fees.

The management group buying stock in the new company numbered the top 15 officers, except for Dick Armstrong, president. Armstrong had ample severance pay commitments in his employment contract, and he elected to take the money and move back to the New York area. The management group purchased 14.2 percent of Parentco's stock at the same price paid by other investors, but Dr Pepper lent each of them half of the purchase price at favorable interest rates. The largest management participant was Foots Clements, who bought 6.7 percent of the Parentco for $2.0 million. He received $3.5 million in the merger from the sale of his stock and options.

The breakdown of common stock ownership is as follows:

Holders	Percentage of Parentco Equity to be Purchased	Source of Funds		Aggregate Purchase Price
		Cash	Loans from Parentco	
Investors associated with or affiliated with Forstmann Little	49.5%	$15,035,000	$ 0	$15,035,000
MBO partnership[1]	35.0	10,640,000	0	10,640,000
Management group	14.2	2,162,500	2,162,500	4,325,000
Subtotal	98.7	27,837,500	2,162,000	30,000,000
Equity reserved for issuance after consummation of the merger	1.3	400,000	0	400,000
Total	100.0%	$28,237,000	$2,162,500	$30,400,000

[1]And certain other officers and employees of Dr Pepper who will purchase an equity interest in Parentco.

A superficial look at the transaction might lead to the conclusion that it is overleveraged and fraught with risk. Certainly the debt could not be serviced out of cash flow alone. A summary of Dr Pepper's operating results follows.

	Year Ended December 31,					Nine Months Ended September 30,	
	1978	1979	1980	1981	1982	1982	1983
Operating Results							
Net sales	$275,279	$297,131	$339,547	$370,613	$516,136	$392,432	$423,526
Operating profit	41,414	42,446	48,204	51,782	39,094	40,948	34,297
Net earnings	$23,866	$23,964	$26,933	$29,944	$12,474	$16,546	$13,987
Balance Sheet Data							
Working capital	$32,212	$35,741	$30,597	$35,289	$60,500	$71,575	$61,663
Property, plant and equipment, net	50,538	58,373	74,174	85,736	132,061	130,068	136,586
Total assets	$110,057	$126,258	$149,829	$168,319	$358,884	$340,094	$369,484
Capitalization:							
Total debt	$539	$949	$8,993	$10,723	$130,795	$123,917	$130,178
Deferred taxes and credits	3,572	4,757	5,661	6,356	8,374	9,659	9,388
Stockholders' equity	88,893	99,741	111,911	125,952	153,595	163,817	153,814
Total invested capital	$93,004	$105,447	$126,565	$143,031	$292,764	$297,393	$293,380

One quickly notices that the company could not even pay interest expenses on the $610 million of debt out of operating profits. Profits before interest expenses in 1983 amounted to an estimated $48 million compared to pro forma interest expenses based on a prime rate of 13 percent of $88.3 million. Also, principal repayments on the bank debt of $165 million were due March 31, 1985, only 13 months after the merger, with another $135 million due in 1986, $100 million due in 1987, and the remaining $90 million due in 1988.

Forstmann Little had, of course, planned to sell certain assets to rapidly repay the debt. Before the ink was dry on the merger, Canada Dry was sold to RJ Reynolds Industries for an announced $175 million. Dr Pepper had estimated that the market value of its 10 domestic bottling plants would range from $250 million to $325 million, and the value of major real properties at $106 million. Forstmann Little sold its bottlers and attendant real estate for over $275 million and reduced its bank debt to approximately $80 million 15 months after the deal closed. At that time, it retained real estate holdings worth in excess of $50 million.

The ability to repay the bank debt out of asset sales placed the risks of the deal in a different perspective. The deal moved from "how can they possibly service the debt" to "how can they possibly not succeed." Since there was little remaining debt to service, the transaction looked like a sure win proposition.

In February 1986, Forstmann Little agreed to sell the company to Coca-Cola for $470 million. These plans were dropped after the move was opposed by the Federal Trade Commission. In August 1986, Forstmann Little agreed to sell Dr Pepper to an investment group for $416 million. Investors included Shearson Lehman, Hicks & Haas, a Dallas private investment partnership, and certain senior officials of Dr Pepper. The sale required Forstmann Little to pay off the remaining debt of $155 million for a net to investors after expenses of about $260 million.

The internal rate of return for the MBO partnership was approximately 31 percent. The MBO partnership was the mezzanine investor, which included 10 corporate pension funds syndicated by Forstmann Little. Their investment included $120 million in subordinated debentures and $10.6 million in common stock equal to a 35 percent interest in the equity.

The $15 million common equity investment made by investors affiliated with Forstmann Little would be worth $128.7 million. This amounts to an excellent 8.3 × gain in less than three years. Management equals that return on their at risk investment but doubles it on their actual cash outlay because half of their investment was leveraged by a loan from Dr Pepper. Clements' share of the pie would be $17.0 million, not bad even by Texan standards.

Dr Pepper was a company whose public market value was substantially lower than the private market value of its assets. The sale of the low profit Canada Dry and bottling plant assets for over $450 million substantially exceeded the $325 million market value of the entire company prior to the announcement that the company was considering selling out. By structuring a deal to capitalize on the high private market value of its least productive assets, Forstmann Little was able to pay a premium for the stock and remain with the highly profitable core asset, worth $260 million net of debt less than three years after the buyout. This creative financing provided excellent returns for all of the investors, including an approximate $200 million increase in the value of Dr Pepper's stock in 1984.

WOODWARD & LOTHROP, INC.

The LBO of Woodward & Lothrop is a story of a company getting pushed into play and finding a white knight to rescue it. A group of old family stockholders believed the price the white knight offered was too low, and a terrific fight ensued. The question of value centered around the company's considerable real estate properties. Both parties hired experts whose opinions conflicted. The battle was fought with newspaper ads and proxy solicitations in both courtrooms and boardrooms. The outcome was generally favorable to all parties but especially to management. It is a clear case of how management took advantage of an unfriendly attempt to sell the company and emerged with a once-in-a-lifetime opportunity to make over $100 million.

The battle started when stockbroker Ron Baron managed to accumulate over 20 percent of Woodward & Lothrop stock for himself and his clients. When the fighting, suits, and countersuits ended, the LBO of Woodward & Lothrop, one of Washington's oldest retailers, left almost everyone a winner.

Armed with his stock leverage, Baron approached Ed Hoffman, Chairman of Woodward & Lothrop, to suggest that the company consider an LBO at $55–$60 per share. Baron's proposal would include employment contracts and equity interests in the new company for the company's officers. Baron had based his target price on a rough calculation of what the real estate and accounts receivable could be sold for, or used as collateral, for financing.

As it turned out, Baron's estimates were pretty much on the money. When Woodward & Lothrop refused to pursue his proposal, Baron tried to find another company to bid for the stock. He and his clients owned enough stock to tempt a potential corporate suitor, and they intended to push the company into selling out. The company was on notice that the battle was on.

Woodward & Lothrop began in 1890 when Samuel Woodward and Alvin Lothrop opened the Boston Store in downtown Washington, DC. It was noted for such innovations as allowing returns and marking all items with prices. The company changed its name to Woodward & Lothrop when it moved into a new, larger location in 1902. Woodward & Lothrop was family managed for more than 75 years and had begun to lose its competitive edge in the 1960s. Market share declined further in the 1970s when Neiman-Marcus, I. Magnin, and Bloomingdale's all invaded Washington. The greater Washington area, with its highly paid and stable government workforce, is considered perhaps the top department store market anywhere.

Ed Hoffman took over as CEO in 1969 and began extensive store reno-vations and redirection of merchandise strategy. By the early 1980s, Wood-ward & Lothrop had 17 stores in the Washington area, and sales topped $400 million in 1983. Woodward & Lothrop owned approximately 64 percent of its store space, compared with an average of 24 percent for eight other leading department store chains. The value of its real estate holdings had grown to exceed substantially the value of the company's stock in the marketplace. In fact, in the first quarter of 1983, the stock sold down to where the entire company had a stock market value of $84 million, compared to real estate values that were appraised a year later at $293 million. To Ron Baron and others, this meant the company was substantially underutilizing its assets.

When Baron began to hunt for a corporate raider, Ed Hoffman fought back. In February 1984, the company sued Baron, alleging that Baron and others were secretly assembling a control block of stock with the intent of selling this stock to the company or a third party at a substantial premium, without filing with the SEC a required Schedule 13D which would disclose that he and affiliates owned more than 5 percent of the common stock.

The same day Woodward & Lothrop sued Baron, company directors granted the top three officers "golden parachute" severance pay contracts, which en-titled them to severance benefits if, after a change of control, the company terminated the officers other than for cause, disability, or retirement. The sev-erance contracts included components for salary and bonus, and stock per-formance shares and stock options.

At $57\frac{5}{8} per share, the severance contracts would have amounted to a pay-ment of $9.1 million for the top three officers, of which Ed Hoffman's share was $4.3 million. For a company that earned only $15.5 million the prior year, these amounts appeared excessive to some of the old Woodward & Lothrop shareholders. The press had heavily criticized the $4 million golden parachute on which Bill Agee pulled the ripcord after Allied Corporation took over Ben-dix Corporation. However, Bendix had more than 10 × the sales of Wood-ward & Lothrop and more than 12 times the net worth.

Since the last grandson of the founders retired from the company in 1980, many family members disapproved of some of Hoffman's moves. They had openly opposed a stock option plan proposed at the 1981 stockholders' meet-ing and called to indicate their dislike of the golden parachutes granted by the board on February 17.

A. Alfred Taubman was one of those Baron contacted in his efforts to get Woodward & Lothrop to sell out. Taubman owned two shopping centers in which Woodward & Lothrop stores were located, and he had become friends with Ed Hoffman. Taubman was also an aggressive acquirer of other busi-nesses. The *Forbes Four Hundred Issue* in 1984 listed him this way:

A. ALFRED TAUBMAN

Real estate, art. Bloomfield Hills, Mich., Palm Beach, 60. Divorced, remar-ried (former Miss Israel); 3 children. Started construction firm on $5,000 loan

1951; built 200 gas stations for pal Max Fisher. Developed shopping centers, saw big money was in ownership; now controls 19 upscale shopping malls; noted for high revenues. Led Irvine Ranch buyout 1977; huge profit when resold to D. Bren. White knight for Sotheby's 1983 (bought 60 percent), Woodward & Lothrop department stores (D.C.) 1984. Also, 100 movie screens; 800 fast-food outlets (franchised); plus art; stocks. "The best opportunities are in improving what you already have." Net worth at least $600 million.

After Baron contacted him, Taubman indicated to Hoffman that he was interested in making a bid if Woodward & Lothrop was for sale. Hoffman wanted to get informal board approval to find a friendly buyer and received it after the board meeting on March 30. It seemed evident that Baron was not going to give up and that seeking a white knight was appropriate. Board members informally agreed, and Hoffman contacted Taubman. The push was on, and Hoffman and Taubman met the next day to talk strategy, price, and terms. They agreed to have their respective investment bankers, Oppenheimer for Taubman and Goldman, Sachs for the company, negotiate the deal.

In addition to Baron, three other potential bidders had approached the company; Wesray, a firm specializing in an LBO and headed by former Treasury Secretary William E. Simon; a group of local investors led by Washington lawyer Robert Linowes; and Carter Hawley Hale, a department store chain that Baron had contacted. Al Taubman, though, was management's choice, and Goldman, Sachs agreed to negotiate exclusively with Taubman in exchange for Taubman's pledge that his bid would be his top price. The company had no legal obligation to negotiate with others to seek a higher price.

A deal was struck, and a formal offer was made to the board on April 30. In attendance were nine attorneys, four of whom were outside directors; three from Skadden Arps, counsel for the company; the special counsel for Hoffman, Mulligan and Mullin; and the company's general counsel. The price offered was $59 per share or $220 million, backed by a bank commitment letter. The offer was contingent on the company's granting to Taubman an option on all the Woodward & Lothrop authorized but unissued stock, and the offer was good only until 5 P.M. that day. An option to buy stock at the offer price is not unusual, as it enables the offeror to recover his expenses and commitment fees if a higher offer is made. Taubman could then exercise his option at $59 per share and sell these shares at the higher offer price. Customarily, the option is for 10–15 percent of the outstanding stock, and a NYSE rule limits listed companies from granting options for more than 18 percent of the outstanding stock. However, Woodward & Lothrop traded over-the-counter and was not subject to the NYSE rules. The Taubman demand amounted to 32 percent of the stock after the exercise of the option.

Despite having no prior information on the buyout proposal, no real estate appraisals, and the unusually large option demand, the board agreed to sell this 94-year-old company after only 2 hours, 25 minutes of deliberation.

It takes two-thirds of the stock to vote approval of a merger in Washington, DC. Thus, giving Taubman an option on almost one-third of the stock, were he able to exercise the option and become a stockholder of record to vote on a competing proposal, gave him a virtual veto on any higher offers. The option was quite legal although highly unusual in amount, and altogether crucial in the outcome.

Goldman, Sachs told the board that it believed the $59 offer was in the upper range of fairness, based largely on financial comparisons with other retailers and retail acquisitions.

The board voted to accept the offer, but the fight was not over and neither was the shouting. The board scheduled the stockholder vote on July 31, and anyone owning the stock on June 21 would be allowed to vote. "This is a hell of an offer," the *Washington Post* quoted Ed Hoffman as saying. Not everyone agreed. Predictably, the old family shareholders were skeptical of the sudden turn of events and decided to meet to investigate the offer. They formed the shareholders protective committee. Its members, all from founding families of Sam Woodward and Alvin Lothrop, controlled 15.1 percent of Woodward & Lothrop stock. Two grandsons of the founders, A. Lothrop Luttrell, former chairman of the board, and Andrew Parker, former vice-chairman of the board, were directors of the company and supporters of Ed Hoffman. They were not invited to join the shareholders protective committee.

Key members of the committee sued the company, senior management, and Taubman on May 30, alleging that the director's fiduciary duties were breached by entering into the merger agreement and by awarding the very substantial golden parachute termination agreements.

The company countersued, charging the committee members with soliciting proxies without filing written proxy materials with the SEC, claiming that committee members made false and misleading statements to shareholders to obtain their proxies, and lastly, alleging that they filed a materially false and misleading Schedule 13D. The committee filed a counterclaim to the company's suit, and so the legal sparring continued.

The shareholders protective committee also hired six independent real estate appraisers, all located in the Washington, DC metropolitan area, to appraise Woodward & Lothrop's properties. The committee also retained Wheat, First Securities to render a fairness opinion when the appraisals were completed. These actions led to a mailing by the committee to all shareholders on July 12, soliciting their vote in opposition to the board of directors. The solicitation stated that Woodward & Lothrop's real estate, including equipment, was carried on the books at approximately $126 million and that its independent appraisers had appraised the fair market value of the real estate excluding equipment at approximately $293 million. The book value of the equipment was approximately $53 million, so the book value of the real estate alone was $72.3 million versus the appraised value of $293 million. The solicitation further pointed out that the lock-up option to purchase approximately 32 percent of Woodward & Lothrop shares granted to Taubman by the company effectively deterred other potential bidders from bidding for the company's stock. Moreover, they claimed that the financial benefits received by the top three executives were excessive.

The solicitation described in detail the appraisal method used in valuing each property and indicated that many of the appraisals used the income approach, which requires sales per square foot to calculate. The company refused appraisers' requests for the company's actual gross sales figures for each of its stores. Thus, the appraisers had to estimate sales per square foot and in some cases were wide of the mark.

The aggregate appraisal value for all of the company's real estate of $293 million, net of estimated taxes that would be due if the properties were sold, produced total net assets per share for Woodward & Lothrop of more than $76. Largely based on these appraised values, Wheat, First Securities advised the shareholders' protective committee that the $59 offer was unfair. Wheat's opinion letter dated July 3 stated,

> We have reviewed and analyzed current fair market value appraisals of Woodward's real estate holdings prepared at your request by independent real estate appraisers and we have considered the information respecting Woodward's real estate under the caption "Certain Projections of Future Operations and Other Information" in Woodward's Proxy Statement dated June 28, 1984. We have visited certain of Woodward's retail locations and service facilities, both independently and with certain of the appraisers retained by you, and we have discussed the appraisals with certain of such appraisers.

Goldman, Sachs used the normal valuation approach employed to value operating companies. This approach assumes that the primary value of real estate as an ongoing company is its ability to generate earnings in the company's operations. Using this approach, Goldman, Sachs concluded that $59 per share was fair to the shareholders.

The Goldman, Sachs opinion letter, dated June 28 or six days earlier, stated,

> We have not conducted any appraisal of the Company's real estate assets and we have been advised by the Company that no appraisals of the current market value of the majority of such assets exist. The company has not prepared or requested us to prepare a valuation of such real estate assets on a liquidation basis and the company has not requested us to analyze and we have not analyzed the company on such a basis.

The qualification that Goldman, Sachs made in its opinion regarding the valuation of the real estate on a liquidation basis rendered the opinion of questionable value. Goldman, Sachs' failure to consider the liquidation value of the real estate normally would have been rectified by a higher bid in a free market, but Taubman's option along with management's opposition inhibited other potential bidders.

In its opinion letter, Goldman, Sachs said they had been advised by the company that no appraisals existed, but the committee's appraisal did exist on the date of Goldman, Sachs' opinion letter and management should have known it. Management had refused to cooperate with the appraisers in their requests for actual and projected gross sales figures on a per square foot basis, physical condition information, property expense experience, taxes, lease terms, and other related data. Nevertheless, using reasonable estimates and assumptions, the appraisers believed they were able to obtain substantially all of the information they deemed necessary to make their appraisals.

In response to a demand filed in Superior Court by the shareholders protective committee that the board of directors invalidate the merger agreement, the board appointed a special committee composed of three nonmanagement directors to review and investigate demands. They were Judith R. Hope, attorney; Lloyd E. Elliott, president of George Washington University; and Walter E. Washington, attorney and former mayor of Washington, DC. The special committee hired two real estate appraisers and an investment banker to advise it. The special committee's real estate experts found that because the shareholders committee's appraisers lacked store-by-store gross sales data and information on taxes, maintenance charges, lease, and deed terms, the appraisers overestimated the income stream that the stores produced. It also concluded that the appraisers' estimate of the operating stores producing rental revenues of 4–5 percent in annual gross sales could not be supported, and that a rental rate of 3 percent of gross sales would have been more appropriate. Using the more conservative rental rate of 3 percent produced a substantially lower portfolio valuation and led the special committee to conclude that shareholders committee's appraised values were overstated by at least 30 percent.

All of the controversy over whether or not the real estate was worth $293 million could only have made the Manufacturers Hanover Trust happy for it was the lead bank in committing to a $284.5 million term loan facility to finance the buyout. The acquisition financing totaled approximately $305 million and was detailed this way:

Sources of Funds

Term loan facility and credit agreement	$284,500,000
Contributions from A. Alfred Taubman	20,000,000
Cash of the surviving corporation	288,000
	$304,788,000

Application of Funds

Payment for common stock	$227,479,000
Payment upon settlement of options	4,029,000
Payment upon redemption of preferred stock	1,253,000
Repayment of outstanding indebtedness	60,600,000
Fees and expenses	11,427,000
	$304,788,000

The senior debt to equity ratio of 14.2:1 was exceptionally high and made possible only by the high value of the real estate portfolio. A more typical financing structure would have contained a mezzanine level of subordinated debt of $30–40 million, and total subordinated debt and equity of $50 million. This would have reduced the senior debt to equity plus subordinated debt ratio of 5.1:1. To achieve a targeted internal rate of return of 25 percent annually, mezzanine investors would need to be allocated approximately one-third of the equity, assuming a 14 percent current yield and an exit P/E ratio in five years of 10 $\times$.

In addition to the term loan facility, the banks agreed to provide a $150 revolving line of credit, consisting of $25 million for working capital purposes and 85 percent of eligible accounts receivable not to exceed $125 million. The entire proceeds of the revolver secured by accounts receivable must be used to reduce the principal due on the term loan. The loan agreement also required that the first $150 million in loan repayments not come from accounts receivable financing or operating cash flow.

In recognition of the high leverage and availability of sale and leaseback of real estate, the bank required a rapid amortization of its debt. Based on a projected closing at the end of July 1984, $50 million was required 18 months later and another $50 million 12 months later. At the end of the fourth year, approximately $179 million of the $275 million debt was required to be repaid, and the entire debt was due in five and one half years. The company's projected internally generated cash flow fell far short of meeting the debt amortization schedule. Based on the company's projections of operating earnings, the cash buildup over the 1984–88 period, including the net proceeds of $25 million on the sale of the North Block real estate, fell more than $177 million short of meeting the debt repayment schedule, and thus required the company to sell and lease back much of its valuable real estate or to refinance the bank loan to meet its schedule of principal payments.

To further ensure a refinancing to meet debt payments, the bank required Taubman to be subject to an equity call if the first four principal repayments totaling $150 million were not met. If the principal amount of $50 million due January 31, 1986 was not repaid, Taubman would be subject to an equity call of up to a $40 million maximum. In addition, Taubman was required to personally guarantee interest obligations of up to $10 million.

Taubman agreed to the equity call and interest guarantee as a means of increasing his return on his investment. Whereas he was at risk for a total of $60 million, he only invested $20 million before the exercise of his stock option. He was able to retain all of the equity except the option he gave top management for 20 percent of the equity. Ed Hoffman was granted an option by Taubman to purchase 8 percent of the common stock for $2.0 million. David P. Mullen, president and CEO; and Robert J. Mulligan, vice-chairman and chief administrative officer, were each granted options on 6 percent of the company for $1.5 million. These options were exercisable over a 10-year period and vested at a rate of 20 percent each year. The total of the three options would require a $5 million equity contribution and would represent 20 percent of the total equity when added to Taubman's $20 million investment. Upon the exercise of the options, Hoffman, Mullen, and Mulligan would incur a tax liability on the difference between the option price and the fair market value of the common stock as determined by the board of directors. To enable the option holders to pay these taxes, which are subject to ordinary income tax rates, the company will pay the three option holders via a stock appreciation right, cash equal to the taxable gain on the options. If the top income tax bracket remained at 50 percent, half of the cash payment under the stock appreciation right would go to taxes due on the payment itself, and the remaining half would go to the payment on taxes due on the ordinary income gain on the options.

Taubman required that Hoffman, Mullen, and Mulligan be at risk for their share of the $50 million equity call and interest guarantees. They are obligated to pay in relation to the percentage of stock held directly if any of their options have been either exercised or vested. This requirement meant that the three top executives together must personally guarantee $2 million in interest payments and be subject to an equity call totaling $8 million if principal payments were not made over the next five years. Since interest payments could be made comfortably out of cash flow, and the first $150 million in principal payments could be generated from the sale and lease back of the retail stores, there appeared to be little risk that Taubman or top management would be required to make good on the $40 million equity call and interest guarantee.

Less than a year after the buyout, the company refinanced its bank debt and completely eliminated the equity call and interest guarantee. It sold $130 million, $14\frac{3}{4}$ percent 10-year subordinated notes in a registered public offering. Thus, whereas the common stock was privately held and not subject to reporting requirements under the Exchange Act, the subordinated notes were publicly held and the company agreed to furnish annual and quarterly financial statements. In addition to the subordinated notes, the company sold $132 million of fixed rate first mortgage notes and borrowed $36 million under a new revolving credit loan from banks to refinance substantially all of the remaining senior debt. Thus, the company borrowed against its real estate to repay its senior debt rather than sell it and lease it back. As a result, the company was not obligated to pay capital gains and recapture taxes on the real estate, and it retained the benefits in any future rise in their values.

Despite the fixed interest rates on the subordinated notes of $14\frac{3}{4}$ percent compared to an 11 percent floating rate ($9\frac{1}{2}$ percent prime plus $1\frac{1}{2}$ percent) at the time of the sale of the notes, the annual additional interest under the refinancing package amounted to only $3.0 million more than the floating rates actually experienced in the first quarter of 1985. Although the banks undoubtedly wanted to retain their high priced loans, Manufacturers Hanover received an arrangement and initiation fee of $5.75 million, topping Goldman, Sachs' fee of $1.5 million for representing the company, and Oppenheimer's fee of $2.2 million for representing Taubman.

When the shareholders protective committee on July 12 mailed its solicitation to the Woodward & Lothrop shareholders urging that they vote against the merger, all stockholders of record on June 21 were eligible to vote on the merger at the special stockholder meeting scheduled for July 31. This date passed, and Taubman did not exercise his option, which would have given him 32 percent of the voting shares. Thus, the committee, with its 15 percent of the votes, only needed to obtain another 19 percent of the votes to defeat the merger. Put another way, for the Taubman offer to gain acceptance, the company needed 79 percent of the remaining shares to vote in favor of the merger; not all of the remaining shares would be voted. At that time, however, no better offer was in sight.

As the vote neared, the company took out a full page ad in the *Washington Post,* declaring that the "dissident stockholders" had overstated Woodward & Lothrop's real estate by $117 million and that Goldman, Sachs had said the $59 per share was fair. The ad claimed that the stock option for the top three executives was necessary to obtain the financing of the merger. The following day, July 25, management and Ron Baron jointly announced that the company's suit against Baron would be dropped in return for his support of the Taubman bid.

On Wednesday, July 25, attorneys for the shareholders protective committee requested that, despite the fact that shareholders were deluged with material from both sides, the shareholders did not have accurate information from the company about the Taubman offer and the basis on which it was negotiated. The federal court agreed that proceeding with the vote would compel the shareholders "to make a vital investment decision based on incomplete and potentially misleading information." The court ordered postponing the shareholders' vote after a scheduled hearing on August 6. The shareholders protection committee wanted the vote delayed because it had finally found someone willing to make a higher bid. He was Monroe G. Milstein, president of Burlington Coat Factory Warehouse.

On July 26, Milstein made an acquisition offer to Woodward & Lothrop for $64 a share. The offer was conditioned on Woodward & Lothrop shareholders' rejection of the Taubman offer that was scheduled to be voted on by the shareholders five days later. It also conditioned that the option granted Taubman be terminated, that financing be completed on terms acceptable to Milstein, and that the company give him access to pertinent information that he would keep confidential. The shareholders committee agreed to give Milstein the first $1 per share over $59, and 50 percent of all over $65 per share on the 562,114 shares that the group owned if he would submit a proposal offer to buy Woodward & Lothrop.

The Milstein proposal indicated that he had hired Prudential-Bache Securities Inc. to help arrange financing for his proposal, and that they expected financing to be available if the Taubman offer was rejected.

The board had to take the Milstein proposed offer seriously if the financing was arranged, and the proposal became a firm offer. Milstein obtained bank commitments for his financing a few days later, and Taubman responded on August 8 by exercising his option on Woodward & Lothrop stock for $103.8 million, giving him approximately 32 percent of the total shares then outstanding. Since the court had ordered a postponement of the shareholder vote scheduled for July 31, the board set a new date of September 11 for the shareholder vote. This allowed Taubman another opportunity to exercise his option to vote his shares on the merger proposal. Greeted with this news, Milstein cut his offer to $62.40 per share in a letter to the special committee of the board delivered on August 14. It also stated that if the lock-up option recently exercised by Taubman was invalidated, the price would revert to $64 per share. The $62.40 per share offer was not an actual reduction in the money offer but a mathematical adjustment to the $64 per share offer in consideration of the new shares that Taubman had just acquired by the exercise of his option.

The special committee had several alternatives at this point. It could recommend that the board abrogate the Taubman offer and accept Milstein's offer. This action would leave Taubman with $6 million profit on his options. The committee could also decide to stand by the company's agreement with Taubman despite the lower price. Since Taubman controlled almost one-third of the company's stock, he had enough to vote down any other merger proposal under DC law. If Taubman voted against the Milstein offer after the company had abrogated the Taubman offer, the shareholders could be left without any offer, not even Taubman's $59 per share. The third option open to the special committee was to say that both offers were fair to the shareholders. Attorneys for the special committee, however, doubted that it would be legal under DC law to offer shareholders a choice and to permit them to vote on both offers at the special shareholders meeting, now scheduled for September 11. Since the last alternative might have been illegal, and since acceptance of the Milstein offer would likely be defeated and could result in no offer if Taubman refused to extend his offer due to expire on September 30, the special committee recommended and the board so voted that the company would stick by the Taubman agreement despite being $3.40 per share lower than the Milstein offer.

On the day of the shareholders' vote, both sides felt that the vote would be extremely close. The meeting opened in a hostile environment, with Hoffman defending the company's support of the Taubman offer and lawyers for the shareholders protection committee urging its defeat. The balloting was to close at 5:00 that afternoon. It was clear that the traders and arbitrageurs who had representatives at the meeting held enough stock to swing the vote for or against the Taubman proposal. This reality apparently pushed Taubman into negotiating a higher price, and the shareholders protection committee finally agreed to support the Taubman deal at $60.50 per share. The company would also agree to pay the Stockholders Committee $2.7 million to defray its considerable expenses. So the Taubman offer carried and a week later, the deal closed with everybody a winner, even Milstein. In addition to the $562,000 he received from the shareholders protection committee's stock, he apparently bought more than 3 percent of the stock in the open market, on which he made at least a $2 per share profit. With the obligation to Milstein, the shareholders protection committee members only netted 50 cents per share more than the original offer, even with the $2.7 million expense payment they obtained from the company covering legal fees, investment banking fees, appraisal fees, proxy solicitor fee, printing costs, and other expenses. Perhaps more important to committee members was the fact that they won a small victory of sorts by forcing the final purchase price up by $1.50 a share and leaving Hoffman somewhat bloodied. Many of the remaining shareholders enjoyed a rise in the stock from its low of 22\frac{1}{2}$ in April 1983 to 60\frac{1}{2}$ in September 1984, or a 2.7 times increase in a dull stock market.

What will Al Taubman's victory likely mean to him financially? If one applies a value formula of five times EBIT plus free cash less outstanding debt, the operating company would be worth approximately $280 million in 10 years. Reasonable people can and have differed over how much additional value to ascribe to the company's real estate. If the company rented all of its property and had no bargain leases, its value could be reasonably estimated using the above formula at $280 million in 10 years. Reducing the real estate values by 30 percent to reflect rents of 3 percent of gross sales and increasing this amount by the company's estimate of annual sales growth of 6.5 percent, produces real estate values in 10 years of $300 million, net of estimated capital gains taxes and ordinary income taxes on recapture. This is the amount of cash that the company could be expected to raise from the sale of its properties plus the refinancing of its bargain leases, without adversely affecting its operating cash flow. Adding this value to the value of the operating company produces a value of $580 million. On this basis, Taubman's 80 percent would be worth $464 million in 10 years on a cash investment of $20 million. He was at risk for $60 million for a year due to the equity call; however, this risk was removed by the subsequent public sale of subordinated notes. The equity call was in lieu of obtaining $40 million in mezzanine capital that would have required giving up perhaps one-third of the company for mezzanine investors to achieve a targeted internal rate of return of 25 percent. Thus, Taubman was able to increase his profit by $150 million by agreeing to the equity call and interest guarantee of $40 million but without increasing the size of his cash investment.

Management received an even better deal. It now gets to look at all the cards before making its bet. At the end of year five, management will be fully vested on its option to buy 20 percent of the company for $5 million, but it does not have to exercise this option for another five years. Initially, management was also fully obligated for 20 percent, or $10 million of the $50 million equity call, but the risk of having to fund this obligation was removed after one year. Since management received almost $9.2 million in the merger as a result of the sale and settlement of their shares and options, management should have sufficient personal assets to exercise its $5 million options 10 years later. The value of management's option at the end of 10 years should be $116 million. The company will also give management sufficient cash to pay the taxes due to the exercise of the options. Hoffman, Mullen, and Mulligan can thank Ron Baron for throwing them into the briar patch. They cashed in $9.2 million on the sale and are able to continue running Woodward & Lothrop without any harassment from stockholders. In 10 years, their $5 million option on Woodward & Lothrop stock could be worth $116 million.

KINCAID FURNITURE COMPANY, INC.

The Kincaid Furniture LBO was the best alternative management could find to provide the family stockholders with liquidity at the highest price attainable. Whereas the company desired to remain independent, it contacted a long-term suitor but found the price offered was too low. It explored going public but found the market would not value its earnings high enough. The LBO solution attained the highest price of the three alternatives, gained complete liquidity for the family's shares, and allowed the company to remain independent.

The company suffered through a recession following the buyout, but the sound structure of the financing enabled it to maintain substantial cash reserves and to remain profitable. When the earnings recovered, Kincaid seized the opportunity to go public in a hot new issue market. Amazingly, the public market valuation was over 3.5 × the private market valuation on the buyout. This clear example of how value was created by the LBO is the focal point of this case.

The Kincaid Furniture Company was founded in 1946 by Wade Kincaid in Hudson, North Carolina. Wade was 35 years old and a foreman at one of the Broyhill Furniture plants. He began by making cedar wardrobes at home at night and selling them off the back of his truck on weekends. He was approached by a Broyhill salesman who asked if he could make a bedroom suite that Broyhill had recently dropped from its line. Wade oversaw the production of the bedroom suite for Broyhill and figured he could make it for himself with a small amount of additional equipment. The Broyhill salesman then produced an order for 2000 of these suites and the Kincaid Furniture Company was launched in business.

Wade was aided in the start-up phase of the company by his father and was eventually joined by a brother, sister, brother-in-law, and three sons. The business grew slowly over the next 25 years until the early 1970s when it began to grow significantly in both sales and profits. By this time, the company was owned by 22 Kincaid family members who knew the company had grown to be a valuable asset but were unable to enjoy the benefits of their wealth. There was no market for the stock, and the company had never paid a dividend. At the gentle prodding of some of the family stockholders, Wade sought to provide a market for the stock in 1973 by taking the company public. However, before the registration statement was filed with the SEC, the market values of furniture stocks plunged in anticipation of the sharp recession in 1974 and 1975, which particularly affected the furniture industry. Kincaid's sales rose from $17.5 million in 1975 to $33.3 million by 1978. Earnings slumped to $250,000 in 1975 but rose to $1.6 million in 1978. Wade Kincaid again decided to provide liquidity for the family stockholders and reviewed his options. This time, the company was faced with the need for a major plant expansion, and again, a public offering seemed the logical solution. The public market values for furniture company equities, though, remained low, and Wade Kincaid sought other alternatives. Selling out to another furniture company was considered, but after conversations with potential buyers, it became clear that book value was the highest price any company was willing to offer. In December 1979, book value was $11.4 million, which was only 4.1 times 1979 earnings. Not only was this price unacceptably low, but Wade also preferred to have the company remain independent if possible. A number of his family members worked there, and he wanted to see two of his sons succeed him in running the company.

Wade then explored the LBO alternative and through an introduction by a local banker, negotiated the tentative sale with a New York investor group. As the New York group proceeded to arrange the financing, the necessary chemistry between the buyers and sellers was found to be lacking. At this time, Wade Kincaid was approached by an investment banker who recommended that he talk to Forstmann Little. Ted and Nick Forstmann and Brian Little had recently formed their company to specialize in LBOs and had raised equity funds for this purpose. Although the new firm had not yet negotiated a deal, the partners were quite experienced in investment banking. Nick Forstmann had experience in LBOs with KKR. This time, the chemistry between the Kincaids and Forstmann Little worked, and Wade elected to accept the Forstmann Little offer, which was slightly higher than the prior one. The price was 154 percent of book value, or 54 percent higher than could be obtained in a sale to another furniture company. The transaction closed on February 14, 1980.

The company's special niche in the furniture industry is the production of medium priced solid wood bedroom and dining room furniture in the American-Traditional style. The furniture is constructed with solid woods, principally cherry, oak, and pine, and does not contain any chipcore woods, plastic, or veneers. Solid wood furniture production requires special expertise in woodworking as well as wood selection, treatment, and processing. It is difficult to attain good quality at moderate price points. Kincaid has excellent production capability, largely attributable to its experienced, hard-working workforce. Kincaid typically maintained a substantial backlog of orders, which enabled it to benefit from long production runs and provided the employees with steady employment. This resulted in a low turnover of workforce when layoffs owing to slack times were commonplace in the furniture industry. These factors enabled the company to produce an outstanding value, which gained it market leadership in the medium priced solid wood sector of the industry. Kincaid held the biggest market share of this niche of the furniture industry.

The purchase price of $17.6 million cash was 7.9 × net income and 3.3 × operating income. This price was full compared to other furniture equities and provided total liquidity for the long-patient family stockholders. The family was able to continue to run the business as before, and management members purchased 15 percent of the stock in the new company. The Kincaids wanted to maintain a business as usual posture to the trade and local community, and few people outside the company knew that the buyout had occurred. When customers inquired, they were told that the company had undergone some financial restructuring involving the purchase of stock from some of the old family shareholders.

The source and applications of funds for the transaction were as follows:

Sources of Funds

Bank credit line	$ 2.0
Bank term loan	4.5
Senior notes-insurance companies	8.0
Senior subordinated notes-insurance companies	3.0
Common equity	3.3
	$20.8

Applications of Funds

Common stock purchase	$17.6
Repayment of debt	1.0
Reserved for new plant expenditures	1.6
Fees and expenses	.6
	$20.8

Manufacturers Hanover provided the bank financing, and Teachers Insurance and Allstate Insurance provided the longer term debt. At the time of the buyout, banks were less aggressive in LBO financing than in later years, and insurance companies were favored for the long-term debt portion of the financial package. The advantages of insurance company loans were that they were truly long-term, 15 years in the Kincaid financing, and they were at fixed interest rates. This was particularly appropriate for a company like Kincaid whose products were highly postponable, big tickets items largely bought on credit. High interest rates depressed housing activity and the demand for furniture, and made credit purchases substantially more expensive.

The timing of the Kincaid financing was fortunate as the prime had just begun its historic surge, which peaked at $21\frac{1}{2}$ percent. Kincaid's blended fixed interest rate was 11.7 percent on the insurance company notes, whereas the bank debt interest rate floated at $\frac{1}{2}$ percent over prime. High interest rates in 1980 caused the furniture business to become quite soft, and Kincaid's sales in the first year after the buyout were flat. Profit margins suffered, however, as the company was forced by competitive pressures to introduce lower priced suites with thinner profit margins. As a result, the company's net income dropped to $891,000 from $2.7 million, before nonrecurring charges related to the acquisition. Operating earnings dropped almost in half, and large interest expenses further depressed earnings. Had the interest rate on the insurance company loans floated at $1\frac{1}{2}$ percent over prime, the company would have suffered a loss before expense deductions related to the buyout. The company had a substantial financial cushion to weather this storm in that it secured a $1.6 million reserve to build a new plant. With sales flat and demand generally weak, the new capacity was not needed, and the financial cushion offered comfort until the recession ended.

The acquisition of long-term financing from insurance companies fixed at 11.7 percent appeared to be extremely favorable when the prime topped at 20 percent less than a year later. However, at the time the loans were committed, the deal looked favorable to the insurance companies. Interest coverage based on 1979 earnings was 3.01 ×, and the insurance companies acquired stock and warrants equal to 31 percent of the total equity. Management purchased 15 percent, and the remaining 54 percent was purchased by a Forstmann Little partnership.

The company's financial performance improved in fiscal 1982 as income from operations increased to $4.9 million versus $2.7 million in fiscal 1981 (50 weeks) on a sales increase of 28 percent. Fiscal 1983 showed further improvement with operating earnings rising to $6.0 million on a 13 percent sales gain. In 1983, the new issue market heated up, and furniture stocks made a rapid recovery from cyclically depressed levels. Taking advantage of this window of opportunity, Forstmann Little took Kincaid public in July 1983.

The remarkable thing about this event was the higher valuation of earnings the public afforded the company compared to its private market valuation almost four years earlier. The buyout was accomplished at 7.9 × earnings and 154 percent of book value. The company had explored the possibility of selling out or going public, and found that neither of these opportunities offered a price as high as the buyout price. Also, there were two buyout groups competing for the company, with Forstmann Little the high bidder. Thus, the valuation of 7.9 × earnings was the highest the private market was willing to pay in late 1979. The public market valuation of the new issue in July 1983 was 17.0 × earnings, a 115 percent increase over the private market valuation three and a half years earlier. The company's financial profile in 1979 compared to the trailing 12 months ended April 30, 1983 is as follows:

	Year Ended	
	December 1, 1979	April 30, 1983
Statement of Income Data	(000)	
Net sales	$35,938	$51,762
Income from operations	5,264	5,948
Net income	2,749	2,272
Earnings per share	1.06	0.85
Balance Sheet Data		
Working capital	8,375	8,535
Total assets	16,177	25,099
Long-term debt	1,000	11,410
Stockholders equity	11,441	8,532
Value of company on buyout	17.900	
Value of company on pre-offering		37.700

Comparison of the income statement and balance sheet data would not suggest that any increase in value in 1983 was justified over 1979. Sales had increased an average of 13.5 percent, but operating margins declined from 14.6 to 11.5 percent. This resulted in a modest average annual increase in operating earnings of 4.0 percent. As a result of substantially higher interest expenses of almost $1.6 million, 1983 net income declined to $2.3 million from $2.7 million in 1979. Long-term debt was $10.4 million higher and net worth $2.9 million lower in 1983 than in 1979. Using the same multiple of operating earnings as realized on the buyout and adding free cash and deducting debt would produce a private market value as of April 30, 1983 of $9.6 million. The pre-offering value of the IPO was $37.7 million, which represented a creation of value over the private market value of 3.9 ×.

It is difficult to find rational reasons for this huge step-up in value. The sponsorship by Lehman Brothers in a hot new issue market probably accounts for much of the higher value. The market multiple of other furniture stocks also contributed nicely. The public market generally values most cyclical businesses at a low multiple of peak earnings, anticipating a cyclical decline, and puts a high multiple on depressed earnings anticipating a cyclical recovery. The market multiple for furniture stocks followed this pattern in late 1982, putting a high multiple on cyclically depressed 1982 earnings. As earnings began to recover in 1983, the multiple on furniture stocks began to trend down. Kincaid caught the end of high furniture multiples with its IPO in July 1983. Lehman was able to apply the still high furniture multiple to Kincaid's earnings, which had already reflected most of their cyclical recovery. The company was halfway through the year, which proved to be the company's peak earnings year of the cycle.

Lehman sold the new issue at a premium to other furniture stocks. This aggressive pricing was based on the company's growth niche as indicated by its record and its backlog of $24.4 million compared to only $5.4 million a year earlier. The accountants assisted in the projection of a growth stock image. The earnings per share shown in the prospectus portrayed a strong growth record, despite much less rapid sales growth.

The company actually earned $1.06 per share in 1979 before the buyout. However, the accountants restated 1978 and 1979 as if the acquisition had occurred on the first day of fiscal year December 2, 1978. This caused the 1979 earnings of $1.06 per share to be restated to $0.05 per share and helped create the illusion that the company was growing very rapidly when in fact it was recovering nicely from a recession. The declining interest expenses resulting from lower interest rates and debt repayment only added leverage to the rapid recovery in earnings. As a result, Lehman was able to price the stock at 17 × trailing earnings compared to the furniture stock multiple of approximately 15 ×. The multiple of Kincaid's estimated earnings of $1.10 per share for the then current fiscal year was 13.2 times. Actual earnings came in at $1.05 per share and declined to $0.68 per share in fiscal 1985. The stock tumbled from a high of 16\frac{1}{4}$ following the offering but continued to hold a premium market multiple compared to the furniture group.

Forstmann Little's equity partnership, Kincaid Partners, was the beneficiary of the higher public market valuation and leverage in the capital structure, obtaining a 9.5 × return on a third of their investment in three and a half years. They had established their position at $1.42 per share, and the $14.50 issue price netted them $13.50 per share after the underwriters' discount. The remaining two-thirds of their initial investment was sold on a secondary stock offering in June 1986 at a net price of $13.83 per share. The insurance company's internal rate of return over the six-year period spanning 1980–86 was 28.9 percent. Management's 15 percent ownership was valued on the IPO at over $6.5 million or over 10 × their investment. Management sold no shares on the IPO and in an unusual display of confidence, actually bought stock on the offering.

Clearly the buyout served the Kincaids well. The family stockholders received their desired liquidity at a good price, and the company remained independent under family management. As a result of the public offering, the company was also able to partially unleverage its balance sheet and secure funds needed to build a new plant and grow in the future.

	Predecessor Company		Kincaid Furniture Company				
	Fiscal Year Ended		Fiscal Year Ended			Three Months ended	
	December 2 1978	December 1 1979	January 31 1981	January 30 1982	January 29 1983	May 1 1982	April 30 1983
Earnings per share	(0.02)	0.05	0.17	0.57	0.83	0.21	0.23

| | Predecessor Company | | Kincaid Furniture Company, Inc. | | | | |
| | Fiscal Year Ended | | Fiscal Year Ended | | | | |
	December 2, 1978 (52 Weeks)	December 1, 1979 (52 Weeks)	January 31, 1981 (50 Weeks)	January 30, 1982 (52 Weeks)	January 29, 1983 (52 Weeks)	January 28, 1984 (Unaudited)	February 2, 1985 (Unaudited)
State of Income Data							
Net sales	$33,291	$35,938	$34,388	$43,972	$49,532	$55,320	$60,772
Income from operations	4,755	5,264	2,661	4,943	5,962	7,189	5,389
Interest expense	180	171	2,126	2,173	1,841	1,370	
Pretax income	4,529	5,241	648	2,834	4,198	6,195	
Provision for taxes	2,205	2,492	229	1,385	2,000	2,892	
Net income (loss)	2,324	2,749	418	1,449	2,198	3,303	2,312
Earnings per share			0.17	0.57	0.83	1.05	0.68
	December 2, 1978	December 1, 1979	January 31, 1981	January 30, 1982	January 29, 1983	January 29, 1984 (Unaudited)	February 2, 1985
Balance Sheet Data							
Working capital	$ 5,955	$ 8,375	$ 8,782	$ 9,031	$ 9,006	$ 9,673	$13,375
Total assets	13,339	16,177	23,675	23,993	25,008	29,872	40,996
Long-term debt (less current portion)	1,182	1,000	15,226	13,749	12,402	7,143	13,618
Stockholders' equity	8,691	11,441	4,264	5,713	7,911	16,970	19,282

GUILFORD INDUSTRIES, INC.

The LBO of Guilford Industries is the story of a New England textile company which, after years of struggling as a producer of traditional apparel fabrics, found a growing niche business in the mid-70s and began to prosper. In 1981, its president decided to sell out to diversify his family's assets but desired to keep the company independent. Complicating the sale was the necessity of financing a 3-year capital spending program which exceeded in amount the asking price for the company. The LBO was skillfully structured to accommodate the heavy capital requirements but to do so required substantial initial equity. By LBO standards, leverage was a very low 2.6 to 1 but the investors' returns proved substantial due to the leveraging of rapidly growing earnings. The company is a good example of how the financial restructuring and a successful equity offering created wealth.

Guilford Industries for many years was a sleepy supplier of traditional woven fabrics to the apparel trade. Located in Guilford, Maine, the company in 1974 smartly recognized that fabrics used in the office interiors industry offered good growth potential. The growing popularity of the open plan office systems, which are panel-enclosed work stations, uses fabric to cover the panels to enhance the acoustical properties and aesthetics of the system. The company's sales of panel fabric grew from less than $1.0 million in 1975 to approximately $55 million in 1984. This was aided greatly by the growth in the market from an estimated $65 million in 1975 to over $1.0 billion in 1984. By completely dedicating itself to designing and producing panel fabrics, the company established itself as the leading supplier of these fabrics. It also produces upholstery fabrics, wall coverings, ceiling fabrics, and window treatments to coordinate with its panel fabrics in the open plan office, but these account for only 5 percent of sales.

In late 1981, H. King Cummings, age 65, founder and CEO of Guilford, decided to sell the company for estate planning purposes. The company was largely owned by the Cummings family and was especially illiquid because its resources had been largely dedicated to finance its growth. The company was enjoying a record year with sales reaching $40.8 million, up 38 percent over the prior year. Net income had jumped from $534,000 in fiscal 1980, to $1,888,000 in fiscal 1981, and surged again to $2,452,000 in fiscal 1982. The company's book value had almost doubled from fiscal 1980 to $8,567,000 in fiscal 1982, but long-term debt soared from $1,210,000 to $5,057,000.

King Cummings had three main objectives in the sale of the company. He wanted the company to remain independent, he wanted family members not involved in the business to receive all cash, and he wanted assurances that the company would have available capital to finance anticipated continued growth. In fact, the three-year capital expenditure program begun in 1981 called for spending $15.5 million, or almost twice the company's net worth. Cummings set the price for the company at $13 million of which $10 million had to be cash. Although this price represented a very reasonable 5.3 times earnings and 2.4 times EBIT, the price was 152 percent of book value and textile companies rarely trade higher than book value.

Considering the need for $10 million cash to purchase the stock, to refinance most of the $5.0 million long-term debt, and to provide assurances of the availability of over $15 million of capital to finance projected growth, Guilford did not appear a prime candidate for an LBO. Usually companies that are growing faster than their internally generated funds can support either go public or sell out to a larger company with substantial capital resources. However, at this time, the public market was not a viable alternative because of poor market conditions for new issues and it was Guilford's wish to remain independent. This left the door open for the Thomas H. Lee Company, buyout specialists, founded by Tom Lee in 1974. Lee won out over many other bidders and investment bankers because Lee was able to meet the financial challenge and satisfy the company's desire to remain independent. To meet the financial requirements, the deal was structured with very low leverage by LBO standards. It is, of course, more difficult to get a high return on investment with a large equity base. However, the success of the Guilford buyout proved that a low leveraged buyout of a growth company can be highly rewarding to the investors.

The Lee Company did an extraordinarily thorough job of investigation of Guilford and its business prospects, expending over 100 worker days in the process. They spent countless hours with Guilford's management, met with key customers, attended trade shows, and interviewed textile industry consultants concerning production alternatives. Through this careful analysis, the Lee people became convinced of the strengths of the company's business and of its future growth potential. The process also provided the company with a better understanding of its customers' needs and resulted in an improved capital spending plan.

The Lee Company was also careful in selecting other investors. It discussed the deal with several large insurance companies, a group of smaller insurance companies, and various venture capital companies before selecting PruCapital as a coinvestor and lender. PruCapital, a part of the Prudential Insurance Company of America, has long been active in the field of LBOs. The Lee Company was so confident of the merits of the deal that it provided $12.5 million of its own funds to close the deal while awaiting the PruCapital investment approval process.

The $13.0 million purchase price was financed as follows:

Source of Funds

Floating rate senior notes (PruCapital)	$ 3,500,000
Seller's 10% senior notes	1,000,000
18% subordinated notes (PruCapital)	4,000,000
Seller's 12% subordinated notes	2,000,000
Lee Co. equity	2,500,000
PruCapital equity	2,500,000
Total	$15,500,000

Use of Funds

Guilford stock purchased for cash	$10,000,000
Guilford stock purchased for notes	3,000,000
Excess cash for growth	2,500,000
Total	$15,500,000

Of Guilford's $5.0 million of pre-acquisition term debt, $2.0 million consisted of low rate industrial revenue bonds. The remaining $3.0 million secured debt was replaced with unsecured debt, and a $7.5 million line of credit with three commercial banks was obtained. Thus, the $7.5 million line of credit and the $2.5 million excess cash provided $10 million of the three-year $15.5 million capital expenditure plan.

The company's operation performance since the acquisition has been excellent, as shown on the opposite page.

Whereas sales declined 8 percent in the first year following the buyout as a result of generally poor economic conditions, the company experienced strong profit improvement. The profit improvement was attributed to good cost controls and manufacturing efficiencies, resulting from the capital equipment program. Operating profit margins rose to 20.4 percent from 13.2 percent in the prior year. Despite a more than doubling in interest expense, net income rose from $2.5 million to $2.9 million. The company was also able to take advantage of an improved new issue market and went public in February 1983 at $6.25 per share (adjusted). This price was approximately 6 × what the investors had paid for the stock only 10 months earlier. The value of the company on the offering was $29.4 million. The stock proved to be the best performing IPO in 1983, selling at issue price at 10.7 × trailing 12 months earnings and enjoying a more than doubling of earnings per share in fiscal 1984. Sales increased 53 percent in fiscal 1984 and operating profit margins increased to 26.1 percent, an almost unheard of margin for a textile company. Net income rose from $2.9 million to $7.0 million, and earnings increased from $0.67 to $1.32 per share.

The IPO provided the company with $4.3 million in new capital and allowed the selling shareholders to sell $1.6 million of their stock. The stock never traded below issue price of $6¼ (adjusted for a 100 percent stock dividend), and the price more than doubled by late summer. Taking advantage of this price increase, Guilford made a second offering in August 1983 at $14.50 per share, this time raising $5.1 million for the company. Selling shareholders netted $7.6 million from the deal. The value of the company on the second offering had risen to $74 million. The two stock deals enabled the company to raise a total of $9.4 million in new equity in the two years following the buyout. Capital expenditures over this period amounted to $14.1 million, and additional working capital needs required another $7.2 million in capital. Internally generated cash flow over these two years equaled $14.6 million, and

Guilford Industries, Inc.
Consolidated Statements of Income
(In thousands)

| | Predecessor Guilford | | | Guilford Industries, Inc. | |
| | Fiscal Years Ended | | | Fiscal Year Ended | |
	February 3, 1980 (53 weeks)	February 1, 1981 (52 weeks)	January 31, 1982 (52 weeks)	April 3, 1983 (53 weeks)	April 1, 1984
Net sales	$24,093	$29,621	$40,836	$37,571	$57,648
Cost of sales	20,452	22,428	31,568	25,332	37,079
Gross profit	3,641	7,193	9,268	12,239	20,569
Selling, general, and administrative expenses	2,330	3,121	3,860	4,571	5,538
Operating profit	1,311	4,072	5,408	7,668	15,031
Other income, net	(23)	20	44	161	224
Interest expense	380	528	1,115	2,354	1,940
Income before income taxes	908	3,564	4,337	5,475	13,315
Income taxes	374	1,676	1,885	2,584	6,305
Net income	$ 534	$ 1,888	$ 2,452	$ 2,891	$ 7,010
Average number of shares outstanding				4,312,000	5,319,000
Earnings per common and common equivalent share				$ 0.67	$ 1.32

the company issued an industrial revenue bond of $3.0 million to acquire an integrated textile mill. The balance sheets on the opposite page show the results of these dramatic changes in the company's financial condition.

Before the buyout, the company's long-term debt amounted to 37 percent of total capitalization, and cash and marketable securities totaled only $550,000. Two years later, long-term debt stood at 38 percent of total capitalization, and cash and marketable securities amounted to $7.8 million. Net worth was $8.6 million before the buyout, dipped to $5.0 million on the buyout, but rose to $24.3 million two years later. Earnings rose from $2.4 million in the year prior to the buyout to $7.0 million two years later. The company had a third stock offering in June 1984, with all the shares sold by shareholders and none by the company. The stock sold at 12.1 × trailing 12 months' earnings; the value of the company at that time was $84.5 million.

In short, the company greatly increased its production capability and earning power, and strengthened its balance sheet two years after the buyout. All of this financial improvement occurred on top of having to finance the $13.0 million buyout. These outstanding results were produced in a very favorable market for panel fabrics but were also aided greatly by good financial structuring, which provided the resources and incentives for management to do the job.

The return on investment for all participants has been excellent. PruCapital invested $10 million of which $2.5 million was for the purchase of common stock. Following the third registered sale of stock, PruCapital had received in aggregate $9.5 million from stock sales and held 550,000 shares as of June 1984. If it sells these shares by the end of fiscal 1987 for an average price of $20 per share and if its $7.5 million in loans to the company are prepaid in June 1985 as seems likely, PruCapital's internal rate of return on investment will be 48 percent. This return greatly exceeds its target return of 700 basis points over the rate of a straight loan or a similar credit.

King Cummings also has profited handsomely from the structure of the buyout. Cummings received $2,088,733 cash and $3,000,000 in sellers notes for his share of the $13 million purchase price of the buyout. He alone accepted notes as part payment for his stock. He insisted that a $1.0 million 5-year note be secured with a letter of credit but agreed to subordinate a $2.0 million 8-year note to all of PruCapital's $7.5 million loans. For this agreement, Cummings was granted a warrant to purchase 300,000 shares of stock at $2.50 per share. He has already sold 100,000 shares obtained via the warrant, netting $1,265,000. If he sells the remaining shares under the 10-year warrant for an average price of $20 per share, he will net another $3.5 million on his shares. If he is able to sell all of his remaining stock at $20 per share, he will have netted approximately $7,257,000 to add to the $5,088,733 he received from the sale of the predecessor company.

Tom Lee took perhaps the biggest risk. He personally loaned the company $11.0 million to close the deal in April 1982 while PruCapital was obtaining approvals for their participation. When PruCapital invested its $10 million in

Guilford Industries, Inc.
Consolidated Balance Sheets
(000's omitted)

	Predecessor Guilford			Guilford Industries, Inc.	
	Fiscal Years Ended			Fiscal Year Ended	
	February 3, 1980	February 1, 1981	January 31, 1982	April 3, 1983	April 1, 1984
Assets					
Current assets					
Cash and cash items	$ 356	$ 563	$ 550	$5,286	$1,878
Marketable securities					5,883
Accounts and notes receivable (net)	77	319	496	3,469	6,342
Due from factor	172	628	1,510		
Funds in trust for capital expenditures					
Inventories	3,842	5,185	6,327	4,970	7,873
Prepaid expenses and total current assets	62	85	203	101	157
Total current assets	4,509	6,780	9,086	13,826	22,133
Property, plant and equipment	3,482	4,167	8,562	14,770	24,162
Other assets	244	518	795	1,663	2,556
Total assets	$8,236	$11,454	$18,443	$30,259	$48,851
Liabilities and stockholders' equity					
Current liabilities	$2,197	$3,464	$4,334	$4,893	$8,356
Long-term senior debt	1,210	1,358	5,057	6,265	8,597
Long-term subordinated debt				5,800	5,600
Obligations under capital leases				380	138
Long-term income tax liability				293	212
Deferred income taxes	492	474	485	421	1,653
Total liabilities	3,889	5,285	9,876	18,052	24,556
Stockholders' equity	4,337	6,169	8,567	12,207	24,295
	$8,236	$11,454	$18,443	$30,259	$48,851

113

May 1982, the company repaid Tom Lee $10 million, and he contributed the $1.0 million balance of the loan to the capital of the company. Tom Lee and his partners invested approximately $2.2 million for 55 percent of the common stock of the company. The Lee partners have sold stock on each of the three public offerings and, with other sales, netted approximately $9.0 million as of June 1984. If their remaining shares are sold for $20 per share, the Lee group will have gotten $38.5 million for their $2.2 million investment. Of this amount, Tom Lee will receive about $28.6 million. Assuming the sale of the remaining unsold shares takes place in fiscal 1987, the Lee group will have enjoyed an internal rate of return of 110 percent.

These excellent returns were obtained with low initial leverage at the outset. Of the $10 million cash portion of the purchase price, $5.0 million was equity, the largest percentage of equity of any of the cases examined in this book.

Since the $5.0 million initial equity was approximately 2.0 × the prior years earnings, and if those earnings were adjusted to reflect the added interest expenses as a result of the buyout, the initial equity was established at approximately 2.8 × earnings. The market capitalized earnings at the time of the third public offering at 12.1 ×, thereby providing P/E expansion leverage of 4.3 ×. The company's ability to almost triple earnings in two years provided a further leveraging of the initial equity and enabled the market value of the initial equity to rise 12.8 × in a little over two years. It was Tom Lee's recognition of the company's potential operating leverage, which could cause a good return on investment to become an excellent return, that enabled him to commit to a low leveraged initial capital structure. The company's earnings gains are not a recovery from depressed levels but real gains on top of record results. That the company has emerged far larger, stronger, and better capitalized than before the buyout is a testament to excellent vision, good financial structuring, and management prowess.

PERFECT FIT, INC.

Perfect Fit is a company that underwent two LBOs and one public offering in a four-and-a-half-year period. The company itself was unexciting and slow growing but had established a niche in a competitively stable market. The initial LBO provided the original family owners with the highest, most liquid price available for their stock. The public offering followed, which supplied new capital to strengthen its balance sheet. The second LBO took out the public shareholders at a modest profit, enabling management to emerge as owners of 86 percent of the stock. This case demonstrates that an LBO is an excellent solution to the problems of maximizing stock values for the original shareholders. It also shows how ownership can be effectively transferred to management at an affordable cost.

Perfect Fit's first LBO took place in May 1981 in order to effect an orderly change in ownership at a price reflecting the true value of the company. The company's chairman, Ephraim Block, had turned 65 and sought a way to provide liquidity to his family's 60 percent ownership of the company. Whereas a public market existed for the company, then known as PRF Corporation, it had traded at very low prices compared to its respectable record of increasing sales and earnings. From fiscal 1976 to fiscal 1980, sales rose from $30.5 million to $53.5 million, and net income increased steadily from $2.0 million to $4.2 million. Its balance sheet was strong, showing $4.9 million in cash and only $371,000 in debt, most of which was a $7\frac{1}{2}$ percent industrial revenue bond. During the three years prior to the initial buyout, the stock averaged selling at 4.0 × earnings. At the time the initial buyout was announced, the stock was selling at $2\frac{7}{8}$, or only 3.3 × the latest 12 months earnings of $0.87 per share. As the board of directors explained, there was "a lack of an appropriate correlation between market prices for common stock and PRF's pattern of increasing sales and net profits."

The low valuation of the common stock was partly due to the company's unexciting business. It made a line of mattress coverings, bedspreads and comforters, draperies, sheets, and pillowcases sold under the nationally advertised brand names of Bed Sack, Bedjacket, and Custom Corner. The Block family control of the common stock also tended to retard interest in the stock. Of the stock's total market value (of $12.8 million) at the time of the buyout, only an estimated $4.3 million worth was held by some 3100 public stockholders, or an average of $1,400 per stockholder. The public was a minority shareholder in a business largely family owned and operated. A third reason for the low market valuation was damage to its reputation resulting from action taken in 1975 to reclassify its stock and rescind a stock purchase agreement. At that time, the company had two classes of stock, with the insiders holding Class A stock and the public holding common stock. The company wanted to reclassify the Class A and convert it into common stock. The company also sought to rescind an agreement that obligated the company to purchase, and the estate of Ephraim Block to sell upon his death, 80 percent of his stock for a price not to exceed $1.5 million. The SEC sued the company in 1976, charging that the company had violated SEC proxy rule and the Securities Exchange Act of 1934. The company agreed to a consent decree, which provided a procedure for accomplishing the conversion of the Class A stock and a rescission of the purchase and sale agreement on Ephraim Block's stock.

In 1978, after the board formally rescinded the agreement to purchase stock from Block's estate, the company was hit with two stockholder suits attempting to reverse the consent decree. The agreement to buy 80 percent of Block's stock from his estate for $1.5 million effectively valued the company at $4.4 million. Since the company had earned $3.5 million in fiscal 1978, the year prior to the suit, the company was worth considerably more than $4.4 million. Thus, the suit contested the rescission of the agreement because the agreement was quite favorable to the shareholders. These law suits only added to a number of legal actions in which the company was involved. In 1977, the company sued Congoleum Corporation for misrepresentations and omissions in connection with the company's purchase of Congoleum's Edison division. Congoleum countersued, and the action dragged on for four years in court.

The company also brought action against Acme Company, charging infringement on its Bed Sack trademark. Acme countersued for defamation and, incredibly, a jury found against the company and awarded Acme damages of $7.5 million. The court, however, set aside the award, and after a retrial, the jury absolved the company of any liability.

Considering the company's legal entanglements and the impression that the company was run primarily for the benefit of the Block family interests, it is little wonder that the public showed a lack of interest in the stock. Ephraim Block, having reached retirement age in 1981, decided that only by selling out could he realize the true value for his 42.3 percent interest in the company. He had attempted to sell to Riegal Textile Corporation in October 1979 for $27 million, but the deal was called off by mutual consent. Block then was introduced to Charterhouse and in June 1980 agreed to sell them the company for $30.5 million. The deal was structured as a sale of assets because the purchaser did not wish to assume some of the company's liabilities, principally the potential liabilities and expenses in connection with ongoing shareholders' lawsuit.

The sale of assets obligated the company to pay taxes for depreciation recapture and investment tax credit recapture, and expenses in connection with the transaction and pending litigation. The company adopted a plan of liquidation in conformity with Section 337 of the Internal Revenue Code, which required that all assets of the company be distributed to shareholders within a year. Since it was unlikely that all of the pending litigation and tax matters would be settled within one year, a liquidity trust was established to receive its remaining assets before the 1-year period expired. This trust then held these assets for the pro rata benefit of the company's shareholders. The initial liquidating distribution to shareholders was approximately $25.6 million, or $5.75 per share. The remaining $4.9 million, or $1.10 per share, was withheld to pay taxes and to cover expenses and liabilities of winding up operations and litigation. The stockholders' suit was settled in 1984 at no material loss to PRF Corporation.

The asset purchase was made by a company organized for that purpose. It was financed as follows:

Secured bank loan	$20.5
Subordinated debentures	1.0
Series A preferred stock	2.0
Common stock	7.0
	$30.5

The new owners of the common stock were as follows:

Lintor B. V., a Netherlands corp. wholly-owned by	
The Charterhouse Group Ltd.	49.0%
Individual executive employees of	
The Charterhouse Group Ltd.	7.4
Electra Investment Trust Ltd.	26.0
Joseph Vitale, Perfect Fit president	10.0
Others	7.6
	100.0%

At the time of the buyout, Charterhouse was a holding company for investments made in over 100 operating companies. It was based in the United Kingdom, and its stock is traded on the London Stock Exchange. Electra Investment Trust is a publicly owned U.K. investment trust.

Joe Vitale, Perfect Fit's president, acquired his 10 percent interest in the new company for a total of $10, whereas the other shareholders paid $7.0 million for the remaining 90 percent interest. Electra bought an additional $2.0 million in preferred stock. Joe Vitale's stock purchase was subject to forfeiture if he left the company. If he left immediately, the company would be required to pay him $250,000 for his freed shares, with the remaining being forfeited. If he remained for a year and nine months, he would receive $400,000 or book value, whichever was higher, for his freed shares, and his remaining shares would be forfeited. If he remained another year, the minimum amount he would receive for his shares would be $700,000. Although this arrangement provided Vitale with a substantial ownership position at essentially no cost, it caused him to incur a substantial tax liability. As a result, over the first three years following the buyout, the company made Vitale a $440,000 noninterest bearing loan to enable him to pay his income tax liability.

In May 1984, three years after the buyout, the company made a $5.0 million public offering, underwritten by Drexel Burnham, Oppenheimer and Company, and Charterhouse Japhet. Approximately $4.0 million of the net proceeds went to the company to reduce debt by $3.7 million. As a result of the offering, total debt was reduced to $5.7 million, and shareholders' equity increased to $19.0 million. The offering was 400,000 units priced at $12.50 per unit, consisting of 400,000 shares, and 400,000 warrants to purchase common stock at $14.50 per share for two years and $16.00 per share thereafter. The stock traded as high as $10\frac{3}{4}$ following separation of the warrant three months after the offering and slumped to a low of $6 in late 1984. Following the public offering, earnings in the first quarter of fiscal 1984 were almost triple the prior year, but the second and third quarters showed a drop in earnings, causing disappointment in the stock. For the year, earnings were $1.49 per share versus $1.34 for 1983 but slumped to $0.31 per share versus $0.36 per share in the first quarter of 1985.

On May 11, 1985, the company announced that it had received a merger proposal from a company formed by Joe Vitale and other members of management, which would pay $12.25 per share for the publicly traded shares and $11.2539 for each restricted share. Warrant holders would receive $0.75 for each warrant. The day prior to the announcement, the stock bid at $10 and the warrants at $⅝ bid. The second LBO closed on November 8, 1985, capping a rather eventful four and a half years.

Typically, after going private on an LBO, a company increases its profit margins by eliminating the costs of being publicly owned and becoming more cost conscious in order to pay down the large debt load. The before and after profit picture for the company is as follows:

	Predecessor Company		Successor Company			
		9 Months	8 Months			
	1979	1980	1981	1982	1983	1984
Sales	100.0%	100.0%	100.0%	100.0%	100.0%	100.0%
Gross profits	30.1	27.9	29.5[1]	30.3	29.6	28.5
Sales, general, and administrative	14.8	15.1	14.9[1,2]	17.1[2]	17.2	16.5[2]
EBIT	15.2	12.8	14.6[1,2]	13.2[2]	12.4[2]	12.0[2]

[1]Adjusted for inventory write–down resulting from the asset write-up on the merger.
[2]Adjusted for fees and amortization of unearned compensation resulting from the buyout.

The expected higher profitability was evident in the period immediately following the buyout, as EBIT improved to 14.6 percent from 12.8 percent. However, in the four years following the buyout, EBIT as percentage of sales never reached the level achieved in 1979, two years prior to the buyout.

The fees referred to in the second footnote of the above table were for consulting and financial advisory fees paid to some of the new stockholders. These fees were as follows:

	1981	1982	1983	1984
Charterhouse Group	$280,000	$550,000	$575,000	$407,000
Electra Investment Trust	63,000			
Arthur M. Spiro[1]	70,000	116,000	57,000	
	$413,000	$666,000	$632,000	$407,000

[1]The fees and salary were combined. Mr. Spiro served as vice chairman of the company following the buyout until he resigned in June 1983.

These fees are very large for a company of this size. The fees paid to Charterhouse and Electra are in part a means of getting an annual return on their common stock investment and of having these payments deductible from pre-tax income by the company. Any dividends paid on the common stock would not have been deductible for tax purposes. If $100,000 of the fees paid to Charterhouse were earned as claimed annually and if the balance of the fees represented a return on their equity investment, the effective average yield on Charterhouse's investment of $3,815,000 was 9.5 percent.

Analysis of Value

From 1979 to the 12 months ended June 1985, sales grew 39 percent, aided by acquisitions. Earnings before interest and taxes, however, declined from $8.6 million in 1979 to $8.3 million in the 12 months ended June 1985. The value of these earnings has remained relatively stable, following the big initial jump in 1981 due to the first LBO. Prior to the announcement of the first LBO, the market valued EBIT at slightly over 1 ×, or $8.6 million. This value jumped to $26.3 million on the initial LBO as shown in the table below:

	Value of Company		
	On Initial LBO	Pre-Public Offering	On Second LBO
	May 1981	May 8, 1984	November 8, 1985
Value of earnings	$26.3	$34.5	$32.5
Add free cash	4.6	2.2	5.0
Less debt	.4	9.5	7.0
Value of equity	$30.5	$27.2	$30.5
EBIT	7.6	7.9	8.6
Earnings value to EBIT	3.48x	4.36x	3.76x

The value of the equity is the value of earnings, plus free cash, less debt. On both LBOs, separated by four and a half years and a public offering, the value was the same at $30.5 million. The value of the equity dipped to $27.2 prior to the IPO because of a decline in free cash and an increase in debt. Earnings actually were valued 31 percent higher on the public offering than on the initial LBO, which partially offset the decline in cash and increase in debt. The above table presents a picture of relatively stable values; however, the debt to equity ratios have experienced wide swings over this period as shown below.

Over the 5-year period ending November 1985, the ownership has changed radically three times. First, the Block family and the public shareholders sold to Charterhouse and affiliated investors, which, after sharing the ownership with the public, sold out to the management group on the second LBO.

Charterhouse's investment in the initial LBO of $3.8 million was worth $13.9 million when it sold on the second LBO four and a half years later.

Debt to Equity Analysis
(Millions)

	Prior To First LBO November 1, 1980	On Initial LBO May 1980	Prior To Public Offering December 31, 1983	Post Public Offering May 8, 1984	Prior To Second LBO June 29, 1985	Second LBO November 8, 1985
Debt						
Term¹	0.4	$17.6	$8.5	$5.7	$3.4	$17.4
Factored accts. rec.						10.0
Industrial rev.					3.7	3.7
Subordinated		1.0	1.0			2.0
Total debt	$.4	$18.6	$9.5	$5.7	$7.1	$33.1
Net worth	23.2	9.0	14.9	19.0	25.1	4.5
Debt to equity ratio	1:54	2.1:1	1:1.6	1:3.3	1:3.5	7.4:1

¹Includes current maturities.

Charterhouse also received consulting fees of almost $2.1 million during this period. Adding its consulting fees, the Charterhouse's internal rate of return was 36.8 percent. Electra's investment of $5.0 million was a combination of $2.0 million common stock, $2.0 million preferred stock, and $1.0 million in a subordinated note, repaid with the proceeds of the IPO. Electra's internal rate of return on its total investment was 27.1 percent.

Joe Vitale got the best deal of all. For $10, he bought 250,000 shares of stock on the initial LBO, worth $2.8 million on the second LBO. This cheap stock arrangement did cause him to pay substantial taxes, due as his shares were released from installment forfeitures. The company loaned Vitale $440,000, interest-free, to pay these taxes. The Vitale family took their 8.7 percent ownership, and with the addition of $673,294 cash, purchased 64.7 percent of the fully diluted equity of the company on the second LBO. The ownership of the company on the second LBO is as follows:

	Shares of Stock Exchanged	Cash	Percentage Ownership
Joe Vitale	250,000	$ 14,167	59.4
Vitale family	6,400	644,933	5.3
Other management (15 people)	25,722	659,127	14.5
Chemical Equity, Inc. and Bankers Trust New York Corp.		2,000,000	20.8
Total	282,122	$3,332,421	100.0%

Assuming the stock will again be worth $30.5 million in five years, the Vitale family interest will be worth $19 million. Of this amount, Joe Vitale's $18.1 million share was purchased without any meaningful equity investment. To purchase his 59 percent ownership on the second LBO, he exchanged his 250,000 shares plus $14,167 in cash.

In summary, Joe Vitale completely bootstrapped his ownership position, from a modest optionholder worth $45,000 on the initial buyout to the position of 59 percent controlling stockholder, which should be worth over $18 million in five years. This is an excellent example of how an LBO is an effective solution to the problems of realizing full value for the original shareholders and transferring ownership to management.

METROMEDIA

The catalyst for the Metromedia LBO was management's desire to buy out the public shareholders. The top four officers succeeded in increasing their ownership from 29.2 percent to 81.5 percent, and top management was also able to cash in their stock and options, net of reinvestment, for over $120 million.

This LBO was the first large deal to give the public stockholders substantial amounts of discount debentures as part of the purchase price. To accommodate cash flow, the debentures paid no interest for five years and therefore, were originally issued at a discount of approximately two-thirds of their face value. The initial market value of the discount debentures provided over 20 percent of the value of the total purchase price.

Metromedia refinanced its bank debt with junk bonds five months after the LBO. It then agreed to sell its businesses for almost three times the total value of the LBO. These moves demonstrate the financial flexibility of a highly leveraged company no longer required by public ownership to play the reported earnings game.

The Metromedia story could have been written by Horatio Alger. When John Kluge became chairman of the board and president in 1959, he was 44. The 4-year old company consisted of three television stations, one radio station, and an outdoor advertising company.

In 1983, Metromedia owned and operated seven television stations in major U.S. markets; seven AM and six FM radio stations, virtually all in major U.S. cities; five radio paging companies; a Texas-based regional long distance telephone service; and the Harlem Globetrotters and the Ice Capades.

On the balance sheet, Metromedia looked like anything but an ideal LBO candidate when a proposal was put together in the fall of 1983. The eventual buyout in June 1984 was so multilayered that it set a record for both size and complexity. The fees were big, too. However, the company's aggressive management engineered the sale of its core businesses and all investors received big payoffs in approximately two years.

Kluge was born in Germany in the midst of World War I in 1915, and he moved with his parents to Detroit when he was 8 years old. A high-achieving student, Kluge entered Columbia University on an honors scholarship and graduated in 1937. Four years after joining a Detroit paper-converting business, he was vice president and part owner.

When World War II broke out in 1941, he enlisted in the U.S. Army, rising quickly to the rank of captain, attached to military intelligence. After the war, he sold his interest in the paper company and moved to Washington. There, he cofounded radio station WGAY and launched his legendary career in broadcasting.

Sixteen years later, he was running Metromedia.

Metromedia began as the DuMont Broadcasting Corporation, which took over the broadcasting division of Alan B. DuMont Laboratories in 1955. DuMont began operations with two television stations—WITG in Washington, DC, and WNEW-TV in New York City. The company grossed only $5.6 million that first year and was unprofitable. DuMont added New York radio station WNEW in 1957.

Kluge's aggressive management pushed growth through acquisition. In 1960, the company purchased Foster & Kleiser, now the nation's largest outdoor advertising company. DuMont changed its name to Metromedia in 1961 and added ABC-TV affiliate KMBC-TV in Kansas City. In 1963, Metromedia bought television station KTTV and radio stations KLAC (AM) and KMET (FM) in Los Angeles. It further diversified by acquiring the Ice Capades.

Metromedia introduced the concept of two-way radio in 1965 and in 1966 began coproducing television shows, including the award-winning National Geographic Society specials and *The Undersea World of Jacques Cousteau*. The company built new videotape production facilities in Hollywood in 1968 and purchased two television stations in major markets in 1972—WTCN-TV in Minneapolis-St. Paul and Cincinnati's WXIX-TV.

The company expanded further into family entertainment in 1976 with the purchase of the Harlem Globetrotters. It added KRIV-TV and KRLD (AM) in Houston in 1978. In 1982, the company reached its limit of seven television stations with the acquisition of Boston's WCVB-TV.

Metromedia upgraded to larger markets in 1983, acquiring KNBN-TV in Dallas and WFLD-TV in Chicago, selling WTCN-TV in Minneapolis-St. Paul to make room for Chicago and WXIX-TV in Cincinnati to make room for Dallas. Metromedia thus was represented in 7 of the nation's 10 largest broadcast markets, including the top 3. All of its stations were independents except for the ABC affiliate in Boston. Stations in Chicago, Dallas, and Houston are UHF; the remainder are VHF.

An independent station generally pays higher program costs and achieves lower ratings than does a network-affiliated station. However, Metromedia held an advantage over other independents because it produced some of its own programs and could attract other leading television producers by enabling the programs to be aired in 7 of the top 10 markets.

Metromedia owned and operated seven AM and six FM radio stations, virtually all in major U.S. cities. The company entered the telecommunications business in late 1982 with the acquisition of five radio paging companies. Three more paging companies were acquired in 1984, and the company acquired a Texas-based regional long distance telephone service in 1983.

Foster & Kleiser, the company's outdoor advertising business, maintained about 45,000 displays in 19 metropolitan regions. Metromedia sold the outdoor advertising displays along with related site leases and working capital assets to Outdoor Advertising Associates, a Metromedia-created organization, for $485 million in 1982. Outdoor Advertising Associates was a limited partnership whose corporate general partner was owned by Metromedia. The general partner operated the business for a management fee and reimbursement of expenses. Bear, Stearns sold Outdoor Advertising Associates to investors in limited partner interests. Capitalization was $350 million bank borrowings, $70 million in a seller's note, and $65 million partnership capital. Changes in tax laws in 1982 allowed faster tax write-offs of the displays. That and the deductibility of interest on heavy indebtedness augmented the investor returns.

For Metromedia, the sale of its outdoor ad display to Outdoor Advertising Associates was an excellent way to raise $415 million in cash and $70 million in notes. This unexciting, nongrowing business was sold for 22.8 times earnings. The partnership, in fact, became a minor cause celebre because it was one of the largest partnerships formed as a tax shelter created by the resale of existing property.

Metromedia also sold and leased back certain real estate assets for $129 million in 1983. To shelter earnings from taxes, the company acquired tax leases for $123 million in 1981, resulting in tax savings through 1983 of $191 million, with an estimated $100 million tax savings being carried forward. Excess cash was used to make acquisitions and repurchase Metromedia stock in the open market. From 1980 to 1982, Metromedia repurchased more than 18 million shares for approximately $390 million.

Metromedia was hardly an ideal candidate for a $1.48 billion LBO from a balance sheet point of view. The April 1, 1984 balance sheet showed little cash and working capital of only $12.4 million. Net worth was $198.1 million. Long-term debt more than tripled that at $657.9 million. Even adding back deferred income taxes of $146.3 million to net worth brought the total to $344.4 million, only 52 percent of long-term debt. Worse, if intangible assets of $613.2 million are deducted, tangible net worth was a deficit of $415.1 million.

However, broadcasting properties are worth far more than their book values, and they are highly marketable. Here is what happened.

Bill Thompson of Boston Ventures Management approached Kluge in August 1983 about the possibility of an LBO. Thompson had taken over the special-industries lending unit of the Bank of Boston made famous by the late Serge Semenenko, a Russian-born Harvard M.B.A. who extended loans to movie studios, loans that many banks shunned. Thompson retained much of Semenenko's influence in Hollywood and expanded special-industries into cable television and venture capital. After Thompson left the Bank of Boston in 1983 to set up his own venture capital operation, he kept his contacts with John Kluge. Kluge said no to Thompson's overtures in August 1983 but met again with Thompson that November.

Metromedia announced on December 6, 1983 that Kluge and Boston Ventures had submitted a proposal calling for Metromedia stockholders to receive $30 per share in cash and $22.50 principal amount in so-called discount debentures. The stock closed the day before at $24.50 on the NYSE. The proposal specified that the management group would own 81.5 percent of the new company after full dilution. The management group was Kluge; Robert Bennett, senior vice president of broadcasting and production; George Duncan, senior vice president of telecommunications; and Stuart Subotnick, Senior Vice president of finance and administration.

Metromedia's board appointed a special committee, consisting of directors who were not company officers and not involved in the buyout proposal, to advise the board on what action to take. The committee engaged Lehman and Bear, Stearns as financial advisers and recommended that Metromedia retain Skadden, Arps as legal counsel. The committee especially needed a professional opinion on the value of those discount debentures. These unusual securities pay no interest for five years, then pay 16 percent for the remaining nine years of life.

Lehman and Bear, Stearns each advised the committee at a January 31, 1984 meeting that the proposal was fair from a financial point of view. Both Lehman and Bear, Stearns expected the discount debentures to trade in a range of $440–470 for each $1,000 debenture. (At the close of the transaction, the debentures were trading on a when-issued basis at $339, putting their value at $7.63 per $22.50 principal amount offered per share. This put the total value of the offer at $37.63 per share.)

The buyout or merger agreement was signed following that meeting.

Nine separate class action suits against Metromedia challenged the proposal shortly after it was announced. Lawyers often urge that shareholders bring such actions in hopes of settling the suits before the buyout closes. The nine suits were joined and settled in March 1984, giving the shareholders a painless warrant worth perhaps $0.39 per share and requiring Metromedia to pay a $0.19 quarterly dividend before the merger. Metromedia would also pay $900,000 in fees to the lawyers initiating the action, possibly the motivating factor behind the suits in the first place.

The special committee agreed to the settlement terms, and following the April 30, 1984 meeting, signed a restated merger agreement.

Acquisition Corporation, the acquiring company, agreed to use its best efforts to obtain equity and debt funds totaling $1.43 billion. Since the proposal was subject to obtaining the financing, it had not been elevated to the status of a firm offer. To do that would require payment of commitment fees, but it also would permit the offeror to make demands, such as the granting of warrants to purchase stock at the offer price to protect himself against financial loss if he is outbid. Kluge and his management team were so in command of the board that the board agreed to go forward on a proposal rather than a firm offer.

The proposed financing was structured as shown below.

Sources of Funds

Bank loans	$1,139.2
Discount debentures	184.1
Equity investment by the institutional investor	125.0
Cash investment by the management group ($18.6 million less $6.6 million to be loaned to the Management Group)	12.0
Equity investment by the partnership	10.0
	$1,470.3

Uses of Funds

Payment of $30 per share to holders of Metromedia Common stock (other than 4.5 million shares owned by Mr. Kluge)	$ 724.3
Discount debentures	184.1
Repayment of term debt	489.7
Payments for options	42.2
Estimated costs and fees	30.0
	$1,470.3

Manufacturers Hanover Trust Company structured the revolving credit loan facility, which allows for borrowings up to $1.3 billion at any one time. The revolving credit commitment has this rapid amortization schedule:

	Reduced To (Millions)	Approximate Interest Rate[1]
Initial commitment	$1300	$1\frac{1}{2}$%above MHTC rate
June 30, 1985	1100	$1\frac{1}{4}$% above MHTC rate
December 31, 1987	850	$\frac{1}{2}$-1% above
December 31, 1989	550	$\frac{1}{2}$ to the MHTC rate
December 31, 1990	365	MHTC rate
December 31, 1991	180	MHTC rate

[1]An additional standby fee of $\frac{1}{2}$% was also placed on the unused portion of the revolving loan.

Prudential invested $125 million in redeemable preferred stock and warrants for the equity portion of the financing. An equity investment partnership committed for $10 million nonvoting common stock and management put in the balance of the equity. Kluge made a tax-free swap of 4.5 million shares of Metromedia common stock, plus $9.6 million cash for 75.5 percent of Acquisition Corporation after dilution. The stock Kluge contributed was worth approximately $169 million based on the value of the offer but was booked at its book value on the new balance sheet. The common stock entry on the new balance sheet is $50.4 million, which includes Kluge's 4.5 million shares and $28.6 million in cash purchases by management. Acquisition Corporation initially believed it had sufficient equity with cash and market value of Kluge's stock equaling about $200 million. When it realized Kluge's stock would be booked at cost, however, it hastily arranged Prudential's $125 million preferred stock investment.

Prudential's $125 million investment had warrants to purchase 15.5 percent of the common stock, and the nonvoting common investors' $10 million investment amounts to 3 percent of the common.

Prudential's redeemable preferred stock had a dividend rate of 10 percent, rising to 15 percent for each quarter if it is in arrears. Metromedia had the right at any time to issue 14 percent junior subordinated debentures in exchange for the preferred. This feature allowed the company to switch from dividends paid with aftertax dollars to interest paid with pretax dollars. Since the company did not anticipate paying any taxes for several years because of tax leases, higher deductions afforded by asset write-ups, and the amortization of the original issue discount on the discount debentures, this exchange was unlikely to occur for several years. The value of the warrants was based on a formula that is essentially 10 × operating cash flow, plus free cash, less debt. There was also an agreed minimum value that valued the warrants at $130 million after the fourth anniversary of the buyout, rising annually by $30 million to $280 million following the ninth year. In each of the fourth through eighth years following the date of the buyout, the company had the right to call up to one-third of the warrants at the higher of the value formula or the minimum value.

The investment of $10 million in Class A nonvoting common by the Boston Ventures-sponsored partnership gave the partnership a 3 percent interest after dilution of the warrants. After seven years, the partnership had a put, and the company had a call on at least 20 percent of these shares. The purchase price is based on a formula similar to the one used to value the warrants.

Metromedia's 6000 common stockholders received $22.50 face amount of discount debentures, which were listed on the American Stock Exchange shortly after the buyout.

Holding the discount debentures has a serious disadvantage for the taxpaying stockholder. The original issue discount—the difference between the debentures' face value and their initial trading value—constitutes ordinary income for tax purposes. The holder of a $1,000 discount debenture must attribute to his ordinary income the amount of the discount (approximately $660) spread over five years, despite having not received any interest income during that period. As a result, many taxpaying holders have sold these debentures to tax-free accounts. These debentures traded at 33–35 percent of their face value during the first six months of trading even though both Lehman and Bear, Stearns predicted that they would go for 44–47 percent.

Stockholders also received warrant debentures that were created to provide some small value to settle the class action suit before the buyout. In the buyout offer, each share received one-half of warrant to purchase warrant debentures. One whole warrant entitled the holder to buy $25 principal amount of the warrant debentures at 95 percent of their face value. The value of the one-half warrant at the time of the buyout was $0.39.

Fees totaling $29.9 million were standard for the size of the deal. Most of that went to Manufacturers Hanover, which received fees of $14.5 million. Boston Ventures received $4 million for assembling the deal. Lehman and Bear, Stearns, received $4.7 million and $2.5 million, respectively. The legal fees amounted to $3.4 million and were well-earned except perhaps the $900,000 that went to plaintiff's attorneys in the class action suits.

The expected returns for the investors were originally based on the following projection of operating cash flows:

Operating Cash Flows[1]
Actual—1983
Projected—1984-1990
(Dollars in millions)

	1983	1984	1985	1986	1987	1988	1989	1990
Broadcasting								
Television	109.5	136.0	125.4	151.3	180.9	218.8	250.3	286.4
Radio	17.2	22.3	28.0	34.3	42.0	50.8	58.0	66.2
Total	126.7	158.3	153.4	185.6	222.9	269.6	308.3	352.6
Telecommunications								
Paging	16.1	40.0	50.8	63.2	78.6	97.9	111.1	125.7
Long distance service	5.3	15.6	16.9	21.0	26.3	33.9	38.8	44.4
Cellular	(.1)	(3.9)	4.4	18.6	32.4	51.3	59.0	67.9
Total	21.3	51.7	72.1	102.8	137.3	183.1	208.9	238.0
Outdoor Advertising								
Management	10.6	12.4	16.2	20.5	25.2	29.0	33.4	38.2
Entertainment								
Film production and syndication	(0.6)	4.0	9.9	11.9	14.1	17.9	20.4	23.3
Touring shows and skating rinks	4.4	4.8	4.5	4.7	4.8	5.9	6.6	7.3
Total	3.8	8.8	14.4	16.6	18.9	23.8	27.0	30.6
Corporate	(14.0)	(27.0)	(30.8)	(33.8)	(34.5)	(35.6)	(41.0)	(47.3)
Total	148.4	204.2	225.3	291.9	369.8	469.9	536.6	612.1

[1]Operating income plus depreciation and amortization of intangibles after corporate eliminations.

These projections are instructive for several reasons. First, since television and radio broadcasting properties generally sold in 1983 for 10 times cash flow, Metromedia's broadcasting properties were perhaps worth $1.27 billion at the end of 1983. This compares to the bank loan funding of the buyout of $1.14 billion and total loan commitment of $1.3 billion. In addition, the telecommunications and entertainment businesses could bring more than $500 million if sold.

Company officers believed they would need to dispose of assets, producing aftertax proceeds of at least $300 million, to meet a net worth requirement of a credit agreement with the banks and a prepayment of $200 million by June 1985. Company management assumed that one or two television stations would be sold to a limited partnership, with Metromedia retaining control as general partner. Accordingly, operations yielding the $300 million after taxes were eliminated from the projections in 1985, except for fees assumed to be received by the general partners of 5 percent of revenues.

However, the company did not want to sell broadcasting properties to meet the bank's credit agreement. Any sale of these assets would have resulted in significant tax liabilities, and an outright sale would have reduced the audience coverage of its television stations as a group, thus making it more difficult for the remaining stations to attract new programming. The company consulted with several investment banking firms and commercial banks and decided to restructure the company and its debt with the use of high yield securities, or junk bonds.

Drexel Burnham, the undisputed leader in junk bond financing, structured a dazzling array of debentures and managed the public offering of these debentures. As a result of this financing, the company raised $1,268 million, repaid the bank debt in full, and eliminated the need to sell broadcasting properties.

The offering included zero coupon senior notes and adjustable rate participating subordinated debentures. Whereas the effective average interest rate on the new securities was 15.4 percent compared to the rate at that time of 14.9 percent on the bank borrowings, the effective cash interest rate on the new debt was 10.3 percent resulting in lower cash interest expense of over $50 million per year until 1989. This is because the zero coupon debentures required no cash interest, and the adjustable rate debentures paid lower cash interest in the early years. Also, another cash savings of $290 million will be achieved because of the rescheduling of principal payments.

Metromedia was betting heavily on substantial improvement in the profitability of the telecommunications and entertainment businesses to meet its earnings projections. Cash flow for telecommunications was expected to rise from $21.3 million in 1983 to $238 million in 1990, an elevenfold increase. Much of that was based on the predicted success of cellular radio and the growth in paging. Entertainment cash flow was projected to grow from $3.8 million to $30.8 million over this period. Television cash flow was projected to grow at an annual rate of 21.9 percent after 1984, a big year because of the elections and Olympics. Cash flow projections for the company's non-broadcasting properties appeared optimistic, but its assumption that television property could be sold at 10 times operating cash flow proved very conservative.

In a bombshell announcement in the spring of 1985, Kluge agreed to sell the company's core business, its seven television stations, for $2.0 billion. The buyer was Rupert Murdock, Australian newspaper scion, who wanted to add television broadcasting properties to his communications empire. The purchase price was 14.7 × projected 1984 operating cash flows. This was $640 million more than a price based on the more conventional standard of 10 × operating cash flow.

Here is a pioneer in the broadcasting business, acclaimed by his peers as innovative, a man who built his broadcasting company by skillfully buying radio and television stations first in smaller markets, then making them more profitable, and finally trading up to larger markets. Here is a man who has a reputation for not overpaying and who probably knows better than anyone the true value of his television properties, selling out completely to an individual with no experience in television broadcasting. As one analyst put it, "Kluge's never done a dumb deal." Kluge did not have to sell because he had taken care of his near-term financial needs with the junk bond financing. One can quickly conclude who got the best end of that deal.

The sale of the television properties was part of a plan adopted in February 1986 to completely liquidate Metromedia. By electing a plan of liquidation, the company had 12 months to sell or transfer all assets to a newly formed partnership, thereby avoiding capital gains taxes at the corporate level.

The sale of the television properties provided Metromedia with $544 million in cash and the buyer assumed all of the publicly held junk bonds that had a value at maturity of $1,920 million and a net value less discount of $1,374 million at year-end 1985.

In March 1986, Metromedia and Outdoor Advertising Associates, L.P., a limited partnership that owned Metromedia's Foster & Kleiser outdoor advertising division, sold its business to Patrick Media Group for $710 million. The sale provided $559 million to the limited partners who had purchased these assets for $485 million in 1982, and $81 million in cash and $70 million stated value of Patrick Media's preferred stock to Metromedia.

In mid-1985, Metromedia sold the Harlem Globetrotters and Ice Capades to International Broadcasting Corporation for $30 million. This sale was followed by the sale of nine of its radio stations and Texas State Networks for $285 million to an investor group headed by Carl C. Brazell, President of Metromedia Radio, and Morgan Stanley & Company.

In July 1986, Metromedia agreed to sell its cellular telephone and paging business for $1.65 billion to Southwestern Bell. Metromedia had projected at the time of the LBO that this business would have operating income of $81.8 million, but actual results of its telecommunications business showed a loss of $8.8 million in 1985. Metromedia's cellular and paging business was the largest in the United States, but most analysts agreed that Metromedia got the better end of the deal.

Assets remaining following the announced sales included Network I, a Florida based long distance telephone service company and an 80 percent interest in Fugazy Express, a franchiser of minilimousines and provider of helicopter service. These assets have a total value estimated at $35 million.

The grand total of the value of Metromedia's assets sold was approximately $4.1 billion. Including assets retained, the total is approximately $4.15 billion. This compares with the value of the common stock on the LBO of $1.08 billion. Including the repayment of debt and expenses, the LBO financing totaled $1.47 billion.

What has the liquidation of Metromedia meant for the investors? After closing on the sale of the television properties for $2.0 billion, Metromedia repurchased all the shares and warrants held by Prudential, Boston Ventures, and two former executives. Prudential received $214.2 in cash for its $125 million investment, an internal rate of return of approximately 35 percent for its investment held less than two years. Boston Ventures' $10 million investment was repurchased for $21.5 million for an internal rate of return of approximately 47 percent.

The stock interest of Robert M. Bennett and George H. Duncan, senior vice presidents, Broadcasting and Production and Telecommunications, respectively, was repurchased when the television properties were sold. Each received $11 million for his $3.0 million investment, of which $1.6 million was loaned them interest free by Metromedia. These loans were exchanged for notes due without interest in February 1993. In addition, Bennett's and Duncan's employment agreements providing annual salaries of $675,000 ending in 1994 were terminated and replaced with consulting agreements providing annual consulting fees of $1.0 million ending March 1993.

Following the repurchase of stock and warrants, only John Kluge and Stuart Subotnick remained as shareholders, holding 97.4 percent and 2.6 percent, respectively. Adjusting the 1985 balance sheet for all of the transactions involving the sale of businesses and the repurchase of stock left the net value of Metromedia before taxes of approximately $1.68 billion. Subotnick's share equals approximately $43 million, a handsome return on his $3.0 million investment. Kluge's interest is valued at approximately $1.64 billion, but he had the most at risk. He bought his stock interest with stock and cash worth almost $180 million. He also received $19.6 million for his stock options and sold in the open market his remaining 2.71 million shares before the buyout for an estimated $100 million. He, too, received an interest-free loan of $1.8 million from the company and raised his annual compensation to $1.5 million.

Kluge's interest in the company of $1.64 billion equates to $364 per share on his 4.5 million shares he owned when the buyout closed. The stock was selling at $24.50 when the announcement was made, giving him appreciation in his stock of 14.9 ×.

This LBO has proved to be a fabulous deal for all concerned. The shareholders saw a more than 50 percent increase in the price of their stock. The banks, investment bankers, and lawyers earned substantial fees. Although the banks were repaid in only five months, they earned high interest rates and good fees on the loans. The outside investors netted outstanding returns. Two members of the management group made 3.7 × their investment and Subotnick's return before taxes exceeds 14 ×.

John Kluge, before his 72nd birthday, had assets worth over $1.8 billion. That made him one of the four richest people in the United States. The majority of the 400 richest people, according to *Forbes* magazine, attained that status through inherited wealth. Kluge reached it "the old-fashioned way. He earned it."

MULTIMEDIA, INC.

The Multimedia deal was initiated by management and the founding families who controlled over 40 percent of the stock. The sharply increased private market values of television, radio broadcasters, and cable television companies were not fully reflected in the public market values of the parent companies such as Multimedia. Metromedia and Wometco, companies similar to Multimedia, took advantage of this disparity in values and went private via LBO transactions. The success of these deals alerted other potential bidders to the underlying values, and when management and the founding families of Multimedia put the company in play, three other bidders entered the picture.

In the face of bids at higher prices, management and the founding families switched to a proposal whereby all shareholders could elect to cash out completely or retain from 79 to 88 percent of their ownership in the restructured company. This unusual feature clouded the valuation comparisons with other offers and enabled the board, with the blessing of fairness from its financial advisor, to put the proposal to a successful shareholders' vote.

The recapitalization merger will never become popular with the likes of KKR and Forstmann Little because it substantially dilutes the new equity. Up to 80 percent of the new stock is acquired by old shareholders and management, leaving only 20 percent of the equity for new shareholders. In the typical KKR and Forstmann Little deals, these percentages are reversed, with no more than 20 percent of the equity going to old shareholders and management. The recapitalization merger also avoids the need for large investments of mezzanine capital from the pools of pension funds assembled by the buyout specialists. Instead, the public is enticed to take the mezzanine layer of subordinated debentures. As a result, few will champion the virtues of the recapitalization merger, and its popularity will probably never be widespread. It is, however, a structure to be considered in situations where controlling stockholders can hold off higher competing offers long enough to let the stockholders vote to retain a future equity interest.

In the spring of 1984, management began to consider a proposal to take Multimedia private. Metromedia and Wometco, both heavily in broadcasting, had successfully completed LBOs that demonstrated that the private market value of broadcasting properties was substantially higher than the public market value of the parent holding companies.

The company, based in Greenville, South Carolina, was organized in 1968, but its predecessor newspaper company dates back to 1888. The company publishes 14 daily and 29 nondaily newspapers, owns and operates five television and eight radio stations, produces television programming, and serves approximately 269,500 cable television subscribers in four states. The company had enjoyed 96 consecutive years of profitable operations.

Multimedia management consulted with Goldman, Sachs, which was asked to structure an LBO proposal and to approach certain commercial banks to arrange the financing. However, a sudden three percentage point rise in the prime rate during the late spring of 1984 halted consideration of the proposal. Discussions were renewed in December 1984, following a decline in prevailing interest rates. In late January 1985, Goldman, Sachs received a commitment letter from The Chase Manhattan Bank for the financing, and on February 1, 1985, the company announced it had received a merger proposal from management and certain members of the founding families of the company. The proposal was for $37 cash and $25 stated face amount of a new issue of subordinated discount debentures. The value of the offer was in the $48–49 range per share. This compared with the price of $44 per share the day prior to the announcement. The $48–49 price was higher than the stock ever traded; however, it was still well below the private market value of the company's properties.

The banks that had committed to finance the LBO proposal required the company to obtain appraisals on its major properties on a going-concern basis. As of June 1985, the appraisals indicated a range of asset values of $1,016–1,113 million. Adding to these amounts the company's free cash and deducting its debt produced a private market value ranging from $57–63 per share. Whereas potential outside bidders did not have access to these appraisals, they could arrive at a fairly accurate estimate of value by knowing what values the market put on comparable newspapers, television and radio stations, and cable television subscribers. The disparity between management's initial proposal of $48–49 per share and the private market value of upward to $63 per share resulted in proposals from three outside bidders at prices ranging from $60–70 per share.

The board appointed a special committee of independent directors to review any proposals and to advise the board on what course of action to follow. The special committee consisted of George H.V. Cecil, president of Biltmore Dairy Farms, Inc., and William D. Sellers, Jr., chairman and CEO of Baggett Transportation Company. A third member, Richard T. Dugan, retired chairman and CEO of Cincinnati Bell, resigned from the special committee due to illness. The special committee retained Skadden, Arps as special legal counsel and Brown Brothers Harriman & Company (BBH & Co.) as financial advisor.

The special committee met on March 15, 1985 to consider the terms of the original proposal submitted by management and the founding families. The committee requested that the original proposal be modified and improved, which resulted in the contemplation of a revised proposal. Before such a revised proposal was made, Wilson C. Wearn, chairman of Multimedia, was telephoned by William E. Simon, former U.S. Treasury Secretary and the current chairman of Wesray Capital. Wesray was an active participant in LBOs, most notably in the highly successful LBO of Gibson Greeting Cards. The Wesray proposal was for $60 per share in cash, with both management and the founding families given the opportunity to participate in the transaction. Management would be permitted to purchase 15 percent of the stock of the acquiring company immediately and then allowed to purchase additional shares over the next five years. The founding families would be given the opportunity to purchase 20 percent of the stock of the acquiring companies and the right to elect the majority of the board of directors. The Wesray proposal also indicated that Drexel Burnham had been engaged to arrange the financing and that could be placed within three days. The founding families expressed no interest in the Wesray proposal, but in light of it, the founding families and management abandoned their revised proposal. Instead, they submitted a recapitalization proposal that would give the company's stockholders the opportunity to elect to receive either all debentures or part cash, part debentures, and an equity participation in the recapitalized company.

The special committee met to consider the recapitalization proposal and to determine the founding families' position with respect to the Wesray proposal. The founding families, who owned over 40 percent of the shares, remained in opposition to the Wesray proposal. Since South Carolina law requires that mergers be approved by at least two-thirds of the company's outstanding shares, the Wesray proposal would not succeed. Based on this reality and on the oral opinion of BBH & Co. that the recapitalization proposal was fair from a financial point of view, the special committee determined that it would be in the best interest of the company shareholders that they be given the opportunity to accept the terms of the recapitalization proposal. On April 15, 1985, the board voted unanimously to accept the recapitalization proposal and sent a press release on its action. The fight, however, was far from over.

On April 10, 1985, the company received a letter from Lorimar, a company primarily engaged in the production of television programs, proposing the acquisition of the company for $61 per share cash. The Lorimar proposal was subject to financing but indicated that its investment banker, Drexel Burnham, expressed a high level of confidence in its ability to arrange such financing. The ubiquitous Drexel Burnham seemed to be retained by both Wesray and Lorimar to finance competing proposals. Wesray called to clarify how Drexel Burnham could wear two hats. It wore its white hat with Wesray, who had indicated it would only proceed with its proposal on a friendly basis. Since Wesray's proposal had been rejected, Drexel considered itself free to put on its black hat to represent Lorimar, which had not required friendly acceptance. Wesray informed the company that Drexel Burnham indicated that if the Lorimar proposal were not accepted by the company, Lorimar would make a tender offer. Since Drexel Burnham pointed out that Lorimar could not proceed without its assistance, Wesray indicated to the company that if Multimedia accepted the Wesray proposal, Lorimar would be precluded from making a tender offer. Wesray indicated it was prepared to increase the cash price to $62 per share and to buy 1.6–1.7 million shares, which when added to the shares held by management and the founding families, would prevent an unsolicited tender offer from succeeding.

The company determined to stay the course and announced on April 11, 1985 that it had received the Lorimar proposal and stated that the company was not being sold to either Wesray or Lorimar.

Since these offers could be viewed as higher than any of the options to be offered to shareholders under the recapitalization proposal, BBH & Co. informed the special committee that it was reevaluating its preliminary oral fairness opinion delivered to the full board on April 5, 1985. BBH & Co. also recommended that the recapitalization proposal be improved in certain respects.

Before these changes were agreed to, Jack Kent Cooke entered the bidding. Cooke met with Wilson Wearn, chairman, and Walter Bartlett, president and CEO, indicating that he was willing to acquire the company at a per share cash price approximately $1–2 more than the price of the highest outstanding proposal. Cooke was estimated by *Forbes* magazine to have a net worth in excess of $600 million and apparently did not need Drexel Burnham to arrange his financing. Again, the company stood firm and issued a press release that representatives of the founding families remained committed to the recapitalization proposal. The press release also said the board had authorized management to secure a $300 million line of credit for the purpose of share repurchases if deemed appropriate. Cooke then announced that he owned more than 9.7 percent of the shares and intended to make an offer to buy the company.

Three days later, on April 29, 1985, management and the founding families submitted to the board a revised recapitalization proposal, which the special committee reviewed and reported to the board with the following recommendation:

The Revised Capitalization Proposal is fair in and of itself to the Company's shareholders [(other than the Management Investors and the Founding Families)]. The [Special] Committee is prepared to recommend that the Revised Recapitalization Proposal be submitted to a vote of the shareholders. However, the [Special] Committee cannot recommend that the shareholders vote for the Revised Capitalization Proposal but rather the shareholders should make up their own minds based on all information available to them. The [Special] Committee is aware of three competing offers from third parties. The financial terms of the three competing offers, as understood by the [Special] Committee, may or may not be better than the Revised Recapitalization Proposal. [BBH & Co.], the [Special] Committee's financial advisor, has shown the [Special] Committee a range of hypothetical values for the Revised Recapitalization Proposal based on differing assumptions as to the fully distributed market value per share of the [New] Shares. Although some of the hypothetical values were in excess of the highest alternative cash offer, more of such hypothetical values were less than the highest alternative cash offer. Since the three competing offers are not available to the shareholders, the [Special] Committee need not decide which is the best offer.

The special committee recommendation was predicated on the oral advice of BBH & Co. that the terms of the revised recapitalization proposal were fair. The committee also was advised that the shareholders agreement, signed by members of the founding families who owned 42 percent of the shares, was legally binding in South Carolina and consequently could defeat any merger proposal. Based on the special committee's recommendation, the board unanimously authorized the execution of the recapitalization agreement and directed that the agreement be submitted for a shareholders' vote at a special shareholders meeting. It also provided that the founding families and management investors would agree not to elect the highest valued option, which was the option to receive all discount debentures in the recapitalization merger.

Nine days after the recapitalization agreement had been executed, Cooke, in a letter to the board, indicated that a corporation controlled by him was prepared to enter into a merger transaction at a price of more than $65 per share, subject to the shareholders' rejection of the recapitalization plan. The founding families reiterated that they remained committed to the recapitalization proposal and stated that they had no interest in the Cooke proposal. Several representatives of the founding families delivered letters to the chairman, avowing that the recapitalization merger "affords all shareholders of the company, not just the founding families, the opportunity to continue as investors in the ongoing corporation."

On May 22, 1985, the directors determined that no further consideration should be given to the Cooke proposal. Cooke resorted to the courts and succeeded in obtaining a temporary restraining order in connection with the merger. This order was dissolved on June 17, 1985 by the South Caroline court. On July 15, 1985, the Cooke group announced it intended to commence a tender offer for 40.4 percent of the stock at $70.01 per share cash. The Cooke group already owned 9.76 percent of the stock, so the addition of 40.4 percent would give Cooke control with 50.2 percent of the outstanding shares.

Under the recapitalization proposal, a corporation called MM Acquiring Corporation was set up to acquire the shares, after which MM Acquiring Corporation would be merged into the company. MM Acquiring had received commitments from various institutional investors to purchase approximately 2.4 million of its shares for $10 per share. The purpose of the sale of these shares was to provide equity funds for the recapitalization merger and to enable Multimedia shareholders to elect to retain an equity interest in the company and receive capital gains tax treatment on the transaction. Responding to Cooke's intention to tender for 40.4 percent of the stock at $70.01 per share, MM Acquiring negotiated an agreement with the Cooke group to purchase its 9.76 percent ownership at $70 per share and agreed to pay $1.7 million for Cooke's expenses. This provided Cooke with an estimated $25 million profit.

This action caused BBH & Co. to reevaluate its oral fairness opinion and the special committee to rethink its recommendation delivered to the board on April 29, 1985 with respect to the recapitalization agreement.

The MM Acquiring Corporation listed a number of reasons why it bought out the Cooke group's stock. Foremost among these is that if all shares were tendered, less than 45 percent of the shares would be purchased for $70.01 per share. Whereas the Cooke group stated that following the tender it would extend a cash and securities offer of the same value as the cash offer for the remaining shares, MM Acquiring believed the Cooke group would have no legal obligation or economic incentive to do so. It also believed the Cooke group would have difficulty financing the purchase of the remaining shares and would require a significant amount of time to obtain FCC approval, if obtained at all. If Cooke was unable or unwilling to offer the remaining untendered shares, a similar value in cash and securities, proration of tendered shares at $70.01 could result in a total value of less than $70.01 as the remaining shares not accepted in the tender could subsequently be obtained at a lower price. This possibility enabled BBH & Co. to reaffirm its prior oral fairness opinion and the special committee was able to restate its prior recommendation. BBH & Co. pointed out in its fairness opinion that Cooke's tender proposal at $70.01 per share was higher than the $52.46 cash alternative of the revised recapitalization proposal but was "not directly comparable with the consideration available to shareholders pursuant to alternatives (I), (III), and (IV) of the revised recapitalization proposal, the future value of which will depend on, among other factors, the future value of the equity of the recapitalized Company."

In its recommendation to the board, the special committee acknowledged that although it was aware that various competing offers had been received by the company, "these offers are not currently available to the company's shareholders. Accordingly, the committee has not compared the revised recapitalization proposal with the competing offers to determine which is the best offer. The committee does not recommend that the shareholders vote for or against the Revised Recapitalization Proposal and continues to believe that the company's shareholders should make up their own minds based on all information available to them." Based on this recommendation, the board once again unanimously determined that the company's shareholders should be given the opportunity to vote on the revised recapitalization proposal. The shareholders overwhelmingly voted to approve the recapitalization merger at a special meeting on September 20, 1985.

Following the public announcement of the original proposal received by the company on February 1, 1985, four separate class actions were brought against the company. Named in the suits were the directors and special committee members. These suits charged that the consideration was grossly inadequate, that the defendants had participated in the perpetration of a fraud upon the members of the class, and that the defendants had aided and abetted each other in a breach of their fiduciary duties. These suits were consolidated by the South Carolina court. An agreement was reached on April 7, 1985, but the Cooke group litigation forestalled a settlement. The court then consolidated the Cooke group's litigation with the original shareholder litigation. After the MM Acquiring Corporation bought the Cooke group's shares at $70 per share, the plaintiffs in the original shareholder litigation filed an amended complaint, which joined the members of the Cooke group as defendants. They charged, among other things, that the premium paid to the Cooke group was a discriminatory corporate distribution and that the purchase of the Cooke shares was intended to entrench the company's management.

Settlement was subsequently agreed upon, which added a fourth option for the shareholders in the recapitalization proposal and provided for costs, including reasonable attorneys' and experts' fees.

From what began as a relatively straightforward offer to purchase stock at $37 cash and $25 stated face amount of debentures evolved into a complex array of options that few stockholders would or could fully comprehend. In order to increase the value of the options and to satisfy both investment bankers and litigants, the final proposal was oddly structured in terms of dollar amounts of cash and debentures. The value of the four options is shown on the opposite page.

Management investors and certain members of the founding families agreed not to elect Option I. This option was made available to 3.2 million shares. Excess shares that elected this option were converted pro rata to any of the other three options that the stockholders elected. Because Option I offered the highest value to the shareholders and also the right to purchase common shares in the recapitalized company, approximately 92 percent of the shares not held by management, the founding families, or the Cooke group elected Option I. Since the company limited Option I to 3.2 million shares, and over 7.6 million elected Option I, the company accepted 41.9 percent of the 7.6 million shares electing Option I and prorated the remaining 4.4 million shares. The prorated shares were given Options II, III, or IV as specified by the shareholders, or Option II (all cash) if no default election was made. If a shareholder failed to respond to the option election request, the stockholder was given Option III.

The debentures that were received by shareholders electing Option I began trading on the American Stock Exchange on a when-issued basis at 51 or $510 per $1,000 debenture shortly after the proxy statement was mailed to the shareholders. The new shares similarly began trading over the counter at 15\frac{1}{4}$ per share. Thus, the shareholders could compute the value of the options prior to their election.

The debentures were structured to accommodate the company's cash flow and to appeal to institutional investors; they are high risk, high yield deben-

Value of Options

Option	As Offered	Resulting From Proration	Actual Year-End 1985
I $125 debentures plus right to purchase for $5.27 in cash, 0.527 of a new share of common stock[1,2]	$63.75 2.77	$63.75 2.77	$69.69 5.87
Total value	$66.52	$66.52	$75.56
II $39.90 in cash	39.90	52.46	52.46
$29.73 debentures	15.16		
Total value	$55.06	$52.46	$52.46
III $34.63 in cash	34.63	47.19	47.19
$29.73 debentures	15.16		
$ 5.27 stock[2]	8.04	8.04	15.87
Total Value	$57.83	$55.23	$63.06
IV $34.10 in cash	34.10	46.66	46.66
$29.73 debentures	15.16		
$ 5.80 stock[2]	8.85	8.85	17.47
Total value	$58.11	$55.51	$64.13

[1]A nontransferrable right expiring September 17, 1985, to purchase either 0.527 of a new share for $5.27 in cash or 0.580 of a new share for $5.80 in cash.

[2]The stock's initial trade of 15\frac{1}{4}$ valued the right at $2.77 assuming the 0.527 election and $3.85 assuming the 0.580 election. At year-end 1985, the stock closed at 30$\frac{1}{8}$, valuing the right at $5.87 assuming the 0.527 election and 7.47 assuming the 0.580 election.

tures, commonly referred to as "junk bonds." However, appraised value of the assets as of June 30, 1985 exceeded the pro forma debt, assuming fair market value of the debentures of $240 million or half of the stated face amount, by a range of $111–208 million. The debentures are unsecured, subordinated general obligations of the company due in 2005. No interest will accrue or be payable on the debentures prior to July 1, 1990, on which date interest will accrue at the rate of 16 percent per annum and be payable each six months beginning December 31, 1990. The debentures are subject to mandatory redemption through a sinking fund, which will redeem 10 percent of the issue annually beginning on June 30, 1996.

The debentures bear "original issue discount (OID)" which for federal income tax purposes will be included on an accrual basis in the gross income of the holders in advance of the receipt of cash payments on the debentures. Taxpaying holders will be required to take the following amounts of OID into income tax years 1985–1990 even though the first actual payment of interest will not be received until December 31, 1990:

Series A—Per $125 Debenture
($80 Million)

	Initial Value	Original Issue Discount
1985	$65.94	$ 2.49
1986		10.71
1987		12.39
1988		14.34
1989		16.58
1990		9.18

Series B—Per $125 Debenture
($400 Million)

	Initial Value	Original Issue Discount
1985	$65.00	$ 2.47
1986		10.67
1987		12.35
1988		14.31
1989		16.57
1990		9.19

Because of this adverse tax treatment for individuals and taxable institutional accounts, many taxpayers sold their debentures to nontaxable institutional accounts in open market transactions. Whereas the OID is taxable income to the debenture holder, it is a noncash, pretax deduction for the company, substantially aiding the company's cash flow. The amortization of the OID saves the company $110 million in taxes through 1990.

The sources and uses of funds of the financing are as follows.

Sources of Funds

Credit agreement	$665,000
Debentures (assumes issue price of 50% of face amount)	240,000
Common stock (value of shares and cash)	110,000
Cash in the company	26,401
	$1,041,401

Uses of Funds

Redemption of shares	$940,241
Repayment of existing debt	78,660
Estimated costs and fees	22,500
	$1,041,401

The $665 million credit agreement is a 10-year commitment, with annual reductions beginning at $15 million in the first year and escalating to $120 million in the tenth year. The repayment schedule, however, accommodates the expected cash drain caused by the cash payment of interest on the debentures in the sixth year. Debt repayment, due in the sixth year, drops to $25 million from $45 million in the fifth year. The interest rate on the credit agreement varies with a ratio of all indebtedness to operating cash flow; it begins at prime plus $1\frac{1}{4}$ percent. As the ratio improves with the repayment and the increase in cash flow, the rate drops largely in $\frac{1}{4}$ percent increments until it reaches prime. Interest rate options based on the Eurodollar rate and the CD rate are also available. The company was required by the banks to enter into rate protection agreements covering at least $332.5 million for a minimum of four years. This arrangement may be interest rate swaps, interest rate insurance, or fixed rate debt. The lead bank on the credit agreement is Chase Manhattan, whose transaction fees amounted to $\frac{2}{3}$ percent, or $4.45 million. Goldman, Sachs received the largest fee, $9.0 million, followed by legal fees estimated at $5.5 million, and BBH & Co.'s fee of $1.675 million.

Equity Financing

The initial equity was $110 million, consisting of 11.0 million shares at $10 per share. The majority of the equity was provided by shareholders electing Options III or IV, or exercising their rights to purchase stock in Option I. Some management investors and certain others contributed their shares to the capital of MM Acquiring Corporation; however, other management investors plus new investors purchased shares of MM Acquiring at $10 per share. It sold approximately 1.2 million of its shares to institutional investors at $10 per share, including 424,300 shares to Goldman, Sachs and 394,860 shares to Phil Donahue, whose television show is produced by and highly profitable for the company. Salomon Brothers also agreed to purchase up to 1.2 million additional shares. These agreements enabled the shareholders electing to acquire stock in MM Acquiring Corporation under Option III or Option I, purchase election A, to receive sale treatment on the transaction and be taxed at capital gain rates rather than as a dividend taxed at ordinary income tax rates. Under Section 302 of the IRS tax code, if the shareholder's ownership percentage immediately after the recapitalization merger is less than 80 percent of his ownership percentage immediately before the recapitalization merger, then the redemption is not taxed as a dividend to the shareholder. By selling slightly over 20 percent of the shares of MM Acquiring to new investors, stockholders electing Option III and Option I, purchase election A, will have an ownership percentage in MM Acquiring slightly less than 80 percent of their ownership percentage in the company prior to the recapitalization merger. Option IV resulted in the shareholders percentage in MM Acquiring dropping to approximately 88 percent and would result in the transaction being taxed as a dividend. This option was added in settlement of the shareholder litigation and would result in disastrous tax treatment for the individual shareholders, for whose benefit the litigation was supposedly initiated. However, this option was attractive to corporate shareholders, which can exclude 85 percent of dividend income from taxes, thereby putting their effective tax rate of 6.9 percent on dividends well below their maximum capital gain tax rate of 28 percent.

Benefits of the Recapitalization Merger

The recapitalization merger provided a decisive advantage in the contest for control of Multimedia. First, it put management and the founding families on the side of the angels by sharing with all stockholders the opportunity to obtain equity participation in the recapitalized company. There is always an argument, however weak, that buyouts deprive existing shareholders of the financial benefits resulting from a company's future growth. More importantly, the recapitalization merger made direct comparison of the value of the various competing offers impossible. As BBH & Co. stated in their fairness opinion:

> Since the date of our initial engagement as the Special Committee's financial advisor, three other entities made proposals to acquire the Company in transactions which would have involved payments to the Company's shareholders ranging from $60 cash per share in the first case to, in the final case, $70.01 per share cash for approximately 40 percent of the Company's shares to be followed by a transaction pursuant to which the Company's shareholders would have purportedly received a combination of cash and securities of equivalent value per share. Such amounts are higher than the value of consideration available to shareholders pursuant to alternative (II) of the Revised Recapitalization Proposal and are not directly comparable with the consideration available to shareholders pursuant to alternatives (I), (III), and (IV) of the Revised Recapitalization Proposal, the future value of which will depend on, among other factors, the future value of the equity of the recapitalized Company; this in turn will depend in part on the Company's earnings and cash flow performance and future financial market conditions and, while the Company's equity may have a value higher than that represented by the purchase price of $5.27 for .527 shares, or the purchase price of $5.80 for .580 shares, embodied in the Revised Recapitalization Proposal, we express no opinion as to such value.

If the management and founding families had stuck to their original proposal of cash and debentures, and increased the price to equal the highest value of $66.62 per share of Option I, BBH & Company probably would not have been able to say the offer was fair in the face of another directly comparable higher offer. The special committee, and, in turn, the board, probably would not have recommended acceptance of this offer without the protection of a professional opinion supporting its fairness.

The market for the new shares quickly proved BBH & Co. and the board correct. After initial trading at $15\frac{1}{4}$, the stock rose to $30\frac{1}{8}$ at the year-end 1985, putting the value of Option I at $74.35 per share and the value of Option III at $65.66 per share.

An apparent negative to the recapitalization merger structure is that there is no opportunity to write up assets to shelter operating earnings from full taxes and to show a positive net worth. Since there was not a change in ownership of greater than 50 percent, the recapitalization merger was accounted for as a redemption not subject to purchase accounting. Thus, the historical balance sheet on June 30, 1985, showing net worth of $264 million, was recapitalized after the merger to show a pro forma net worth deficit of $584 million. However, the employment of the discount debentures provided excellent tax shelter in place of the write-up of assets. The amortization of the OID saved $110 million in taxes over the first five years and will even enable the company to obtain a tax refund in the first two years due to projected losses. Since the company was not sold, losses can be carried back against past taxes paid and result in tax refunds. Had the deal been conventionally structured as a purchase and the election to write up assets made, recapture taxes would have exceeded $45 million, payable shortly after the election. As is, the company projects that it will receive a tax refund of $3.9 million in the first two years and pay a total of $44.8 million in taxes in the first five years. The recapitalization merger is therefore superior to the write-up of assets from the standpoint of tax savings over the first five years. Because the OID would be completely amortized in five years, there would be no future tax benefits to the recapitalization merger in contrast to the ongoing depreciation of some long lived written-up assets.

Future Returns for Stockholders

The Multimedia proxy statement prepared for the special stockholders meeting on September 20, 1985 gave the public stockholder a rare look at the future. It contained projections for 1985–95 of revenues and net operating cash flow by the business segment. Based on these projections, future stock values can be calculated. Using the same multiple of operating earnings that was realized in the recapitalization merger, the future stock values are as follows.

Future Multimedia Stock Values
(Millions)

	On Merger	1986	1990	1995
EBIT	$ 85.3	$ 106.4	$ 181.6	$ 330.2
Multiple on recapitalization	11.9x	11.9x	11.9x	11.9x
Value of earnings	$1,018.9	$1,266.2	$2,161.0	$3,929.4
Less debt	78.7	938.3	895.0	480.0
Value of company	$ 940.2	$ 327.9	$1,266.0	$3,449.4
Earnings per share[/]		29.80	115.00	274.20
Value of Option I ($57.23 cash reinvested)		75.79	133.64	237.72
Value of Option III ($47.19 cash reinvested)		65.25	120.82	221.37

[/]Estimated shares outstanding: 1986 and 1990—11.0 million shares, 1995—12.6 million shares.

Thus, the founding families who along with management put the company in play with their initial offer, were able to get cash of $47.19 per share and stock worth $8.04 per their 0.527 fractional share. Their fractional share of stock in 10 years should be worth $144, and if the value of the cash received after capital gains taxes grows at 5 percent per year, their holdings would be worth approximately $221 per original share. This is a compounded annual return of 17.5 percent based on the stock price of $44 the day prior to the announcement of the original proposal. The founding families ownership percentage dropped from approximately 40 percent to approximately 32 percent in the recapitalized company. It is doubtful that the Wesray proposal, which was for $62 cash and offered the founding families a 20 percent equity interest in the acquiring company, would have provided the founding families with a higher long-term return on their investment. This may or may not be the case for management, as Wesray permitted them to purchase 15 percent of the acquiring company immediately and additional shares over the next five years in a stock option plan. Under the recapitalization merger plan, management's ownership rose from 1.3 percent to 4.0 percent. Management, however, does have three attractive option plans under the recapitalized merger. Particularly attractive is the restricted option plan providing 10-year options to purchase 504,498 shares at $1.00 per share. The value of this option was $7.2 million at the initial when-issued stock price. These options, combined with the new key executive options, were worth $8.7 million at the outset of stock trading. All told, the option package amounted to 1.6 million shares, and when coupled with the 438,536 shares management obtained at the outset, would provide management with 16.2 percent of the company after exercise of the options. Management was able to cash out its old shares and options for $7.3 million, net of their purchase of stock in MM Acquiring. Current management's stock ownership in 1995 should be worth $120 million, and the options issued to them would be worth another $213 million before taxes if the stock attains its projected price of $274 per share. If they had to pay 28 percent of the value of the options in taxes, management would realize a total return of $271 million, an excellent 62 × their initial investment of $4.4 million.

The unique and gratifying aspect of the Multimedia deal is that whereas management and insiders are projected to enjoy excellent returns on their investment, the public was also provided the opportunity to retain equity ownership. In fact, the public realized a better deal than the founding families because the latter group agreed not to elect the highest valued option. A public shareholder who elected Option I and chose Option III for its prorated shares would have ended up at year-end 1985 with $27.42 in cash, $28.15 in market value of debentures, and $15.87 in market value of stock. This total value of $69.23, net of the cost of the stock purchased under Option I, compares favorably with both the Wesray and Lorimar proposals and very possibly the Cooke proposal as well. With the Cooke proposal, the difficulty of financing shares not purchased on the proposed tender could have resulted in a value

	Year Ended December 31,					Six Months Ended June 30,	
	1980	1981	1982	1983	1984	1985	1986
	(In thousands, except per share amounts. Parentheses signify unaudited funds.)						
Broadcasting and entertainment	$ 83,281	$ 97,369	$110,509	$125,881	$135,319	$ 64,267	$ 73,770
Newspaper operating revenues	71,332	78,475	82,147	90,659	102,995	48,611	52,116
Cablevision operating revenues	8,950	19,432	32,807	53,180	66,047	$ 32,183	$ 36,482
Total operating revenues	163,563	195,276	225,463	269,720	304,361	145,061	162,368
Operating expenses	107,995	130,481	150,961	181,266	202,014	96,383	109,171
Depreciation and amortization	9,658	12,752	15,446	18,411	21,523	10,838	12,690
Total operating costs and expenses	117,653	143,233	166,407	199,677	223,537	107,221	121,861
Operating profit	45,910	52,043	59,056	70,043	80,824	37,840	40,507
Interest expense	5,834	5,779	6,916	8,198	8,289	4,124	4,170
Loss on investment in joint venture					(11,000)	(1,200)	
Other income, net	1,617	1,569	1,219	3,413	2,632	1,330	2,998
Earnings before taxes	41,693	47,833	53,359	65,258	64,167	33,846	39,335
Income taxes	20,075	22,009	24,385	30,084	30,479	16,077	18,881
Net earnings	$21,618	$25,824	$28,974	$35,174	$33,688	$17,769	$20,454

Unaudited Pro Forma Condensed Consolidated Balance Sheet
June 30, 1985

(In thousands except per share amounts).

	Historical[1]	Recapitalization Merger Adjustments	Pro Forma after the Recapitalization Merger
Assets			
Current assets:			
Cash and cash equivalents	$ 42,202	$(26,401)[2]	$ 15,801
Marketable securities	310		310
Net trade accounts receivable	45,490		45,490
Inventories	7,674		7,674
Film contract rights	5,458		5,458
Other current assets	5,035		5,035
Total current assets	106,169	(26,401)	79,768
Net property, plant, and equipment at cost	175,818		175,818
Net intangible assets	134,414		134,414
Other assets	12,090	1,828	13,918
Total assets	$428,491	$(24,573)	$403,918
Liabilities and Shareholders' Equity (Deficit):			
Current liabilities:			
Current portion of long-term debt	7,556	(7,556)[2]	
Accounts payable and accrued expenses	26,221		26,221
Income taxes payable	15,110	(3,688)	11,422
Film contracts payable	4,198		4,198
Unearned income	8,544		8,544
Total current liabilities	61,629	(11,244)	50,385
Existing long-term debt, excluding current portion	71,104	(71,104)[2]	
Credit agreement		665,000[2]	665,000
Debentures		240,000[3]	240,000 [3]
Deferred income taxes	30,710	436	31,146
Other liabilities	1,188		1,188
Shareholders' Equity (Deficit):			
Common stock	16,688	(15,588)[4]	1,100
Additional paid-in capital	46,037	(46,037)[4]	
Retained earnings (deficit)	201,586	(786,487)[4]	(584,901)
Less treasury stock	(451)	451[4]	
Total shareholders' equity (deficit)	263,860	(847,661)	(583,801)
Total liabilities and shareholders' equity (deficit)	$428,491	$(24,573	$403,918
Book value per share	$15.83	$(68.90)	$(53.07)
Tangible book value per share	$7.76	$(73.05)	$(65.29)

[1] Historical condensed consolidated balance sheet of the company at June 30, 1985.
[2] See the table of sources and uses of funds.
[3] Represents $480 million stated face amount of debentures, with an estimated fair market value of $240 million which may not necessarily be the price at which the debentures will be issued.
[4] Represents changes in shareholders' equity accounts due to the redemption of outstanding shares, the reduction in the par value of the common stock, and the retirement of treasury shares after the redemption.

for all shares lower than provided in Options I and III. By mid-1986, the combined value for shareholders who elected Option I was approximately $82.50.

The stock purchase option gave the public the opportunity to buy stock for $10 per share, which has a projected value in ten years of $270 per share. This is a compounded annual return of 39.2 percent, a rate unavailable in the public markets.

In a reversal of prior market experience where the public market values were well below the private market values for Multimedia, the leveraging of the company via the recapitalization merger resulted in public market values in excess of the private market values. Thus, the deal not only produced a full recognition of private market values for its shareholders but it also resulted in a market premium over these values and led to creating value.

With the employment of the recapitalization merger technique, management and the founding families were able to retain ownership of the company in face of higher all-cash proposals. Management was able to position its equity participation to provide excellent potential returns, and the founding shareholders received substantial cash and retained 80 percent of their ownership in the company. The public got the most cash out and the opportunity to maintain 80 percent of their ownership. The grand result was an excellent price, the fairest of options for the public, and the substantial retention of the company's traditional ownership.

PIECE GOODS SHOPS, INC.

The Piece Goods Shops story concerns a company going private to escape an apathetic stock performance, then using an LBO to triple its value, and finally selling out on another LBO to again triple its value. It began with a company whose stock had a market value of $3.9 million and ended with a sellout for over $60 million. The value was created when the $20 million LBO was sold to another investor group for an estimated $60 million three years later. The original owners' acceptance of a large amount of sellers' notes enabled the initial LBO buyers to highly leverage the equity on the LBO. The final sale provided the new owners with huge returns on their small investment and made management an estimated $15 million on their $150,000 investment.

Piece Goods Shops, Inc. was founded in 1935 by Dudley L. Simms II in Huntington, West Virginia. His two sons, Dudley and John, took over management of the business in the 1960s and aggressively expanded its chain of retail fabric shops. By 1971, the company's 44 shops had sales volume of $9.3 million and net profits of $500,000. In April 1972, the company offered its stock to the public in a hot new issue market, selling 200,000 shares at $13.50 per share. This price was 20 × projected fiscal 1972 earnings and valued the company at $12.8 million versus book value of $1.6 million. Following the offering, the Simms family controlled approximately 68 percent of the company.

The company's retail stores sell fabrics (60 percent), patterns (30 percent), and needlecraft (10 percent) to the home sewing market. It sells first quality goods in leased stores, usually located in strip shopping centers. In 1983, it had 106 stores located in 11 states, with a heavy concentration in North Carolina and Virginia.

In the year following the IPO, the company's stock dropped along with the general market, and in the face of a drop in fiscal 1973 earnings to $0.28 per share from $0.67 per share in fiscal 1972. The stock plummeted to a low bid of $1.00 at the market bottom in October 1974, only to recover to $6.00 in 1975 as earnings jumped to $1.10 per share. The recovery was short-lived as earnings dropped to $0.87 per share in 1976 and again in 1977 to $0.46 per share, causing the stock to drop to a low of $2.00 bid in 1977. Management attributed the earnings drop to margin pressures and large markdowns.

Another depressant to the stock was a $12.5 million lawsuit filed in 1975 by former franchisees of the company. The former franchisees charged that the company manipulated the franchise corporations to weaken them prior to the consolidation of the franchise companies into Piece Goods Shops. They further charged fraudulent mismanagement on the part of the three Simms, mainly relating to private dealings between the Simms and the company which was to the stockholders' detriment. The suit resulted in a qualified opinion by Price Waterhouse and Company in its 1977 audit statement. In 1978, the company made a provision for the settlement of the lawsuit which dropped earnings from $0.87 per share to $0.60 per share. The stock traded as low as $2\frac{7}{8}$ in July 1978, or only 3.3 times net income from operations and 44 percent of book value.

The Simms brothers decided there were no advantages for the company to be publicly owned, as the public market valuation was too low to permit any major financing. A publicly owned company was expensive, particularly since it diverted management from running the business. Furthermore, it gave competition detailed competitive information and increased the likelihood of shareholder litigation which had so burdened them for the past three years. They concluded the best course of action was to have the company tender for the stock and return to a privately owned status.

In October 1978, the company offered to repurchase all of its shares at $7.00 per share, or 8.0 × trailing 12 months operating earnings. The shares closed at $4\frac{1}{4}$ bid the day prior to the offer. There were 298,500 shares held outside the family and available for repurchase. Book value was $6.60 per share, and working capital was $5.22 per share. The price was determined by the board of directors without any outside appraisal or fairness opinion. Fairness rules had been proposed by the SEC but had not taken effect at the time of the tender. The board believed the highest price attainable if it chose to liquidate was $3.00 per share, and the highest price it could sell out for was $5.00 per share. It also observed that the highest price the stock had traded during the past four years was $6.00. So, the $7.00 per share offer looked like a fair price by these comparisons, and the stockholders agreed. The tender was successful, and the company went private in December 1978. The $1.4 million required for the tender was financed half from cash and half from bank borrowings.

During the next four years, the company's sales rose over 80 percent, and net income from operations rose 3.5 × to $2.8 million. The number of stores increased only from 86 to 91, but pretax profit margins rose from 5.2 percent in 1978 to 11.5 percent in 1982. The profit improvement came from lower cost of products sold, and lower operating, general, and administrative expenses as a percentage of sales. Clearly, competitive conditions that had proved difficult for the company in 1976 and 1977 had markedly improved. The company had high inventory turnover, low overhead, and good financial controls.

In 1982, the company was approached by John W. Jordan and David W. Zalaznick of the Jordan Company, a private New York investment firm specializing in LBOs. Jordan believed the company's unexciting, somewhat recession resistant business was well suited for an LBO. Competition was weak and in some locations nonexistent, and the company had exhibited good cash flow and growth characteristics. A deal was struck with the Simms brothers for a purchase of assets for approximately $20 million. By purchasing assets, the buyer did not acquire the liability of the still unsettled lawsuit.

The source and application of funds for the buyout were as follows.

Sources of Funds

Bank revolving loans	$13.3
Sellers' notes	7.0
Equity	0.6
	$20.9

Application of Funds

Purchase of assets	$20.0
Fees and expenses	0.9
	$20.9

The purchaser was a partnership, a form rarely used in buyouts except for the purpose of pairing the investment company with a company with substantial tax loss carryforwards, using those losses as a tax shelter. A partnership is not generally appropriate for companies that are highly profitable or have substantial needs to invest capital. This is because partnerships do not pay taxes, but the individual partners do pay ordinary income taxes on their share of the income. Since individual tax rates were 50 percent at the margin and corporate tax rates peaked at 46 percent, higher taxes would be paid under the partnership format. Net income would, however, save on future capital gains taxes if the company were subsequently sold. Net income would increase the partnership's basis for computing capital gains taxes. However, if the partnership is in a loss position, the loss is of greater use to the partners to shelter their higher tax rates. In the Piece Goods buyout, the buyer was able to write up inventories to their sale price, less cost to sell them. This write-up amounted to $9.7 million, which when included in costs of goods sold, created substantial reported losses to the partnership. This accounting treatment enabled the partnership to report losses in the first year of approximately $7.0 million, which individual partners used to offset personal income taxes. Each partner was able to use his share of the $7.0 million loss to reduce his taxable income in 1982 and 1983. Thus, the partnership created tax write-offs for its partners in 1982 and 1983, and the company used its untaxed earnings and inventory reduction to reduce its acquisition debt by $7.3 million in the first year following the buyout.

The company continued to show profit improvement the year following the buyout, with income from operations rising from $5.7 million to $8.1 million on a sales gain of only 8 percent. Pretax margins, before interest and expenses, rose to 15.1 percent of sales. This ranked the company as one of the most profitable retail operations of any type in the country. Despite interest expenses increasing by $2.2 million, net income exceeded the prior year's net in a little over 11 months of operations.

The company's income statement is shown on the opposite page.

With this good record, the company filed a registration statement with the SEC in September 1983 to sell 500,000 shares by the company and 1,250,000 shares by selling shareholders. The estimated offering price was between $14 and $16 per share, which would have valued the company before the offering between $56 and $64 million. When it became evident that deteriorating market conditions for new issues would not enable the company to go public at a price within the expected $14–16 range, the proposed offering was withdrawn from registration. The company was going to be incorporated, and stock would have been exchanged for the partnership's interest.

Sales and earnings continued to increase in 1984, but the company remained a partnership despite earning substantial taxable income. In the spring of 1985, the company was sold to an investor group for an unconfirmed price of approximately $60 million in cash and notes. At this price, John Jordan's direct ownership amounted to $9.0 million, and David Zalaznick's shares were worth $6.0 million. These values represented approximately 100 × their investment in the partnership 31 months earlier. A limited partnership set up by the Jordan Company, which owned 47 percent of the stock, received $25.0 million on the sale. Management of the company, consisting of Craven B. Page, chairman and CEO; John L. McBride, president; and Carl N. Boon, executive vice president, purchased a 25 percent interest in the company for $100,000 cash contribution and a $50,000 loan to the purchasing partnership. All three had been with the company for many years, but only Page had been an officer of the company before the buyout, having served as comptroller and then treas-

Statement of Income Data
(000's omitted)

| | Year Ended July 31 | | | | August 21, 1982– |
	1979	1980	1981	1982	July 31, 1983
Net sales	$30,679	$33,708	$40,509	$49,493	$53,534
Cost of products sold	20,389	22,955	26,485	31,843	31,313
Gross profit	$10,290	$10,735	$14,024	$17,650	$22,221
Operating expenses	6,948	7,412	8,445	9,923	11,536
General and administrative expenses	1,165	1,162	1,352	1,675	2,293
Depreciation and amortization	244	274	323	351	326
Income from operations	$ 8,357	$ 8,484	$10,120	$11,949	$14,155
Interest expense	1,933	1,905	3,904	5,701	8,066
	29	35	39	51	2,264
Income before income taxes	$ 1,904	$ 1,870	$ 3,865	$ 5,650	$ 5,802
Provision for income taxes	905	886	1,870	2,790	2,856
Net income	$ 999	$ 984	$ 1,995	$ 2,860	$ 2,946

urer. Each had an 8.3 percent interest in the company, which was worth an estimated $5.0 million in cash and notes on the sale. Each had invested only $50,000 for their stake.

Piece Goods Shops is a good example of how a small company with public ownership can enhance its value via an LBO. The thin public market for the stock had produced an average value for the company of $3.0 million for a five-year period prior to the company going private. This period was marked by a rollercoaster earnings performance, and a lawsuit casting a cloud over the company's public image. It was too small an issue to have institutional interest, and individual investors had been whipsawed by volatile earnings and bad publicity. The wise decision to go private valued the company at $6.5 million. Four years later, the LBO valued the company at $20 million, or three times the going private value. This did not represent any higher value in relation to earnings, as earnings had also approximately tripled during this period. The company's attempt to go public a year after the buyout at values ranging from $63–72 million did represent a quantum leap in value. In fact, the proposed new issue apparently exceeded values investors were willing to pay for the company, but the deal also looked like a bailout for the insiders who were to get 71 percent of the proceeds. The step-up in proposed value on the public offering from the value on the buyout was represented almost entirely by an expansion of the P/E ratio, from 7.0 × on the buyout to a range of 18–21 × on the aborted public offering. This proposed threefold increase in the P/E ratio over the P/E ratio on the LBO represented a substantial creation of value that is difficult to completely explain. Certainly the stock was reborn, unburdened by the heavy baggage it carried in the mid-1970s. Its up and down earnings record seemed to be finished, and its somewhat tarnished image with investors disappeared. The 5-year record was one of rapid growth, showing earnings rising from $999,000 in 1979 to $2.9 million in 11 months in 1983. This spanned two brief recessions during which the company prospered, validating the argument that the company's business prospered during hard times as women turned more to making their own and their children's clothes to save money. Few remembered that earnings had dropped from $0.67 per share to $0.28 per share in the 1974 recession. Its tripling of profit margins from 1978 to 1983 indicated a strengthening of its competitive position and the skill of management.

In addition to attaining the image of a highly profitable growth stock, the company obtained a critical earnings mass, which when capitalized with a growth stock multiple, produced a market value sufficiently large to interest the institutional market. Also, the company had new sponsorship with Prudential-Bache managing the offering, and the market for IPOs of smaller growth stocks was more favorable in 1983 than at any time since the company went private in 1978. All of these things combined to create a threefold increase in value over the price paid for the company on the LBO less than a year and a half earlier. Had the company not sold out in 1982 and attempted to go public again in 1983, it is highly doubtful that the proposed valuation of earnings would have been nearly as high. The company in this instance would not have escaped its past, and it is unlikely that its public offering P/E ratio could have exceeded 12–15 ×. Did the leveraging provided by the LBO further cause the underwriters to push the P/E on the public offering up to 19–21 ×? Certainly the LBO provided some positive elements missing in the old company that added to the perceived value of the company. Whereas the company failed in its attempt to go public in the range of value of $63 plus million, it had the effect of setting the value of the company when it ultimately sold a year and a half later.

The LBO proved enormously profitable for John Jordan and his investors. The investors were able to finance the purchase with only $600,000 in equity because the sellers were willing to take sellers' notes amounting to 33 percent of the financing. These notes were subordinated to the bank financing and thus treated as equity by the banks. The equity was established at a P/E ratio of 0.21 ×, and when it was sold at a price close to 20 × earnings, the initial investors made approximately 100 × their investment in three years.

GLENDALE FABRICS, INC.

The owner/management group of Glendale Fabrics had watched the company they founded 14 years earlier grow to sales of $35 million and net income of $1.3 million. Net worth reached $7.5 million. They decided it was time to receive some liquidity for their now considerable investment and initiated discussions with investment bankers concerning the possibility of going public. The investment bankers did not believe the public market would be receptive to a public offering and suggested an LBO largely financed with sellers' notes. This "friendly debt" financing enabled the equity in the new company to remain small, which was advantageous in several ways. The investment by outsiders in 51 percent of the new company ensured that a competitive return could be negotiated for the repurchase of their stock in five years with the exercise of a put option. The 49 percent of the company offered to the owner/management group was largely purchased by their children, which resulted in excellent estate planning. This low risk LBO provided liquidity and diversification for the owner/management group and enabled them to transfer the ownership of the company to their heirs outside of their estates. It therefore provided an alternative to the estate freeze, which is usually accomplished with a recapitalization of the company using preferred stock to freeze the value in the owners' estates.

The preferred stock estate freeze has, however, lost some of its attraction because the IRS has frequently challenged the allocation of the values between the preferred and common stocks. Typically, upon recapitalization, a large portion of a company's value is allocated to the preferred stock held by the original owners, and a small portion of the value is allocated to the common stock held by the owners' heirs. The IRS, however, has claimed that the common stock has all of the growth potential and thus has a greater value than its allocated value. Also, if the preferred stock carried a below market dividend rate and was noncumulative, the IRS has claimed its allocated value relative to the common stock is further reduced.

In addition to freezing the estate, the low risk LBO also provided liquidity to the original owners but at the cost of capital gains taxes. The preferred stock estate freeze does not trigger any taxes but also does not provide any liquidity for the original owners. Offsetting the taxes in the LBO alternative is the premium sale price that is structured into the deal, enabling the aftertax proceeds to equal or exceed the preferred stock values in the traditional estate freeze. The sellers' notes provided income for the original owners equal to or higher than the preferred stock dividend in the estate freeze, but the interest on the notes is tax-deductible for the company whereas the preferred dividend is not.

To fulfill the principal objective of the estate freeze of having the steadily increasing value of the company accrue to the heirs and not be subject to the original owners' estate taxes, the heirs must gain ownership of the common stock. They do so in the LBO by first acquiring a minority ownership position in the new company, which will become the entire ownership position when the company is able to reacquire its stock from the outside investors. This can be accomplished with a call option granted to the company, subject to future earnings performance targets, or with a put option which provides compelling incentives for its exercise.

In the Glendale case, the sellers were satisfied that the put price formula which maximized the price in the sixth year and declined thereafter would be sufficient incentive to assure the put would be exercised. This confidence emanated from the fact that the heirs' 49 percent ownership could block the sale of the company, and the nature of the business precluded a public offering. Techniques have since been developed that effectively remove all alternatives open to the outside investors except the exercise of the put option. This, then, assures that the entire ownership of the company passes to the heirs of the original owners, completely outside of the owners' estates.

Glendale Fabrics was founded in 1969 to produce specialized fabrics for use in stretch garments. The company had expanded into several closely allied textile businesses in the early 1970s, which eventually proved unprofitable and were discontinued. Its core business remained profitable and well-positioned among the four principal producers, each with a 20–25 percent market share. There were only a handful of major customers, with the top two accounting for approximately 70 percent of Glendale's business. The fear that either of the top two customers would decide to enter the business continually hung over this small niche company and had the effect of holding the return on investment to normal levels. The business was capital intensive, employing high speed machines operated around the clock. There was nothing to prevent further competition from entering the business, except that it took a certain size to be able to service the big accounts, and without big orders, the equipment could not be run continuously and efficiently.

The business had experienced a basic underlying growth throughout the 1970s and early 1980s, which enabled Glendale to increase sales steadily from 1976 to 1983 at a 17 percent compound rate. Earnings had not quite kept pace with sales growth due to a decline in pretax profit margins in fiscal 1983 to 6.8 percent from a 5-year average of 9.4 percent. Some of the margin erosion resulted from a small acquisition that was losing money, and attempts to turn it around proved costly.

After 14 years of successful operations, the owners and operators of the company desired some liquidity for their now considerable investment. The company's initial investment of $457,000 had grown to approximately $7.5 million, and excess cash was accumulating. Management did not want to be acquired by another company and lose control over the company's operations. In any case, it was doubtful that the company could have been sold for a price exceeding book value, despite being only 5.9 × current earnings. The company explored the possibility of a public offering, but considering the fact that the company essentially produced a single product and that 50 percent of sales went to its largest customer and 70 percent to the top two customers, potential underwriters did not believe the stock could be sold to the public at a reasonable price. After declining to take the company public, the investment bankers suggested that liquidity and a premium price might be accomplished with an LBO. The company had over $2.0 million in excess cash and debt of only $683,000. The investment bankers proposed that the price be 150 percent of book value and that the deal be structured with little new equity and a large amount of sellers' notes. The equity would be 51 percent owned by a venture capital investor with current shareholders subscribing to 49 percent. Since the difficulty of achieving liquidity for the outside investors would likely become a problem in the future, the venture capital investor required a put option that gave them the right to sell their shares back to the company. The put price was negotiated at a 35 percent compound rate, peaking at the sixth year and declining thereafter. This equates to a return of 4.5 × the investment in a little over five years, when the put option would likely be exercised. This rate of return seemed high to management, who was confident of the company's long-term viability. However, from the outside investor's perspective, it was limiting its upside return but not its downside risk. The principal company risk of having over half of its business with one customer was investigated by the investment bankers. Top management of the largest customer was questioned about its future plans in the procurement of the type of fabrics sold by Glendale. This most important customer gave assurances of its intentions to continue to purchase its fabric requirements from outside vendors and to divide its purchases among its three principal vendors, including Glendale. With this information, investment bankers were able to convince the venture capital investor that the expected returns on its investment were commensurate with the perceived risks.

The put option prices for shares purchased for $1.00 per share were as follows.

Year Exercised	Stock Repurchase Price
Year 1	$1.00
Year 2	$1.35
Year 3	$1.82
Year 4	$2.46
Year 5	$3.32
Year 6	$4.48
Year 7	$3.32
Year 8	$2.46

By having the put price formula decline after the sixth calendar year, the company hopes to entice the outside shareholders to sell their stock back to the company at that time, and thus the insider shareholders would again become 100 percent shareholders.

The company was offered a call option to purchase the outside shareholders' stock at the put formula price, provided an earnings test was met over a 5-year period. The company's Big Eight tax partners advised against the call option feature, fearing that it could jeopardize the capital gain tax treatment in the transaction. IRS regulations, dealing with constructive ownership for purposes of control, hold that options to acquire stock are considered as stock owned. In this instance, the proposed call options were not exercisable unless the company met a test of increasing cumulative earnings over a 5-year period. The company would hold the position that the shares under option should not be counted as shares owed because the option is valid only if the earnings test were met. Whereas the call option was technically valueless unless and until the earnings test was met, the options would nevertheless have some current value as they potentially represented a right to acquire the controlling block of stock at an attractive low price. They would have a current value much like the market value of an out-of-the-money call option. This current value, when added to the 49 percent interests of the selling shareholders in the new company, could possibly push the sellers' economic interest in the new company to over 50 percent and thereby call into question whether the gain on the initial sale of the stock in the buyout would be taxed as a capital gain or treated as a dividend and taxed at ordinary income rates. The difference in the maximum capital gain tax rate of 20 percent and the maximum ordinary income tax rate of 50 percent would amount to $3.2 million in this transaction. The tax advisors counseled that granting to the company a call on the outside investors' shares would be risking the capital gains treatment of the initial sale of the company, and so the call option idea was dropped.

The financial structure of the buyout was as follows.

Sources of Financing

Bank	$1,000
Sellers' notes	7,744
Cash in company	2,217
Equity	500
	$11,461

Uses of Financing

Purchase of common stock	$11,361
Expenses and fees	101
	$11,461

Only 1 percent of the stock was purchased for cash on the close, which took place on December 28, 1983, with the balance in sellers' notes. The closing date was chosen for the purpose of making 1983 a tax year. Another 29 percent was bought for cash in April 1984, bringing the total stock purchased for cash at 30 percent for a total of $3.3 million. The original note agreement called for redeeming 20 percent of the sellers' notes in October 1984, 25 percent in January 1985, and 25 percent in January 1986. A bank loan commitment for $8.8 million was obtained to fund the scheduled sellers' note redemption. However, in the first nine months following the buyout, the company's operations showed a pretax profit of only $40,000, largely due to losses incurred in a company acquired a year earlier. The company's principal business had remained profitable although that business had been under some profit margin pressure. In view of the relatively poor operating earnings outlook, the management decided to forego the scheduled October 1984 note redemption of $2.2 million and to reschedule the note redemption to $1.1 million in January and July 1985, and $1.4 million in January and July of both 1986 and 1987. The company could borrow all of the 1985 redemption payouts of $2.2 million under the bank loan agreement but expected to have cash flow of $2.1 million in the year-ended September 1985. If earnings continued as projected, borrowings of another $3.0 million would be needed to fund the remaining note redemptions totaling $5.6 million.

The willingness of the sellers to adjust the note redemption schedule to reflect current operating conditions was consistent with the initial planning of the buyout. In order for the sellers to get a price of 150 percent of book value for their stock, they were willing to substantially finance the purchase with sellers' notes. This enabled the financing to be structured with a relatively small amount of equity, or 4.4 percent of the total financing. By keeping the total equity small, the outside shareholders' 51 percent investment was only $255,000. This enabled the outside investors to negotiate a 35 percent compounded annual return upon exercise of the put option, or 4.5 × their investment in five years. Since 4.5 × $255,000 is only $1,142,000, the company would be reasonably expected to be able to finance the put option out of cash flow. Since the company could not be sold without management's consent, as a sale requires a two-thirds vote, and since the public market for the stock will probably remain unavailable, the put will probably be exercised early in the sixth year by the outside shareholders. With this a likely scenario, management, who also held the sellers' notes, was more cautious about borrowing large sums from a bank to fund out their note redemption if this action would endanger the financial health of the company. After all, if and when the outside shareholders are bought out, the remaining shareholders want the company to be financially viable.

The plan of taking 70 percent of the purchase price in sellers' notes and redeeming those notes as earnings comfortably permit is somewhat similar to a company making a large payout in dividends to its shareholders. If Glendale had decided to pay its shareholders $11.3 million in dividends over a four-year period, it could finance the dividends in a similar fashion as the financing of the sellers' notes.

The cost differential of the LBO alternative versus paying similar sized dividends is the cost of buying out the outside shareholders and a tax cost. There would be an interest cost on both alternatives, but interest on the sellers' notes is income to the sellers and could be viewed as a dividend paid with pretax dollars. If the Glendale put is exercised, the company will be required to repurchase the outside shareholders' stock for $1,142,000 as expected in the sixth year. Over the initial five plus years, the company has free use of the $255,000 investment made by the outside shareholders, and it should be worth $375,000 at an 8 percent compound growth rate. Subtracting this amount from the put price of $1,142,000 equals a net cost of the put of $797,000, the present value of which at a 10 percent discount rate is $495,000. Adding the present value of the put to the capital gains taxes of $2.5 million triggered by the sale produces a total cost of the transaction of $3.0 million. This contrasts with the ordinary income tax cost of $5.7 million on similar sized payments if received as dividends. Thus, the net savings of the LBO alternative compared to paying the sale price out as dividends is $2.7 million.

The principal objective of providing liquidity was followed by a secondary objective of effecting some estate planning. The benefits of an LBO in the transfer of ownership to the next generation are often unappreciated. In fact, from an estate planning viewpoint, the Glendale LBO takes first prize. It earns this high status by providing dramatic benefits to all three major objectives in estate planning—liquidity, diversification, and tax saving. The liquidity objective is accomplished at a favorable tax cost by replacing unmarketable stock with cash and relatively short-term notes. The diversification objective is met by changing from a high investment concentration in one small company to a balanced portfolio of higher quality stocks and bonds. However, it is in the area of increasing the value of the owner's family holdings that the LBO offers the most striking benefits. By having one's heirs subscribe to all of the 49 percent ownership offered management in the new company, the original shareholders could transfer their ownership in the company to their heirs completely outside of their estates. In Glendale's case, the new company's equity was $500,000. Glendale's owners were offered 49 percent of this equity for $245,000. These 49 percent owners will become 100 percent owners after the fifth year, when the 51 percent owners put their stock back to the company at the previously negotiated put price. Rather than the original owners purchasing the 49 percent interest in the new company, they could and in some instances did let their heirs purchase it, or they put it in a trust for the benefit of their heirs. In instances where the heirs were unable to fund their portion of the $245,000 purchase price, the original owners gave it to them and this amount was deducted from each of the original owner's unified credit. This is the amount that can be offset against tax liability on taxable lifetime gifts and estate transfers. The amount of gifts exempt from tax in 1987 is $600,000 per individual. Had the two original owners made a gift of the entire $245,000, no taxes would be due because each of the original owners had a unified credit well in excess of the size of their gifts. Although the gifts would reduce the lifetime credit against estate taxes, the gifts themselves reduce the amount of the taxable estates, and the expected appreciation in the value of the gifts occurs outside of the original owners' estates and is therefore not taxed at the top estate tax rate of 55 percent.

To illustrate the effect on estate taxes, two examples are provided, showing the estate values if the original owner dies in 10 years after effecting the LBO contrasted with the owners' continuing their current ownership. It is assumed that on the sale of the stock, state and federal capital gains taxes total 23 percent and that the aftertax proceeds grow at 7 percent per year. It is further assumed that the company's $1.5 million basic earning power will increase by 5 percent per year and that for estate tax purposes, the company's stock is valued at 80 percent of book value.

Estate taxes can be paid with the sale of liquid investments in the LBO example. Without the LBO, the estate would need the company to redeem the stock to pay the taxes. Because the company would be hard-pressed financially to redeem $11.1 million worth of stock, the estate could qualify for up to a 14-year extension of the time to pay these taxes, with only a 4 percent interest rate on the first $345,000 of tax liability and the IRS interest rate on the balance. The company would need to redeem sufficient amounts of the estate's stock annually over a 14-year period to pay the interest and taxes. These repayments reduce the high and low interest loans pro rata.

In the example without the LBO, the book value of the company will be reduced by stock redemptions totaling $20.6 million to pay the estate taxes plus interest on the loan over the 14-year extension. Interest payments would be $1,040,000 over the first five years if the federal interest rate is 10 percent. These payments would decline by $110,000 per year thereafter, as the $1,100,000 annual installments of estate taxes are paid over the last 10 years of the 14-year extension. Assuming the estate had stock redeemed by the com-

Table 5.5   Value of Original Owners' Estate Ten Years Later

	With LBO	Without LBO
	(in millions)	
Cash and securities	$17.5	$ 0.0
Book value of company stock		27.2
Taxable value of estate	17.5	21.8[1]
Federal estate taxes	8.7	11.1
Residual estate	$ 8.8	$10.7

[1]Assumes taxable value of company stock at 80% of book value.

Table 5.6   Value of the Heirs' Estates After Inheritance Ten Years Later

	With LBO	Without LBO
	(in millions)	
Inheritance—cash	$ 8.8	$ 0.0
Book value of company stock owned	$19.7	$27.2
Less present value of taxes and interest		10.5
Total value of estate	$28.5	$16.7

pany under Section 303 to pay both interest and principal, the total amount
of the stock sales would be $20.6 million and the present value of this stream
of payments would be $10.5 million at a 10 percent discount rate. Thus, the
company would be required to pay out every year for 14 years an amount
averaging $1,470,000 to redeem the stock. If one-half or more of the company
is sold during the 14-year extension period, the deferred estate tax payments
are accelerated, making them immediately due and payable. Any LBO would
trigger the immediate payment of the deferred estate taxes, and the LBO sale
would not likely contain enough cash to pay these taxes. A cash buyer of the
company at book value would be difficult to find due to the price (11.3 ×
earnings), slow growth prospects, and the company's narrow customer base.
However, assuming a cash sale for $27.2 million is transacted, $11.1 million
would be earmarked to pay the estate taxes, leaving $16.1 million in cash and
no further interest in the company. This compares with the LBO alternative
as shown in the following table.

Table 5.7   Value of the Heirs' Net Worth After Inheritance Ten Years Later

	With LBO	Without LBO
	(in millions)	
Inheritance—cash	$ 8.8	$16.1
Book value of company stock owned	19.7	
Total value of stock	$28.5	$16.1

The contrasting difference in values is dramatic. This example demonstrates
just how valuable an estate planning tool the LBO can be. By transferring the
original owners' interest in the company out of the original owners' estates
and into the estates of the owners' heirs, all estate tax obligations on the original owners' stock in the company have been bypassed. Moreover, ownership
of the company remains with the original families.

If the original owner should live 20 years after the LBO date, the advantages
of the LBO widen.

Table 5.8   Value of Original Owners' Estates Twenty Years Later

	With LBO	Without LBO
	(in millions)	
Cash & Securities	$33.9	$ 0.0
Book value of company stock owned		59.3
Value of estate for estate taxes	33.9	47.4
Estate taxes	17.7	25.2
Residual estate	$16.2	$34.1

Table 5.9   Value of Heirs' Net Worth After Inheritance Twenty Years Later

	With LBO	Without LBO
	(in millions)	
Inheritance—cash	$16.2	$34.1
Book value of company stock owned	51.8	
Total net worth	$68.0	$34.1

Again, this assumes the company can be sold for book value and mostly cash. The sale price of $59.3 million is reduced by estate taxes of $25.2 million to a residual value of $34.1 million. With the LBO, the company's stock appreciates in the heirs' estates rather than in the original owners' estates, a principal objective of an estate freeze. Unlike an estate freeze, which provides no liquidity, the original owners can enjoy their $8.5 million aftertax proceeds of the sale and watch their investments grow to $33.5 million over 20 years in a safely diversified portfolio. Furthermore, they can enjoy seeing the company they built remain in the families' ownership, knowing it will not have to be sold or shackled with large stock redemptions to fund sizable estate taxes upon their death.

This LBO produced tremendous benefits for the company's owners in every important category. It produced a sale price 50 percent higher than otherwise available; it provided capital gain treatment to the proceeds and gave the owners liquidity and diversification; it transferred the ownership of the company outside of the original owners' estates, and kept the ownership in their families. Because the future growth in the value of the company was not subject to high estate taxes, the families' net worth is estimated in 20 years to be twice what it would have been. Also, everything was accomplished at a very low level of risk because the majority of the debt for the buyout was held in "friendly" hands.

Glendale Fabrics, Inc.
Balance Sheet—Year-Ended November 27, 1983
and November 28, 1982
(000 omitted)

	1983	1982
Current Assets		
Cash and Short-Term Investments	$1,870	$3,159
Receivables	4,569	3,231
Inventories	1,838	1,298
Total Current Assets	$8,295	$7,729
Property and Equipment	9,635	7,245
Less Depreciation	6,483	4,530
Net Property and Equipment	3,152	2,715
Total Assets	$11,501	$10,444
Current Liabilities		
Current Installments on Long-Term Debt	$ 265	$ 118
Accounts Payable	2,003	2,162
Accruals	702	1,030
Total Current Liabilities	$2,970	$3,315
Long-Term Debt	683	256
Deferred Taxes and Compensation	388	419
Total Liabilities	$4,042	$3,990
Shareholders' Equity		
Common Stock	$ 455	$ 458
Retained Earnings	7,004	5,996
Total Shareholders' Equity	7,459	6,454
Total Liabilities and Shareholders' Equity	$11,501	$10,444

Glendale Fabrics, Inc.
Statement of Income—Years Ended November 27, 1983
and November 28, 1982
(000 omitted)

	1983	1982
Net Sales	$35,331	$27,742
Cash of Goods Sold	31,669	23,703
Gross Profit	3,662	4,039
Selling, General and Administrative Expenses	1,323	1,125
Income From Operations	2,339	2,914
Other Income	53	24
Income Before Taxes	2,391	2,937
Income Tax Expenses	1,123	1,353
Net Income	$1,269	$1,584

LADD FURNITURE

The LADD LBO was the result of Baldwin-United strategy to sell this unwanted division for a loss and obtain a tax refund. Baldwin-United intended to convert their sellers' notes into 75 percent of the equity in five years, but instead sold the note back to LADD in the face of steadily worsening financial problems. Operating management increased their ownership by buying out some of the original stockholders who were affiliated with Baldwin-United, and promptly went public to pay back their debt incurred to buy back the Baldwin-United convertible note. The public offering 22 months after the buyout was at a price of 145 × the cost of the original LBO stock in only 22 months. This case illustrates how the management of an unwanted, underachieving division of a large company can engineer an LBO resulting in quick and very substantial gains in their net worth.

The LADD buyout combined good management with good luck to produce a quick fortune. Few have made so much money with so little invested in so short a time. Ironically, the people whose actions helped create the big quick gains made the least by selling out too early.

The fortunate few were the management of the furniture division of Sperry and Hutchinson. Baldwin-United was in the process of acquiring Sperry and Hutchinson in 1981 when it was approached by management proposing a management buyout. Baldwin-United was wheeling and dealing financially, and the prospect of generating cash and a tax refund from the sale of an unwanted division was attractive.

Sperry and Hutchinson had acquired its furniture division piecemeal. David M. Lea and Company was acquired in 1969 for stock. Lea traced its origins back to wood manufacturing operations established in 1869. In 1979, Sperry and Hutchinson bought American Furniture Company, founded in 1927, and Drew Furniture Company, founded in 1955, for $15 million in cash. Sperry and Hutchinson also acquired Daystrom Furniture in 1971 for $18 million. Daystrom commenced operations in 1934. These companies formed LADD Furniture; the name was chosen by taking the first letter of the component businesses—Lea Industries, American Drew, and Daystrom.

In 1981, the company was a vertically integrated manufacturer of wood and metal furniture in the low-medium to high-medium price ranges. American Drew, its largest and most profitable component, produces traditional, country, and colonial styles of wood bedroom, dining room, and living room occasional pieces sold in medium to high-medium price ranges. It had produced a number of the nation's top selling groups, and its leading seller had been produced for an almost unheard of 23 years.

Lea Industries was the second largest and second most profitable component. Lea makes medium-price wood furniture for the youth and adult bedroom market. Daystrom, the smallest of the three LADD Furniture companies, makes metal kitchen, dinette, and casual dining room furniture in the medium-price range. Another division makes plywood, veneer, and wood laminated parts.

Prior to 1981, Sperry and Hutchinson had been controlled by the Beinecke family, but the fear of an unfriendly takeover arose when a block of the family stock held in estate was sold to the Bass Brothers. Sperry and Hutchinson hired Goldman, Sachs to advise on a strategy, and to look for a white knight or a friendly merger partner. These deliberations concluded that several divisions, including the furniture division, fit poorly with the other parts of Sperry and Hutchinson's business and were sale candidates. When Baldwin-United surfaced as a potential acquirer of Sperry and Hutchinson, it, too, wanted to sell the furniture division. Goldman, Sachs evaluated each of Sperry and Hutchinson's businesses and placed a value on the furniture business well below its book value (which included substantial goodwill). Sperry and Hutchinson would realize a substantial tax recovery on the sale by selling the furniture businesses before its acquisition by Baldwin-United. After reaching an agreement with the Beineckes for the acquisition of Sperry and Hutchinson, Baldwin-United met with top Sperry and Hutchinson furniture executives to discuss a proposal to sell the furniture business to its management and other investors. At the initial meeting were Don Hunziker, Sperry and Hutchinson Furniture's CEO; Dick Allen, executive vice president; and three senior officers of Baldwin-United, including Harold Smith, senior vice-president of manufacturing of Baldwin Piano and Organ Company, a Baldwin-United subsidiary. A proposal was developed for an LBO of Sperry and Hutchinson Furniture by seven members of management, plus Harold Smith of Baldwin Piano, James Ault of Baldwin-United, and Hoyt Bray, a friend of Smith's. Of the 5 million shares to be outstanding, the latter three buyers, all friendly to Baldwin, would own 2.6 million shares, or 52 percent, thereby placing control in friendly hands.

The initial proposal called for an equity package consisting of a $2 million cash investment and a $7 million subordinated note convertible into 75 percent of the outstanding shares in five years. The subordinated note was to be provided by NILIC, a Baldwin-United insurance subsidiary. Allen knew that members of his management team would have to borrow nearly all of the $960,000 required to purchase their 48 percent interest, and he realized that to repay these loans with future dividends after taxes would be difficult. He then decided to establish a holding company funded by a $1 million loan from NILIC, $500,000 in loans from stockholders, and $500,000 in equity investment. The holding company would then invest its $2 million in the equity of the LBO. This further leveraging of the equity engineered by Allen resulted in management's having to pay only $480,000 for its stock, half in cash and half in a loan. This allowed for the repayment of 75 percent of the $2 million equity investment by the repayment of debt, rather than with dividends taxable to the stockholders. After considerable negotiation, it was agreed that the $7 million subordinated note was to be convertible into 75 percent of the company after 5 years and that the management team would have a right of first refusal on any subsequent sale of the note.

The final purchase price was funded as follows.

Bank term loan	$20,000,000
Bank revolver	30,300,000
NILIC convertible note	7,000,000
Seller's loan	285,000
NILIC subordinated note	1,000,000
Stockholders' loans	500,000
Stockholders' equity	500,000
Assumption of liabilities	10,600,000
Total purchase price	$70,200,000

The deal closed in September 1981 after the bank financing had been arranged through a group of banks led by Manufacturers Hanover Commercial Corporation. The book value of the assets sold was $89.6 million, providing ample collateral for borrowing $50.3 million on a fully secured basis.

Dick Allen became the chief financial officer of Sperry and Hutchinson Furniture in November 1980. He led the development of a strategic plan, which called for the reorganization of the company into three operating companies as profit centers run autonomously. It also called for elimination of significant overhead costs, management layers, and hourly employees to improve productivity. Though the plan was presented to Sperry and Hutchinson in early 1981, their preoccupation with the sale of Sperry and Hutchinson held up approval on implementation until the businesses were sold in September 1981. However, 1981 was a recession year that especially affected the furniture industry. Despite the cut in expenses, LADD's profits dropped to only $1.8 million for the year ended January 2, 1982, compared with $6.9 million earned in 1978. Sales declined from $162.9 million in 1979 to $141.2 million in 1981. The introduction of heavy debt with interest rates of 2 percent over prime gave management added incentive to cut expenses quickly and deeply, despite the fact that the reorganization and cost-cutting plan was beginning to be implemented at the time of the buyout. In the first 16 months of operation after the buyout, operating earnings totaled $16.3 million, and interest expenses equaled $10.3 million. LADD also cut inventories by almost half and worked at reducing accounts receivables. As a result, it was able to reduce short-term borrowings by $19.7 million in 1982 even while earning only $2.2 million due to depressed industry conditions and high interest expenses.

Because the LADD individual shareholders would own only 25 percent of the stock after Baldwin-United converted its seller's note after September 1, 1986, Allen negotiated for a stock purchase agreement. He argued that being a minority stockholder with no liquidity would be unacceptable to the management group. This agreement allowed a shareholder, after three years or upon retiring at age 55, to offer his shares first to the other stockholders, then to LADD, and finally to Baldwin-United. If the stockholder found no takers, he could then put the stock to Baldwin-United at a price that was the product of the previous year's earnings, times the industry P/E ratio as computed and published by Wheat, First Securities through the efforts of its noted furniture analyst, Jerry Epperson. This stock purchase agreement proved to be of critical importance in determining the future ownership of LADD.

Participating in the sharp market rebound beginning in August 1982, furniture stocks began to anticipate the expected business recovery and rose sharply in advance of actual earnings improvement. That price action produced a furniture stock P/E ratio of 11 times in January 1983, compared with a five–seven × multiple that had prevailed for the previous decade.

When the company's earnings of $2.24 million were multiplied by 11 ×, Lee Weisnicht, a member of management who had reached age 55 and was thus eligible for retirement, computed his stock to be worth $267,000. His investment of $16,550 had been made only 18 months previously. Since the pricing formula locked in the previous year's earnings for the entire year, Weisnicht was fearful that the high P/E ratio multiplier might decline substantially and offset the expected higher earnings in 1983 to produce a lower formula price in the near future.

Weisnicht chose to retire and sell his stock under the Shareholders Agreement. The action was contagious, as all three Baldwin-United nonmanagement shareholders, also having reached the age of 55, decided to exercise their stock purchase agreements. The formula price for their shares totaled more than $3 million. An additional consideration in their decision probably related to Baldwin-United's financial troubles that were beginning to surface. The selling shareholders reasoned that if the other shareholders and LADD were unable or unwilling to exercise their rights to buy the stock offered to them under the stock purchase agreement and that if Baldwin-United's troubles increased, its banks would not allow it to honor the repurchase price of $3.27 million. Thus, there was a real incentive to cash in their shares before the window of opportunity closed or before the value of their investment declined. None of the other shareholders elected to buy the tendered shares, since Baldwin-United would ultimately dilute their ownership with the conversion of the $7 million note. Baldwin-United then asked LADD to buy the stock, but the LADD board decided that the $3 million purchase might jeopardize the future of the company since it would erode all of its equity. Baldwin-United did buy Weisnicht's stock for $266,985, but their banks balked at the remaining $3 million obligation.

LADD had earlier in the spring offered to purchase the $7 million convertible note held by NILIC for $14 million and was turned down. LADD decided to go for it again, offering to pay $17 million in cash for the note and to purchase the stock from the selling stockholders for $3 million under the stock purchase agreement. In addition, LADD agreed to release NILIC from a $20.3 million mortgage loan commitment. NILIC had come under some criticism from the insurance commissioner of its home state of Arkansas because too many of its assets were in securities of Baldwin-United affiliates. Accordingly, the insurance commissioner agreed to the sale of the $7 million note for $17 million cash.

To finance the purchase, LADD explored both the private and public markets and elected to go public, being lured by the high valuation of furniture manufacturers' earnings the market afforded. The company selected Wheat, First Securities to manage the underwriting and moved as quickly as possible to become effective. The principal selling stockholder was AMDALE, an investment company formed by Allen, Hunziker, and John Foster, a LADD officer, to purchase the NILIC convertible note for $17 million. Manufacturers Hanover Commercial Corporation financed the NILIC note purchased by AMDALE, a loan that was guaranteed by the company and by Allen, Hunziker, and Foster. The note was convertible into 75 percent of the outstanding shares approximately three and a half years later. AMDALE requested immediate conversion so it could offer the shares on the public offering and repay the Manufacturers Hanover Commercial Corporation loan to purchase the shares. In return for the immediate conversion privilege, AMDALE agreed to convert the NILIC note into only 26 percent of the outstanding shares. AMDALE's negotiations with LADD were not difficult, as Hunziker and Allen of AMDALE were negotiating with Hunziker and Allen of LADD. The public offering in August 1983 produced for AMDALE sufficient funds to repay the note, pay fees and expenses, and still have $3 million excess funds. AMDALE was later merged into LADD. The principal reason for using the AMDALE investment company approach was to prevent the immediate write-off against net worth of the $10 million premium that the note was purchased for over its face value.

In June 1983, the market peaked, and furniture stocks were no exception to the slow erosion to stock prices generally.

The LADD IPO continued to be in demand and became effective on August 4, 1983 at $14.50 per share. This was 12.9 × trailing 12 months fully diluted earnings per share of $1.12. The offering, after underwriting discount and expenses, netted the company $8.8 million, AMDALE $21 million, and selling shareholders $3.2 million. For the original shareholders, the net gain after all expenses was 134 times their investment, achieved over a period of 23 months. Don Hunziker, who had worked for various predecessors of the company for 26 years, had committed to borrow $160,000 of which $80,000 went to buy 800,000 shares of stock in September 1981, when the outlook for the furniture business was far from rosy. He increased his holdings to 1,283,000 shares through additional purchases from Smith, Ault, Bray, and Weisnicht in April 1983. The additional shares cost him approximately $770,000 but were worth more than eight times that amount on the public offering less than four months later. Hunziker sold 67,500 shares on the offering, netting him $903,000 after discount and expenses. At that date, his remaining holdings were valued at $17.6 million.

Dick Allen, the financial mastermind of the reorganization and leader in negotiations and structuring of the buyout, ended up with stock worth $14.1 million, after netting $903,000 on the public offering. Bill Fenn, the company's president, joined the management team seven months after the buyout and acquired 320,000 shares from Hoyt Bray for $40,720. Bray had agreed at the outset to make up to half of his shares available to future key management employees. Fenn added to his holdings when the Smith group sold in April 1983 and ended up with stock valued at $8.7 million, after netting $595,000 on the public offering. Fenn had held his original stock less than 15 months at the time of the offering.

It is ironic that those shareholders who sought to cash in on what they considered a tremendous profit in a short time suffered the greatest long-term opportunity loss. Lee Weisnicht, who first retired and put his stock to Baldwin-United, received $266,985 for a $16,550 investment. To take this profit at the time was sensible, but had he held his stock, it would have been valued at $2.4 million at the public offering price. Harold Smith made a profit of 16 times his investment, but he left more than $20 million on the table by his early exit. On April 25, 1983, he received $2.02 million cash and a two-year note for $552,000 for his 1.6 million shares. Just 101 days later, these shares were valued at the public offering at $23.2 million. It was Smith, perhaps more than anyone else, who caused the series of events to happen. Among the Baldwin-United executives, he had the greatest appreciation of the value of LADD. He was also constructive in his consulting on manufacturing matters for which LADD compensated him. Baldwin-United was able to absorb the Weisnicht stock put of $267,000, but when Smith followed with an almost $2.6 million obligation, Baldwin-United balked because of its own financial problem. This bind made Baldwin-United receptive to negotiating a solution and enabled LADD to purchase the convertible note and relieve Baldwin-United of its stock repurchase obligations to Smith and the three other sellers. Smith was also in a good position to evaluate Baldwin-United's financial problems, which would have eventually resulted in a worthless put obligation by Baldwin-United. Surely Smith has looked back and wished he had not sold all his shares at $1.61 per share. Without the exercise of his put, however, Baldwin-United might not have sold the convertible note, the financing of which propelled LADD to go public. Smith was also able to take his cash and purchase 42 percent of Baldwin Piano on an LBO from Baldwin-United. It could well be that in the long run Smith holdings of Baldwin Piano will equal or exceed the value of his original LADD holdings. The value of LADD on the public offering was $100 million, which means the NILIC note would have been worth $75 million if it were convertible at that time. This would put a value of $25 million on the remaining 25 percent, of which Smith would have owned $8 million worth with little if any liquidity. Certainly Hoyt Bray cannot feel too bad. He had no active connection with the company whatsoever but agreed to invest $80,000 in the buyout at Smith's urging. In 19 months, he walked away with $400,000, or five times his money.

This, of course, is an unusual story. The generation of capital gains of this magnitude in this short time frame are extraordinary, and fate played a hand in their achievement. However, this buyout demonstrates what opportunities lie in the purchase of an unexciting and unwanted division of a large company by the employment of creative structuring, a sound business plan, and a little bit of luck.

Ladd Furniture, Inc. and Subsidiaries
Consolidated Balance Sheets
(Dollars in thousands, except share data)

	January 2, 1982	January 1, 1983	May 28, 1983 (Unaudited)
Assets			
Current assets:			
Cash	$	$ 611	$ 1,164
Trade accounts receivable	16,249	13,263	18,718
Employee and other receivables	470	375	410
Inventories	26,420	15,099	15,304
Prepaid expenses and other current assets	554	529	549
Deferred income taxes	41	87	87
Total current assets	43,734	29,964	36,232
Property, plant, and equipment, at cost	19,266	19,999	20,179
Less accumulated depreciation	514	2,124	2,796
Net property, plant, and equipment	18,752	17,875	17,383
Timberlands and timber rights, at cost, less applicable depletion	221	125	85
Deferred charges, at cost, less applicable amortization	116	90	80
Total assets	$62,823	$48,054	$53,780
Liabilities and stockholders' equity			
Current liabilities:			
Bank overdrafts	$ 54	$ 0	$ 0
Short-term borrowings	22,981	3,239	3,555
Trade accounts payable	4,693	4,673	5,663
Accrued expenses and other current liabilities	5,025	4,546	5,466
Income taxes	102	2,732	2,689
Total current liabilities	32,855	15,190	17,373
Long-term debt	28,500	28,500	21,552
Deferred compensation	61	145	129
Deferred income taxes	619	1,258	1,486
Total liabilities	62,035	45,093	40,540
Stockholders' equity			
Common stock	500	500	660
Additional paid-in capital		12	6,852
Retained earnings	288	2,449	6,280
	788	2,961	13,792
Less treasury stock			(552)
Total stockholders' equity	788	2,961	13,240
Total liabilities and stockholders' equity	$62,823	$48,054	$53,780

Consolidated Statement of Earnings
(Dollars in thousands, except share data)

	Predecessor Companies		LADD Furniture Inc. and Subsidiaries			
					Five Months-Ended	
	Year-Ended January 3, 1981	Eight Months-Ended August 30, 1981	Four Months-Ended January 2, 1982	Year-Ended January 1, 1983	May 29, 1982 (Unaudited)	May 28, 1983 (Unaudited)
Net sales	$146,140	$93,903	$47,300	$114,824	$45,268	$54,079
Cost of sales	116,703	74,557	36,587	85,823	34,801	39,138
Gross profit	29,437	19,346	10,713	29,001	10,467	14,941
Selling, general, and administrative expenses	22,734	14,792	6,808	16,582	7,001	6,870
Operating income	6,703	4,554	3,905	12,419	3,466	8,071
Other deductions (income):						
Interest expense	2,268	1,333	3,249	7,069	3,497	1,623
Gain on sale of machinery and equipment	(20)	(152)	(60)	(108)	(17)	(2)
Income from settlement of litigation						(238)
Other, net	111	64	(252)	(332)	(155)	(292)
	2,359	1,245	2,937	6,629	3,325	1,091
EBIT	4,344	3,309	968	5,790	141	6,980
Income tax expense	1,790	1,780	680	3,552	532	3,149
Net earnings (loss)	2,554	1,529	288	2,238	(391)	3,831
Net earnings (loss) per common share:						
Primary			0.06	0.45	(0.08)	0.78
Fully diluted			0.06	0.42	(0.08)	0.62
Weighted average number of common shares outstanding			5,000,000	5,000,000	5,000,000	4,917,860

CONE MILLS

Cone Mills was put into play when its retired chairman sold his stock to a company, which acknowledged it intended to gain control of Cone Mills. The company successfully defended itself from the unfriendly takeover attempt by taking the company private with an LBO. With the use of an ESOP, the company was able to obtain tax refunds and increase future cash flows by making substantial ESOP contributions in both common and preferred stock. If the company's 10-year projections are realized, the ESOP will own over 75 percent of the company's equity, thus providing the employees with the incentives and pride of ownership. Cone's use of an ESOP avoided the criticism leveled at Dan River management and others that the use of their ESOP was largely a management entrenchment device. Cone did not use the ESOP financing structure developed by Kelso in which management appeared to purchase stock at a small fraction of the price paid by the ESOP.

Cone Mills, headquartered in Greensboro, North Carolina, is the nation's largest producer of corduroys and has approximately the same leading market share in denims as Burlington Industries. It also produces yarn-dyed and uniform fabrics, greige goods and commission textile dyeing, printing, and finishing services. It has 21 plants in the Carolinas and Mississippi, and employs 10,000 workers.

In 1980, Cone enjoyed record sales and pretax earnings of $730 million and $86 million, respectively, led by the boom in denim sales. In the early 1980s, sales and earnings slumped for both denim and corduroys due to the recession and weak export sales. Sales in 1983 were $688 million, and pretax earnings were $28.6 million.

Cone's size and dominant presence in the textile industry would please Moses and Caesar Cone, its founders. The two brothers from Baltimore first established Cone Export and Commission Company to sell and merchandise textile products manufactured in the South.

The idea to establish Cone Export was conceived as the brothers traveled throughout the South, selling goods from their father's wholesale grocery operation in Baltimore. Because of a shortage of cash after the Civil War, bartering was often the means of exchange. Many of the Cone's customers were multiproduct general stores that were owned and operated by textile manufacturers.

The general stores were often the primary sales outlet for textile products. Realizing the potential of a merchandising and marketing firm to broaden the market for southern textiles, Cone Export was incorporated in New York City by the Cones in May 1891. Cone Export also provided a vehicle in which to liquidate bartered textile inventories.

Now known as Cone Mills Marketing Company (a subsidiary of Cone Mills Corporation), the firm continued to sell and merchandise textiles produced by Cone Manufacturing. Caesar and Moses did not begin actual textile production until 1895, when the first plant was erected in Greensboro.

For the ensuing 50 years, the Cone family continued to strengthen its company through acquisition and construction of additional manufacturing facilities. In 1948, the company began to consolidate operations under Bernard and Herman Cone as independently run mills were merged into the parent, Cone Mills Corporation. Desire on the part of shareholders to diversify their assets and liquify their holdings led the company to go public in 1951.

From the mid-1970s through 1983, Cone had pursued a strategy of equipment modernization. Over $350 million was invested in plant and equipment during this period. Cone was poised to reap the benefits of its modernization program when in October 1983, Ceasar Cone II, retired as chairman in 1973, contracted to sell his 600,000 shares, or 10.9 percent of Cone common stock, to Western Pacific Industries, a company that had just accumulated 333,000 shares to give it approximately 17 percent of the total. In its Schedule 13D filing with the SEC, a requirement once an entity owns over 5 percent of a public traded company, Western Pacific acknowledged it currently intended to seek to acquire control of Cone although it had not formulated any plan or proposal.

Management first learned of Caesar Cone's intentions on October 31, 1983. The company was not given a chance to bid for these shares, as a purchase agreement for $50 per share had already been executed. Although Caesar Cone's sale to Western Pacific provided the catalyst for the ultimate buyout of the Company at $70 per share, he suffered an opportunity loss of $12 million on his 600,000 shares.

Cone Mills' immediate response to Western Pacific's actions was to question the legality of the 13D formally filed with the SEC on November 4, 1983. In its filing with the U.S. District Court in Greensboro, Cone alleged that Western Pacific "violated Section 13(d) of the Exchange Act by falsely denying in its Schedule 13D that it was an unregistered investment company under the Investment Company Act of 1940 and by failing to disclose that, as a result of such status, it was prohibited by Federal law from acquiring control of Cone." Though a legitimate argument, the filing more importantly bought strategic time for Cone.

The day after Cone's District Court filing, Dewey L. Trogdon, chairman and CED, called an emergency meeting of the board of directors. Also invited to attend were Salomon Brothers, Cone's investment banker since 1977, and representatives from the law firm of Cleary, Gottlieb, Stein, and Hamilton. The participants in the meeting identified the eight basic alternatives Cone had:

1   Initiate talks with a third party in regard to a possible friendly takeover.
2   Initiate the above but as a business combination.
3   Negotiate with Western Pacific.
4   LBO of Cone by management.
5   Sale of additional common stock to a friendly third party in an effort to dilute Western Pacific's holdings.
6   Possible acquisition by Cone of another entity.

7 Repurchase Cone common stock held by Western Pacific and make a tender offer for Western Pacific stock.

8 Pursue its present litigation against Western Pacific and make no formal response.

From the proceedings of November 8, Salomon was left with two areas of primary responsibility: to explore potential merger partners for Cone and to determine the financial feasibility of a leveraged management buyout. Realizing now that anything was possible, Trogdon began his own exploration into the possibility of a management buyout.

Trogdon immediately involved Cone executive vice-president and treasurer Joseph F. Bond in the LBO discussions. While Salomon crunched numbers, Trogdon and Bond made contact with several potential institutional lenders and two firms engaged in organizing and investing in LBOs.

Simultaneous to its feasibility studies, Salomon contacted 12 potential merger companies, two of which were textile firms. In addition to its initiated contacts, Salomon also received two unsolicited inquiries as to potential mergers with Cone.

Salomon was unable to negotiate a firm offer for the company although several companies indicated interest. At a November 28 gathering of the same group of directors, bankers, and lawyers that convened on November 8, Trogdon proposed a leveraged management buyout of Cone for $68 per share. The board set up a special committee, consisting of members of the board that were not part of the management group making the proposal.

The special committee met on November 28, and considered the management group proposal, and a written proposal received that day from one of the two LBO firms with which Trogdon and Bond had previously held discussions. The written proposal offered $68 per share and management equity participation. The special committee recommended acceptance of the management group proposal, provided Cone would be able to consider any subsequent offers. It recommended that the other written proposal be rejected because Cone would have to pay a substantial fee if the transaction was not completed and the proposal called for Cone to grant it an option to purchase a large number of shares. The special committee also opined that it was not likely to close without the cooperation of management, and it believed such cooperation was unlikely. Unfriendly LBOs are difficult to finance at best and probably impossible to finance in a business as multifaceted and complex as Cone's.

The management proposal included the top five executive officers who were also directors of Cone and 42 other executive officers and managers. With the establishment of an ESOP, all employees would participate as equity owners in the company. Management was attracted to an ESOP because it was consistent with the company's culture and provided for employee participation. The ESOP also offered a means of sheltering earnings from taxes to enhance the repayment of acquisition debt.

In contrast to the use of an ESOP where the ESOP actually borrowed the money, Cone's method was to make annual contributions initially in preferred stock, thereby avoiding dilution of common shares. This is allowed because the Cone ESOP is unleveraged, or incurs no debt. If the ESOP is the borrower, common stock equity must be contributed to the ESOP. Cone's ESOP permitted it to contribute up to 25 percent of payroll, with a minimum contribution of 10 percent in the initial two years. Thereafter, the minimum contribution is made in the form of common stock, preferred stock, debt or other qualified employer securities, and is a pretax deduction as an employee benefit contribution. The contributions are allocated to each employee over the age of 21, with one year's service in proportion to the employee's compensation. When an employee reaches 65, dies, or is disabled, he receives his vested share. If an employee retires early, he would receive his ESOP interests at the age of 65 or 1990, whichever occurred first. Cone's intention is to offset any taxable income with ESOP contributions in the early years until the debt is substantially repaid. ESOP contributions can be reduced or eliminated altogether if the company can satisfactorily amortize debt from operations. Because the company is endeavoring to apply all of its cash generated to debt service, it desired to pay stock dividends on the preferred stock contributed to the ESOP. If the IRS were to rule that the preferred stock had a market value of less than par, it would allow only this amount of the preferred stock contributions as a deduction for tax purposes. To avoid this, it hired an appraiser for the ESOP, who also advised them on structuring the preferred stock to enable the appraisal to be at par value.

The ESOP became the means by which employees accumulate funds for retirement in the future, as contributions to existing pension plans were ended. Cone purchased annuities to provide for payment of retirement benefits accrued to December 31, 1983. Going forward, the pension plans have been revised and coordinated with the ESOP, and together will give the employees at least what they would have received without the ESOP. The annuitizing of the pension plans permits the return to Cone of the excess assets held under the pension plans of approximately $50 million of taxable income. The ESOP contribution made for 1983 of $37.2 million enabled the company to recover 1980 taxes of approximately $17 million. This recovery of 1980 taxes was not possible after 1983, as losses can be carried back only three years.

The fairness of the $70 sale price was opined by Salomon. Based on Cone's projected 1984 aftertax earnings of $31 million, the buyout amounted to 12.3 × this estimate, a significant premium over other textile P/E ratios. It also represented a substantial premium over its highest traded price of 43\frac{1}{2}$ prior to Western Pacific's involvement. Salomon prepared a hypothetical asset valuation which produced an adjusted book value of $83.64 per share. It took into consideration the undervalued inventory valuation, replacement cost of plant and equipment over book value, and other items undervalued for assets. The board considered the hypothetical book value to be a mathematical exercise that could not be actually realized in a liquidation due to overcapacity in certain areas of Cone's business and the expenses of a liquidation. The board concluded and Salomon agreed that the highest value would be realized in a sale of Cone as a going-concern.

The proposal to purchase all common shares at $70 and to cancel all existing stock options for the $76 per share (the spread between the exercise price and $70, plus a tax reimbursement payment provided by the terms of the options) was predicated upon obtaining proper and necessary financing. Morgan Guaranty was retained to structure the financing and serve as lead bank. The projected need for funds was approximately $465,250,000 and was broken down as follows.

	Requirements
Payment of $70/share of common stock	$381,526,000
Cancellation: purchase of outstanding options at $76/share	15,542,000
Refinance current debt	60,682,000
Expenses[1]	7,500,000
	$465,250,000

[1]Expenses included $4,000,000 for Salomon, $1,775,000 for bank fees and expenses, and $900,000 for legal fees and expenses.

Morgan Guaranty initiated a consortium including nine other banks that were willing to provide both debt and equity financing to Cone Mills' Acquisition Corporation. Led by Morgan Guaranty, the banks committed to take $457 million. Other participating institutions were: Bank of America (San Francisco); Chemical Bank (New York); Continental Illinois (Chicago); First Union (Charlotte); Mellon Bank (Pittsburgh); NCNB (Charlotte); Northwestern Bank (Greensboro); South Carolina National (Columbia, S.C.); and Wachovia Bank (Winston-Salem). Each consortium member took a strip consisting of a like percentage of each of the securities listed below:

Senior revolving credit	$370,000,000
Subordinated term debt	50,000,000
Senior preferred stock (12% cumulative)	25,000,000
Convertible preferred stock	10,350,000
Common stock (banks)	1,650,000
Total bank consortium	$457,000,000
Common stock—management	8,250,000
	$465,250,000

Of the $8,250,000 equity investment by management, $4,761,750 was obtained by the tax-free exchange of 68,025 shares of Cone common held by management prior to the transaction. A significant portion of the balance was funded by purchases of management's stock options for $15.5 million.

Cone Management owns 83.3 percent of the common stock in the new company before conversion of preferred stock. The bank consortium owns the remaining 16.7 percent and controls one out of nine board seats. The only guarantee of control stems from bylaws that allow cumulative voting, resulting in a sufficient number of directors and enabling the banks to elect one director.

The convertible, nonvoting preferred stock, which is owned 100 percent by the consortium members, carries a conversion rate of 10 common to one preferred share. In the agreement with Cone, the stock is convertible only upon a public offering of stock by the private company or the acquisition by another firm of at least 51 percent of the common shares. Upon conversion, the banks will own 60 percent of the founders' common stock and the management group 40 percent. Stock held by the founders, however, could be significantly diluted due to the issuance of new common shares contributed to the ESOP. By law, a full-service banking institution cannot hold any more than a 5 percent voting equity position in another company. For this reason, the 10 banks divvied up the equity shares.

The $420 million was broken down into a revolving credit facility of $370 million and a subordinated term loan of $50 million. Both loans carried variable rates, with the revolver priced at $1\frac{1}{2}$ percent over Morgan Guaranty's prime rate (or $2\frac{1}{2}$ percent over the LIBOR) and the subordinated debt at 3 percent over prime (4 percent over LIBOR). Both loans were unsecured and carried $\frac{3}{8}$ percent annual commitment fees on the unused portions of the lines.

The buyout changed the capital structure of Cone Mills as shown below.

	As of January 1, 1984	Post Merger
Senior debt and deferral items	17.1%	79.5%
Subordinated debt		10.7
Senior preferred		5.4
Participating convertible preferred		2.2
Common stock	82.9	2.1
	100.0%	100.0%

The new balance sheet is heavily weighted with floating rate debt. In an economic environment such as in 1981 and 1982, which experienced both high interest rates and a textile industry recession, floating interest rates could seriously deplete cash flow. To account for this possibility, management negotiated a $30 million cash cap facility whereby the new company will not suffer a cash interest expense of more than 15 percent annually. Should Cone's interest charge exceed 15 percent, the consortium will lend the difference above the 15 percent rate. The cash cap credit facility carries a rate of prime plus $1\frac{1}{2}$ percent and a $\frac{1}{4}$ percent commitment fee on the unused portion.

Fortuitously, when outside forces put Cone into play, the company was operationally prepared. From the mid-1960s through the mid-1970s, Cone pursued a strategy of product line retrenchment. The company continued to participate in those markets in which it had a dominant market share or in which it occupied a specialty niche. Other operations not meeting these criteria were either sold or liquidated. During the mid-1970s through 1983, the company pursued a strategy of equipment modernization.

A third of a billion dollars was invested in plant and equipment during this period. Following the period on modernization, the company's strategy shifted to the efficient and effective management of the company's production facilities, and management concentrated on a market driven strategy of identifying and meeting market needs. It was at this point that the events leading up to the buyout took place. The large capital program supported them, and the implementation of more efficient production coincided with the need to generate cash flow as a result of the LBO.

The Cone buyout was conventionally structured to maximize cash flow and minimize taxes. The annual large contributions of either preferred or common stock to the ESOP was planned to address the tax saving objective. The utilization of the ESOP as an integral part of the LBO structure also had the objective of retaining and motivating employees, and preserving the company's corporate culture. Foremost in structural considerations was maintaining the company's competitive position, accomplished by management's ability to recognize and meet the market's needs with products made by a hard working, motivated workforce using modern equipment. Cone management developed highly detailed strategies to remain a strong competitive factor in a difficult business. It made projections to support the financial structure of the LBO, which assumed that their domestic markets were generally mature and would experience overall growth averaging only 1.2 percent per year. It assumed that retailers would increase their direct imports, which would not only affect textile producers but would weaken their customers as well. It assumed that the Far East would be the most disruptive force in the textile and apparel markets. It assumed that competition for market share would be intense and would shift more to service and price, as more companies modernized and were able to meet high standards of quality and fabric width. It assumed that product prices would keep pace with 5–6 percent inflation and that there would be no recovery in export sales, which were down sharply largely due to the strength in the dollar from 1981–85.

Based on these assumptions, the bank debt can be comfortably serviced. The company was not required to repay any debt in the first year but projected it would generate $110 million available for debt reduction. These funds came from a combination of cash flow from operations, excess pension asset recoveries, tax refunds, taxes sheltered by ESOP contributions, and working capital reductions. Projections indicated an additional $34 million cash flow generated in 1985, placing the total available to meet the scheduled $95 million debt repayment in 1985 at over $144 million. The senior debt should be fully repaid in 1990 along with retiring the $25 million senior preferred stock held by the banks. The projections also show the company accumulating cash of $201 million by 1993, after repaying the subordinated debt when due in 1992.

During the first 10 years, the company projects it will pay taxes at an effective rate of 36 percent. Contributions to the ESOP over the period are projected to exceed $414 million, net of redemptions, and provide the largest single portion of the $640 million projected cumulative cash flow available for debt reduction. As a result of these contributions largely made in common stock, the employees are projected to own 69.5 percent of the equity in 1993, plus $68.5 in preferred stock. The value of this equity, capitalizing operating profit at 4.0 × and adding free cash and deducting debt and preferred stock, is $424.0 million in the tenth year.

Estimated Equity Values

	Estimated Percentage Ownership After Conversion	Capitalization Rate of EBIT (In millions)		
		4.0x	4.5x	5.0x
Management	12.2%	$ 62.8	$ 68.6	$ 74.4
Banks	18.3	94.2	102.9	111.7
ESOP	69.5	357.7	390.9	424.0
	100.0%	$514.7	$562.4	$610.1

Adding the estimated $68.5 million in preferred held by the ESOP and assuming a 30 percent attrition of wage earners over the 10-year vesting period, the value of the ESOP would exceed $50,000 per hourly paid employee. This could prove conservative as a capitalization rate of only 4.0 × operating earnings is the equivalent to a P/E ratio of only 7.7 ×. In the 6-year period prior to the buyout, the company's P/E ratio averaged 7.1 ×, but the P/E ratio for the market in general was low due to high inflation and high interest rates. On the other hand, it will be difficult for the company to meet its 10-year projections after experiencing lower earnings than projected in the first two years following the buyout. In 1985, the flood of imports worsened to the point where the company felt compelled to take out ads in the trade press to proclaim its good financial health. These difficult times have occurred during a period of general economic prosperity. Any weakening of the overall economy would only accentuate the already weak demand and price factors in the textile industry. The picture would brighten considerably, however, if a weaker dollar makes domestic textiles more competitive with imports, or the better enforcement of import quotas in conjunction with the promotion of U.S.-made products succeeds in stemming the flow of cheap textile and apparel imports.

If the company makes its 10-year projection, the consortium of banks will have earned an internal rate of return of 16 percent over the 10-year period, assuming an average prime of 11 percent and equity values based on a 4.0 rate of capitalizing operating earnings. Whereas prime plus 5 percent would be a superior return on a conventional bank loan, this return might appear inad-

Summary Balance Sheets
(Dollars in thousands, except per share data)

	Fiscal Years	
	January 1, 1984	January 2, 1983
Assets		
Cash and short-term investments	$ 10,513	$ 17,164
Receivables net	103,225	69,838
Refundable income taxes	21,951	1,870
Inventories		
Amounts	116,848	114,265
Turns based on sales	5.9	5.3
Other current assets	6,428	4,385
Property, plant, and equipment net	230,291	210,667
Other assets	4,034	5,491
Total assets	$493,290	$423,680
Liabilities and Stockholders' Equity		
Short-term notes payable	$ 28,413	$ 0.0
Other current liabilities	108,944	56,076
Long-term debt		
Amounts	4,871	10,403
Percentage of capital employed	1.4%	2.8%
Deferred items		
Amounts	32,611	21,960
Percentage of capital employed	9.2%	6.0%
Stockholders' equity		
Amounts	318,451	335,241
Percentage of capital employed	89.4%	91.2%
Total liabilities and stockholders' equity	$493,290	$423,680
Working capital	$121,608	$151,446
Book value per common share	57.71	60.95
Number of common stockholders of record	3,172	4,350
Ratio of earnings to fixed charges		7.84x

Summary Statement of Operations
(Dollars in thousands, except per share data)

	Fiscal Years Ended	
	January 1, 1984	January 2, 1983
New sales	$687,776	$608,201
Cost of sales	601,647	536,449
	86,129	71,752
Selling and administrative expenses	56,025	52,667
	30,104	19,085
Other income, net	882	3,375
	30,986	22,460
Interest expense	2,368	1,948
	28,618	20,512
Unusual items	51,019	2,433
Income (loss) before income taxes	(22,401)	18,079
Income taxes (refundable)	(13,645)	5,273
Net income (loss)	(8,756)	12,806
Average number of shares outstanding	5,506	5,530
Per share of common stock		
Net income (loss)	(1.59)	2.32
Cash dividends	1.60	2.20

equate as a compensation for risking 98.2 percent of the total capital in the deal. However, all but $175 million of the banks' total commitment of $457 million was covered by excess pension funds, tax refunds, and working capital valuing inventories at market. Remaining assets included net plant, property, and equipment of $230 million, and extensive land holdings unrelated to the business.

Whereas the employees are likely to be the biggest winners of the buyout, the public stockholders also benefited nicely. For the six years prior to the buyout, the stock traded at an average price of approximately $30 per share. The actual price range during this period was $43\frac{1}{2}$–$19\frac{3}{4}$. The day before Western Pacific filed its Schedule 13D, the stock closed at $45\frac{3}{4}$. The $70 buyout price represented a 53 percent premium on this price and 133 percent premium over the average trading price for the prior six years. This period spanned the highest earnings period of the company's history.

Management benefited from the buyout in two ways. First, it received $15.5 million for its stock options and another $4.7 million in the value of its stock owned. It exchanged its stock and $3.5 million in cash for its $8.250 million investment in the new company. Using the 4.0 capitalization rate for operating earnings, their stock should be worth $62.8 million in 1993. In addition, their participation in the ESOP should amount to over $6 million and provide management with an estimated 8.4 × return on their investment. This is a respectable internal rate of return of 23.7 percent. Although they will have to work very hard to achieve these returns in the difficult market environment for their products, the strong management team should be up to the task. As an officer of Blue Bell, a major customer, stated, "Cone is a leader in the industry. They are a very well-managed company. They have invested properly, are up-to-date technologically, and listen to their customers. These are the keys to survival in a tough business."

DAN RIVER, INC.

The Dan River LBO was initiated as a defense against an unfriendly takeover attempt by Carl Icahn. The stock appeared to Icahn to be substantially undervalued, selling at a low of 4.5 × the prior year's earnings and only 30 percent of book value. The company pursued a variety of ways to defend itself, culminating in a leveraged ESOP purchase of the stock. The structure featured two tiers of stock, one owned by the employees via the ESOP and the other by management. The structure seemed to favor management, which paid almost 11 × less for their stock than the ESOP paid for its stock, but management's stock has no value until the value of the ESOP's stock rises over 50 percent.

It appears that the dual stock leveraged ESOP structure developed by Kelso for LBOs is inherently flawed from an employee relations standpoint. The press often refers to these deals as MESOPS (management enrichment stock ownership plans). The Labor Department also has expressed its dislike for the dual stock structure. For example, it withheld its approval of the proposed LBO of Scott & Fetzer until the financing fell apart. A union official representing some of Scott & Fetzer's employees was quoted in the *Wall Street Journal:* "We saw this as an incredible rip-off of employees. This was a management enrichment program." Management's share of the ownership was also an issue in two other controversial ESOP buyouts at Blue Bell and Raymond International. In both deals, the Labor Department forced management to cut its ownership. In the Raymond deal, the feeling of a rip-off prevailed as *Business Week* reported that unhappy workers referred to Kelso and the Raymond management as "killer bees." At Dan River, some employees have reacted negatively to the deal. A year and a half after the deal closed, amid difficult industry conditions, plant closings, and layoffs, an employee was quoted: "A lot of us feel that we got took."

The Dan River buyout story reads like an old-time melodrama or Western movie shootout. Here was a company "celebrating" its 100th anniversary by closing six plants and eliminating 2000 jobs in the face of recession and rising imports. Smiling in the wings was a corporate raider threatening to take over. However, the good guys won in a dramatic showdown when in an eleventh hour maneuver, the company issued a block of preferred stock and survived a critical stockholders' vote, giving 95 percent ownership to company employees and two retired officers.

In 1982, Dan River was proud of the fact that of the 109 industrial companies founded in 1882, it was the only surviving independent one to be on the Fortune 500 list. The centennial of Dan River's existence, though, proved to be a year of corporate chaos. The company was struggling against rising imports and weak demand due to recession. It was also trying to fight off a determined takeover threat from Carl E. Icahn, a New York corporate raider and arbitrageur who began acquiring the stock when its price fell to a third of book value. Icahn had used similar takeover tactics with Marshall Field, Hammermill Paper, Saxon Industries, and Tappen Company by selling back his blocks of stock at substantial profit after being defeated in his announced goals of taking over the companies. Dan River's reaction to Icahn's tactics was to draw its own guns out of its holsters. "These guys have a history of playing pretty rough," to block takeover threats, one textile industry observer commented.

The company was founded as the Riverside Cotton Mills on the Dan River in Danville, Virginia. It began producing a plaid cotton fabric woven on its 100 looms from yarn spun on its 2240 spindles. In its first 16 years, net profits averaged 15.8 percent of sales. Through expansion and acquisition, the company, called The Riverside & Dan River Cotton Mills as the result of a merger in 1909, operated 13,500 looms and 467,000 spindles by 1925. Demand for textiles was sluggish during most of the 1920s, and the company suffered its first loss in 1924.

During this period, it experimented with a new concept in industrial relations called "Industrial Democracy," which was an attempt to apply the Golden Rule to industrial relations. This experiment was discontinued in 1930 during a prolonged strike by workers in response to reduced wages. The company records include this epitaph: "The demise of the Democracy took place in 1930. No one sang its requiem. Its grave was trampled by strikers." The company struggled throughout the 1930s due to severely depressed economic conditions and did not return to full production until World War II.

Sales hit $100 million in 1948, and the company listed its stock on the NYSE in 1955. A major expansion and acquisition program began in 1956, and by 1965, Dan River had diversified into financial factoring, carpeting, and knitted fabrics. In the early 1970s, the company sold its factoring subsidiary and concentrated on a modernization program that resulted in spending $190 million on plant and equipment during the decade.

In 1982, the company's products were divided into fabrics for apparel, and fabrics and finished products for the home. Apparel fabrics included corduroy, denim, and velour. Home furnishings included sheets, pillowcases, towels, bed covers, and carpeting. Dan River sold its products to garment manufacturers, mail order houses, chain stores, converters, retailers, and jobbers. The largest customers were Levi Strauss for denim, Liz Claiborne for velour knits, and K-Mart for home furnishings.

Modernized facilities combined with strong demand, particularly for denim and corduroy, enabled the company to report record profits in 1979 of $22.1 million on sales of $579 million. Still, the return on investment was only 13.2 percent, creating a major dilemma for textile manufacturers. Large capital expenditures result in unneeded expansion of capacity. Because the new equipment is faster than the equipment being replaced, more goods are produced. The resulting increased production puts downward pressure on product prices which in turn, results in a low return on investment. The investment in modernization must be made to remain competitive but cannot be economically justified in hindsight. In the five years before the LBO, Dan River made capital expenditures of $158.5 million, but its average return on equity was an anemic 6.7 percent.

Poor return has caused textile stocks to sell typically at prices well below their book values per share. Dan River was no exception as its stock price averaged $15 per share in 1982 compared with a book value of $35.11 at year-end 1981. The highest price the stock traded in the 1980–82 period was $23, and it sold as low as 10\frac{1}{2}$ in the third quarter of 1982 when Carl Icahn was buying. Fully diluted earnings had peaked at $3.53 per share in 1979, declined to $3.13 per share in 1980, and fell to $2.34 per share in 1981. The company reported earnings of only $0.27 per share in the first six months of 1982, well below its dividend of $0.56.

The poor results were attributed to extremely poor market conditions caused by the recession and a flood of imported textile products. Imports exceeded six billion square yards compared to the domestic market of 11 billion square yards. Dan River responded by closing six of its plants, permanently eliminating 2000 jobs. Closing these plants and disposing of these properties cost $11.1 million, which was charged to 1982 operations. Losses on the sale of the property, plant, and equipment of the six plants was $8.7 million, offering further evidence as to why textile stocks sell at substantial discounts to book values.

Despite the poor earnings performance and the uncertain outlook for Dan River in the summer of 1982, the company had working capital of $25 per share at year-end 1981. When the stock hit 10\frac{1}{2}$ per share, Icahn figured he could not lose. He filed a Schedule 13D with the SEC on September 14, 1982, indicating his group owned 398,000 shares, or approximately 6.9 percent of the common stock. The filing also indicated that the group intended either to seek control of Dan River or sell its shares, undoubtedly at a nice profit. Later that month, the Icahn group disclosed it had bought 461,500 additional shares for $17.50. These shares had been purchased by Unitex Limited, a Hong Kong textile company, in 1979. Dan River sued Unitex, and the two companies settled the litigation in 1981 with Unitex agreeing not to increase its holdings above 12 percent of the outstanding common stock before December 31, 1984. Dan River agreed to elect Frank S. Cheng, a managing director of Unitex, to its board.

Shortly after disclosing that he controlled 15 percent of the common stock, Icahn met with Dan River's senior officers. He stated his desire to purchase either from the company or through a tender offer additional shares of stock at $16–17 per share to bring his holdings up to 40–50 percent of the total outstanding. He also indicated that after he bought that additional stock, Icahn

Capital Corporation would probably propose a merger, a transaction that would give a debt security for the remaining shares, priced to produce a value lower than the cash price paid for stock acquired in the tender offer. Icahn also offered to give Dan River management long-term contracts and to sell them some or all of the assets of the newly merged corporation in an LBO.

Dan River management refused to deal with Icahn and four days later obtained permission from the Dan River board to sue him. The board further authorized the issuance of 1.7 million shares of Series B preferred stock to a newly created stock bonus plan for the benefit of its nearly 2000 salaried employees other than the directors of Dan River. This stock was entitled to one vote per share, thereby giving management a voting block equal to 22 percent of the total voting shares. This turned out to be critical. More importantly, any person or group owning more than 35 percent of the common stock would need the approval of more than two-thirds of the new preferred to approve a takeover proposal of Dan River.

After Icahn and Dan River filed lawsuits against each other, Icahn began a tender offer on October 25, 1982 and amended it five times over the next two months. The initial tender was for 3.1 million shares at $18 per share, conditioned on the mutual suspension of litigation until after a special meeting of the stockholders for the election of directors. Otherwise, the tender was for 700,000 shares at $15.

Dan River's board met three days later and predictably determined the offer was unfair. The board relied heavily on the opinion of Kidder Peabody that the offer was not fair from a financial point of view, and the advice of counsel that the offer raised questions under the federal securities laws. With each amendment to the tender offer, none higher than $18 per share and each contemplating a debenture for the remaining shares worth $15–18 per share, the board, backed by Kidder Peabody, recommended rejection by the shareholders. The Icahn tender offers expired on January 20, 1983, with the Icahn group owning approximately 29 percent of the common stock.

At the October 28 board meeting, in addition to rejecting Icahn's initial tender offer, the board decided to explore its alternatives, including merger, acquisition, liquidation, and the repurchase of the common stock. The board engaged Kidder Peabody to advise it on these alternatives: They subsequently had discussions with 34 prospective acquirers of Dan River. Before they were supplied a confidential memorandum, each had to agree not to take any action without approval of the Dan River board. Two definitive proposals resulted from these discussions. Hanson Industries, Inc., a subsidiary of the U.K. company Hanson Trust PLC, attempted to buy Icahn's block, but Icahn wanted more than Hanson was willing to pay. Dan River then agreed to sell McDonough Company, a subsidiary of Hanson, 475,000 shares of common stock at $18.50 per share; McDonough agreed not to acquire more than 20 percent of the outstanding common stock unless it offered to acquire all of the stock for $18.50 per share or higher. Most of the shares sold to McDonough had been recently purchased in the open market by Dan River at an average price of $18.01 per share.

A second and ultimately successful proposal began in early December 1982 when Kelso, an investment banker specializing in the use of ESOPs, approached Dan River. After some discussion, Dan River authorized Kelso to study the feasibility of an LBO using an ESOP. Kelso presented a proposal to Dan River management in late December, using an ESOP for the purchase of the common stock at $22.50 per share. On January 4, 1983, Chemical Bank provided written conditional commitments to provide substantially all of the financing necessary to complete the merger at $22.50 per share. The board met that day and approved the Kelso proposal in principle. Kidder Peabody expressed a preliminary conclusion that the $22.50 price was fair and that a price of $25 was not feasible. The Kelso proposal satisfied the principal objections of the board to the Icahn tender offer by proposing a fair price and equal treatment to all holders of each class stock. Icahn's tender offer proposed to give less value in a merger for the untendered shares as an inducement for shareholders to sell to Icahn.

As is customary, the board appointed a special committee of outside directors to advise what action the board should take on the merger proposal. The special committee contacted the management group in March 1983 and asked whether the group would, in light of the recent decline in interest rates, increase the price to be paid for stock. Management said no, pointing out that the company had received no offers since the agreement had been announced and that the best price available in a conventional LBO was in the range of $20 per share. Management further said that the price was fair, that any attempt to get financing for a higher price could endanger the Chemical Bank commitment, and that it could not recommend employee involvement in an ESOP at a price above $22.50 considering Dan River's financial projections. Goldman, Sachs had been retained to advise the special committee and also rendered its opinion that $22.50 was a fair price.

The special committee and the board acted with extreme prudence and caution in its deliberations because the $22.50 price could be viewed as too low when compared to certain financial facts. The price represented a discount of 28.2 percent from the 1982 year-end book value of $31.33 and was lower than working capital of approximately $25 per share. The company also had expended about $28 per share during the past five years on modernization, which could be expected to improve future performance. There was the issue of conflict of interest on the part of four board members, including David W. Johnston, Jr., chairman and CEO, and Lester A. Hudson, Jr., president and chief operating officer, who were purchasing Class B common stock in the newly formed holding company that would own Dan River if the merger were approved. Their purchase price for Class B common stock was $2.06 per share, whereas the ESOP paid $22.50 per share for Class A common stock. The difference in value between the Class B common and Class A common was sometimes glossed over by critics of the deal structure. Although it might appear that management was getting a fantastic bargain, the board mandated that the Class B common would always be worth $21 per share less than the Class A stock, so that initially the Class B was worth $1.50 per share if the Class A was worth $22.50. However, outside appraisers deemed the Class A stock was worth only $14.16 per share, which would render the Class B common mathematically worthless. Management was willing to buy the Class B common only because of the leverage it provided. If the value of the Class A stock were to double its initial price of $22.50 to $45 per share, the value of the Class B would be $24 per share or almost 12 × the initial price of $2.06 per share.

A healthy shareholders' vote was critical for the merger to go through. In his cover letter attached to the proxy statement explaining the vote on the merger to be taken at the stockholders' meeting on May 24, 1983, David Johnston commented that achieving more than two-thirds majority of the vote "will require the enthusiastic cooperation of all Dan River stockholders who favor the merger." Johnston knew that the Icahn group, with its 22 percent of the voting stock, was probably going to abstain in voting on the merger. Therefore, it would require approval by approximately 85 percent of the remaining voting stock to pass.

The final vote count showed approval by 70.2 percent of the voting stock, a margin of victory of only three percentage points. The issuance of the 1.7 million shares of Series B voting preferred was critical in getting two-thirds approval. The Icahn group owned 29 percent of the common stock, but when the board dusted off an authorized but unissued preferred stock, gave it voting rights, and contributed it to an employee benefit plan, Icahn's voting power dropped off to 22 percent. Without this dilution of voting power, Icahn's votes could have defeated the merger proposal.

The deal had survived another close vote when the union voted only 58 percent in favor of allowing pension plans to be used as a source of funds for the merger. The plans were terminated after the merger, fully vesting all benefits. Single premium annuities were purchased to guarantee the payment of the accrued benefits. All of the excess assets held under the plans, approximating $16 million, were contributed to the new ESOP. Another $13 million in funds came from the sale of preferred stock to two other employee benefit plans, namely the profit-sharing plan and the Tax Reform Act of 1982 ESOP (TRASOP). These two benefit plans covered only white collar nonunion employees who accounted for about one-sixth of the workforce. The contributions to the ESOP created a substantial loss for the year, which enabled the company to carry back this loss and recover $20 million in taxes paid in 1979 and 1980. Thus, the combination of tax refunds, excess pension fund assets, and the sale of preferred stock to employee benefit plans generated $49 million, or almost one-third of the funds required to finance the merger.

The principal vehicle used in the financing of the merger was a newly formed

ESOP for the benefit of all employees. A holding company was established to actually purchase Dan River's common stock for $22.50 cash. The use of a holding company enabled the operating company to retain its debt obligations totaling $99.3 million rather than to refinance these debts with higher cost loans. The stock ownership of the holding company is given in the following balance sheet.

	Class A Common Stock	Class B Common Stock	Percentage of Total Shares	Total Class A&B Common Stock
ESOP	$110,000,000		70%	$110,000,000
Management Group (26 people)		$3,600,000	25%	3,600,000
Kelso Investment Associates	748,710	651,290	5%	1,400,000
	$110,748,710	$4,251,290	100%	$115,000,000

Dan River was purchased entirely by its employees, two retired officers, and Kelso. The management group swapped some of its old common stock for Class B common and was loaned $750,000 on a 10-year 9 percent note as partial payment for its Class B stock purchase.

The creative equity structure enabled the management group and Kelso to buy the Class B stock at $2.06 per share whereas the ESOP paid $22.50 per share for the Class A stock. Kelso also paid $22.50 per share cash for its Class A shares, which was substantially more than the ESOP actually paid, using a note worth less than $14.00 per share. The company retained Houlihan, Lokey, Howard & Zukin, Inc. to appraise the values of the common and preferred stocks and to price the Class B stock. Houlihan arrived at the values rather circuitously but logically. First, it appraised the total value of the leveraged holding company at $74 million and the Class A common at $14.17 per share. The board, on the advice of Houlihan, determined that the Class B common is worth $21 per share less than the Class A common. Since Houlihan appraised the Class A stock at $14.17 per share, the Class B had a negative value. Houlihan reasoned that it really was not totally worthless because it effectively gives the holder an option on value after the Class A common stock exceeds $21 per share. Using a modified Black-Scholes option pricing model, Houlihan determined that the fair market value of Class B did not exceed $2.06 per share. How could the ESOP pay $22.50 for its Class A stock that was appraised at $14.17 per share? The answer is that the ESOP pays for it with a 9 percent note, which Houlihan believes is worth at most $13.96 per share. The holding company holds the ESOP note and causes its repayment by making annual contributions to the plan. The low valuation of the note relates to its low interest rate, the lack of acceleration of payments due if principal payments are not paid, the fact that payments can be made only to the extent that the ESOP receives cash contributions from Dan River, and lack of marketability. Houlihan estimated it would take the company seven years to pay the principal and interest on the note if contributions are 10 percent of payroll, which was estimated to grow at 6 percent annually. Thus, all the $110 million principal is to be repaid with tax-deductible contributions to the ESOP.

Since it took $149.6 million to purchase all the Dan River common and preferred stock, the holding company had to borrow $148.9 million from Chemical Bank. The collateral for the Chemical Bank loan was the common stock of the operating company, which was a subsidiary and had $99.5 million of its own debt. Whereas this stock was sold to the ESOP, the ESOP pledged the shares as loan collateral. Shares are released from the pledge as the ESOP's note is paid to the holding company. Chemical Bank insisted that $49 million be repaid in five months and gave the company a $36 million line of credit that could be used to repay the $49 million if there was a delay in getting the refund of income tax and excess pension fund assets. Interest on the Chemical Bank loan to the holding company was set at $1\frac{1}{2}$ percent over the prime rate, and the bank received $500,000 in commitment fees. Kidder Peabody and Goldman, Sachs received fees of $1.49 million and $350,000 respectively. Kelso's fee was $900,000.

Even after repaying $49 million of the Chemical Bank loan, the loan balance was still about $100 million and Houlihan valued the whole company at $74 million. How could a company in which earnings trended downward sharply since 1979 and only had a slight operating profit in 1982 borrow close to $100 million on top of its old borrowings of $99.3 million? The answer is that after accounting for the $99.3 million operating loans, the company had equity of $196.6 million and had averaged $32 million annually in cash generated from operations over the past four years. As long as there was sufficient cash flow, management would make tax-deductible contributions to the ESOP, which would then use these funds to repay its note to the holding company, which would then repay Chemical Bank.

In assessing how the various participants in this buyout are likely to fare, we assumed the company's projections would be achieved. In fact, textile and apparel imports have continued to increase, further depressing apparel fabrics demand and prices, and to a lesser extent, hurting home furnishings. As a result, when the company received an unsolicited bid to sell four of its plants, it accepted and closed another in 1984, which generated some cash but diminished cash flow and potential ESOP contributions. This removed the company from the greige and print fabric business completely, which had suffered greatly from import competition. It is therefore highly doubtful the company will meet its earnings projections. Under the original projections, the Chemical

Bank loan would be fully repaid in five years. The ESOP contributions projected at 10 percent of payroll would exceed average pension plan contributions over the prior three years by 10 ×, and each employee should have an
average of more than $10,000 contributed for his or her retirement benefit.
However, with the sale or closing of five plants in 1984, cash flow was reduced
and the payroll dropped to 8,000 employees.

The value of the company in five years based on the projections is unlikely
to exceed $103.4 million, which is the point at which Class B common stock
begins to have true value. Thus, management and Kelso have to look beyond
five years to realize substantial gains on their investments.

If the value of the company in 10 years is double the $74 million sellout
valuation, the Class A common would be worth approximately $27.50 per
share and the Class B common $6.50 per share. This would increase the value
of the ESOP shares to more than $17,300 per employee if no further contri-
butions are made to the plan after the ESOP note is fully repaid. Kelso's $1.4
million investment would be worth close to $3 million, putting the return at
7.8 percent compounded annually. Management's stock values would increase
over threefold for a compounded rate of return of 12.2 percent. Considering
the risk, neither of these levels of return would be sufficiently high to attract
outside investors. Icahn realized a gross profit estimated at approximately $9.0
million on a total investment of about $28.7 million. However, the profit is
before legal fees, and all is taxed as short-term capital gains. Thus, after taxes
and expenses, Dan River was not a bonanza for Icahn and only enhanced his
unwanted reputation as a hard-hitting corporate raider.

The clearest winners in the buyout are the employees who will receive substantially greater retirement benefits. Ironically, the employees appear to be
the least happy over the deal. Consider that to pay off the ESOP loan, with
interest, $138 million must be contributed to the plan. For the remaining 8000
employees, this amounts to $17,300 per worker. This compares with the 1982
contribution to the pension plans of $836,000 or approximately $700 per
worker. The ESOP replacement for the old pension plan is committed over a
15-year period to contributions of 25 × the rate of the 1982 pension plan
contribution. *Business Week* wrote a cover story in April 1985 entitled,
"ESOPs: Revolution or Rip-Off?" It featured Dan River as an example of
the rip-off. It quotes a union official: "The company (Dan River) stamps its
cartons with a big 'D' and 'employee-owned.' But most of the people realize
that they don't own anything. They're just paying the bill for these big management people to own the company." This comment completely ignores the
fact that the employees owned 99 percent of the Class A stock, which accounted for all of the current value of the company. An industrial engineer is
quoted as saying, "We can never sit down and figure out what we have and
what we don't. A lot of us feel that we got took."

The United Textile Workers' General Counsel is quoted as saying: "If you are going to get into an ESOP, you sure as hell don't want one like Dan River's.''

Business Week says that workers interviewed in Danville expressed open contempt for management. A 28 year-old weaver stated: "Frankly, I wish Icahn would have taken over Dan River.''

These comments perhaps reflect the frustrations and fears of a small number of employees who have seen a shrinkage of the 12,000 workforce by one-third in two and a half years. Undoubtedly most, if not all, of this shrinkage

Selected Financial Data

(Dollars and share amounts in thousands, except per share data)
Year Ended

	January 1, 1983	January 2, 1982	Dec. 27, 1980	Dec. 29, 1979	Dec. 30, 1978
Net sales	$519,124	$634,777	$607,737	$579,199	$530,361
Cost of sales	465,396	545,960	517,511	486,800	456,661
	53,728	88,817	90,226	92,399	73,700
Selling, general and administrative	54,216	53,489	50,797	46,958	41,175
expenses	(488)	35,328	39,429	45,441	32,525
Other income, net	2,109	1,098	1,590	832	689
	1,621	36,426	41,019	46,273	33,214
Interest expense	15,108	16,739	10,697	8,314	9,413
Plant closing costs	11,142				
Earnings (loss) before income taxes and extraordinary gain	(24,629)	19,687	30,322	37,959	23,801
Income taxes	(15,217)	5,147	10,695	15,814	10,429
Earnings (loss) before extraordinary gain	(9,412)	14,540	19,627	22,145	13,372
Extraordinary gain	686				
Net earnings (loss)	$ (8,726)	$14,540	$19,627	$22,145	$13,372
Average common shares					
Primary	5,571	5,678	5,656	5,599	5,600
Fully diluted	6,582	6,337	6,375	6,366	6,388
Per share of common stock Net earnings (loss): Primary:					
Before extraordinary gain	$ (1.76)	2.51	3.42	3.90	2.33
Extraordinary gain	0.12				
	$ (1.64)	$ 2.51	$ 3.42	$ 3.90	$ 2.33
Fully diluted	$	$ 2.34	$ 3.13	$ 3.53	$ 2.15
Cash dividends	$ 0.84	$ 1.12	$ 1.12	$ 1.00	$ 0.76
Depreciation and amortization	21,264	19,440	17,561	15,886	14,867
Capital expenditures	$ 34,832	$35,653	$41,472	$34,811	$21,387

would have occurred regardless of the LBO. Undoubtedly, management has been unsuccessful in educating its employees on how the deal was fair to the employees and how management's stock is worthless unless the employees' stocks' appraised value is increased by almost 50 percent. As a result of the LBO, the employees' old pension funds are safely insured, and everyone with 10 or more years with the company is 100 percent vested under the new ESOP.

In perfect hindsight, Dan River is a deal that probably should not have occurred and could not have been financed under business conditions that existed two years later. Management did not initiate the buyout. It fought back at an unfriendly takeover attempt. By having the nonmanagement employees end up with 70 percent ownership, management thought they were on the side of the angels. Management, however, found themselves sandwiched in between the rock of imports and the hard place of huge debt, and tough measures to cut labor costs needed to be implemented. In this battle for survival, the last thing management needed or deserved is the feeling on the part of employees that "We got took."

Balance sheet
(000 omitted)

	At Year End				
	January 1, 1983	January 2, 1982	Dec. 27, 1980	Dec. 29, 1979	Dec. 30, 1978
Assets					
Cash	$ 3,691	$ 4,097	$ 5,611	$ 5,811	$ 5,106
Receivables, net	82,079	98,975	102,762	91,865	93,056
Refundable income taxes	16,371	1,704			
Inventories	105,673	112,986	101,354	102,543	96,783
Assets held for sale	7,060				
Prepaid expenses	7,490	3,205	3,070	2,193	2,609
Property, plant and equipment, net	180,727	183,354	167,502	146,225	127,748
Other assets	3,673	2,606	2,957	2,191	2,150
Total assets	$406,764	$406,927	$383,256	$350,828	$327,452
Liabilities and Stockholders' Equity					
Short-term notes payable	$ 16,500	$ 18,219	$ 8,545		
Other current liabilities	60,046	53,935	58,768	$ 62,087	$ 52,603
Long-term debt	99,252	101,301	94,013	84,105	89,845
Deferred items	34,397	28,268	24,738	21,231	17,833
Stockholders' equity	196,569	205,204	197,192	183,405	167,171
Total liabilities and stockholders' equity	$406,764	$406,927	$383,256	$350,828	$327,452

LESLIE FAY, INC.

The buyout of Leslie Fay was the result of the aging founder and principal stockholder's efforts to maximize his stock values and minimize his taxes. With the help of some brilliant financial structuring and tax planning, a deal was put together to accomplish both objectives. The crux of the structure was to marry a company that had large net operating losses (NOLs) with a newly formed investment company in a partnership to buy the assets of Leslie Fay. The NOLs were used to substantially offset income taxes, allowing pretax earnings to be used to pay both interest and principal on the acquisition debt. Large earnings gains used up all of the NOLs in only two years, prompting a second LBO at over three times the value of the original deal. The second LBO also was structured with an NOL partnership, but two years later all partnership interests were swapped for common stock and the company had a public offering. All investors profited greatly on both deals and management made two quick fortunes.

How can a company be sold for $54.5 million on an LBO and sell out again for $178.4 million 26 months later?

John Pomerantz could not do anything right, according to his father, Fred Pomerantz. John was to prove Fred wrong on that point as exemplified by his presidency of Leslie Fay, the company his father founded in 1947.

When Fred reached the age of 81 in 1982, he and his wife owned 27 percent of the company and were considering ways of diversifying their investments. They had reached a tentative agreement to sell the company to a group of investors, including Wertheim & Company two years earlier, but the deal fell through in January 1981 when the union's pension fund denied its needed permission.

Then in September 1981, Wilmer J. Thomas, Jr., an independent investment banker, introduced Ira Hechler, the innovative buyout specialist formerly with Oppenheimer and Company, to son John with a proposal to form a group of investors to buy Leslie Fay. The group included top management of the company, plus Harold S. Geneen, former head of ITT, Hechler's wife, and Thomas. Negotiations with Fred Pomerantz led to an agreement to buy assets of the company at $15.50 per share. The tentative Wertheim group agreement a year earlier had been at $10.50 per share, so the shareholders benefited by the company's inability to get the union to agree to the prior sale proposal. In the Hechler proposal, the attorneys devised a way to solve this technical problem, enabling the union to release the company from certain obligations after the buyers agreed to post a bond as security for the pension fund obligations.

The sale netted Fred Pomerantz $14.8 million for his 35 years of leadership of the company he founded. Son John netted a mere $2.6 million in the deal but obtained a 31 percent interest in the new company.

His father warned him that it was foolish to load up the company with all that debt, but John surprised him. John more than doubled the company's earnings in two years, and in the second sale to an investor group in June 1984, his share of the proceeds was $41.1 million. Happily, Fred did not begrudge his son's good fortune in earning in only two years almost three times what it took him 35 years to make. However, it may have been painful for him to learn that Leslie Fay's two other top officers, Walter Leiter and Alan Golub, each netted $12.4 million in the deal. The success of the second buyout only reinforced how right John had been.

Fred Pomerantz took advantage of a wrinkle used by Hechler, when effective capital gains taxes were 49 percent. The selling company sells its assets for cash and becomes an investment company. Anyone choosing not to tender his shares on the sale could elect to do nothing and remain a shareholder in the investment company and thus avoid triggering capital gains taxes. Fred and his wife sold about one-third of their stock before closing which amount was subject to capital gains taxes, and kept the remaining 660,527 shares they owned in the investment company without incurring capital gains taxes. The investment company changed its name to Fayless Investors, Inc., and the new operating company took the Leslie Fay name.

After the buyout, Fayless Investors offered its shareholders the option of redeeming their shares at $15.50 per share or remaining in the investment company. Approximately 73 percent of the stock was redeemed in the first month, leaving Fayless Investors with assets of about $13.2 million. Since Fred Pomerantz and his wife owned more than 50 percent of the stock in Fayless Investors, the company avoided the status of personal holding company for federal income tax purposes by investing its assets entirely in tax-exempt bonds. As an investment company, the tax-free income could be distributed to the shareholders and retain its tax-exempt status. The management of Fayless Investors consisted of the established nine-man board of Leslie Fay.

Leslie Fay is one of the three largest women's apparel manufacturers in the country. It designs and manufactures a broad line of women's dresses, skirts, blouses, and sportswear, and sells apparel under some 23 names. Its "Head" division distributes men's and women's ski, tennis, running, and swimming apparel, and casual and golf wear. Many of the brand names sold are provided by divisions that are operated in many respects as separate companies. The styles produced under the names used by Leslie Fay are generally created by fashion designers employed by the company. The company pays a fee for the use of the brand names, such as "Head" and "Sassoon."

A substantial portion of the apparel is produced at the companies' own plants, but the company also uses a number of independent contractors and imports apparel principally from the Far East. The company sells directly to approximately 14,000 accounts, mostly department stores and specialty stores throughout the United States.

The two buyouts of Leslie Fay rank high in the field of acquisition complexity. The deals were structured mainly to use pretax income to pay both interest and principal on the debt. In the 1982 buyout, the purchase price was slightly below book value so there was no opportunity to write up assets that could then be amortized and depreciated to shelter income from taxes and thereby enhance cash flow. Ira Hechler, Wilmer Thomas, Don Schapiro of

Barrett Smith Schapiro Simon & Armstrong, and Arthur Kalish of Paul, Weiss, Rifkind, Wharton & Garrison, devised a way to save on taxes by pairing the investor group with a company with large NOLs to buy Leslie Fay's assets. The NOLs were then used to substantially shelter income from federal taxes, thus making pretax earnings available to repay the debt.

To make it work, the buyer was created as a joint venture partnership with two general partners, one the investor company called Lesfay Corporation and the other a toy company that was in bankruptcy.

Louis Marx & Company, a former manufacturer of toys and games, filed for bankruptcy under Chapter 11 on February 6, 1980. Wilmer Thomas, who was involved with Wertheim in the original buyout proposal that aborted, persuaded the creditors of Louis Marx & Company to become a general partner in the joint venture partnership in hopes of recovering some cash to satisfy their claims as creditors. The largest creditors were European American Bank & Trust Company and Chemical Bank, followed by McCann Erickson and Texas Instruments. Louis Marx & Company, which changed its name to LMX Corporation after the deal closed, sold Thomas 47.5 percent of its stock for $275,000. Since it was bankrupt, Marx had to borrow from a creditor bank to fund its investment in the joint venture of $500,000.

Lesfay, the other joint venturer, contributed $10.5 million to the partnership, of which $10.0 million was borrowed. Thus, of the total $54.5 million raised in the Hechler deal to purchase Leslie Fay's assets, all but $500,000 was borrowed. This is leverage of the first magnitude.

Lesfay's ownership was divided as shown below:

John T. Pomerantz—CEO of Lesfay	31.2%
Walter I. Leiter—executive vice president	9.4
Alan Golub—senior vice president	9.4
Harold S. Geneen—investor	10.9
Marilyn Hechler—investor	10.9
Subordinated investors	28.4
	100.0%

Control of the joint venture partnership rested in the hands of the five directors appointed by Lesfay: Harold S. Geneen; Willem F.P. de Vogel, representing the subordinated investors; and the three investors from management. Wilmer Thomas and an attorney, Joseph Greenberger, completed the board.

The sources of financing were:

Bank loan	$30,000,000
Subordinated debentures	6,000,000
Equity capital—Lesfay	10,500,000
Equity capital—Marx	500,000
Sales of real estate	5,400,000
Cash on hand	2,100,000
Total	$54,500,000

Chemical Bank was the lead lender on the term loan, which carried an interest rate of prime because senior debt coverage was 5.26 times. Repayment was scheduled in five equal payments beginning in 15 months. In addition to the term loan, the banks agreed to a revolving credit facility of $30 million, provided a credit test was met and contingent on letters of credit of $30 million to facilitate purchase of imports. The senior subordinated debentures paid 19 percent interest, and the junior subordinated debentures had a current yield of 20 percent. Structuring the deal with a high current yield allowed a smaller allocation of common stock to provide a total internal rate of return targeted at approximately 40 percent. Even with the high interest rates on the subordinated debt, total debt coverage was projected at 4.21 times.

Expenses totaled approximately $800,000, of which $350,000 went to Bear, Stearns for rendering a fairness opinion and financial advice.

In addition to substantial stock ownership in Lesfay, the three-man management group participated in a newly created profit fund replacing its old employment agreements. Since the management group already had significant equity ownership in the new company, the profit fund might be viewed as incentive overkill but the combination certainly produced results. Under the old agreement, John Pomerantz received in 1981 a base salary of $225,000 and 2 percent of net pretax profits over $5 million, rising to 3 percent of profits over $15 million. It netted him $455,000 in 1981. The new profit fund extended the employment agreement to 10 years and increased base salaries. The fund provided a base of 7.5 percent of net earnings of the joint venture in excess of $16 million, the percentage rising by 0.75 percent each year until reaching 15 percent in 1992. Under the old employment agreement, John Pomerantz would have earned approximately $910,000 in 1983. Under the new agreement, he earned more than $2.43 million of which $1.63 million was his share of the profit fund.

Projections used to obtain the financing showed operating profits rising from $16.1 million in 1981 to $19.2 million in fiscal 1984. In fact, operating income rose to $36.5 million in 1983, perhaps setting a record for exceeding projections in LBOs. Total pretax income hit $54.4 million in the first two years after the buyout. Since LMX's definite NOL carryforwards were only $40 million (although another $15.7 million of NOLs would be claimed), Lesfay no longer needed LMX as a partner in the joint venture. The partnership agreement assumed it would take four years and eight months to earn enough taxable income to deplete LMX's tax loss carryforwards. However, this point was reached in only two years. LMX was getting 90 percent of the income allocated to its capital account, but was no longer able to provide any tax shelter. This was highly favorable to LMX because the joint venture agreement provided that the 90 percent of the company's earnings that was allocated to LMX from April 29, 1982 to December 31, 1986 would be paid to LMX in equal installments over the ensuing 25 years, with interest of 7 percent on the unpaid balance. The allocation of net income flip-flopped in 1987, providing Lesfay with 90 percent and LMX with 10 percent thereafter.

Selected Consolidated Financial Data of Leslie Fay
(In thousands except for per share data)

	Fiscal Year Ended					Nine Months Ended	
	April 30, 1977	April 30, 1978	April 28, 1979	May 3, 1980	May 2, 1981	January 31, 1981	January 30, 1982
						(unaudited)	
Net sales	$143,157	$168,563	$195,249	$195,401	$236,936	$180,044	$203,057
Income from continuing operations	2,776	5,100	6,963	6,169	8,214	5,265	7,331
Net income	2,317	4,396	6,013	3,031	8,214	5,265	7,331
Net income per share	0.76	1.40	1.92	1.72	2.30	1.47	2.03
Dividends per share	0.38	0.42	0.48	0.48	0.48	0.36	0.45
Book value per share	9.81	10.58	11.64	12.11	13.91	13.20	15.56
Ratio of earnings to fixed charges	2.70	4.38	5.34	2.95	6.60	5.59	8.25

In September 1983, Lesfay and LMX discussed the possibility of consolidating ownership and having a public offering. LMX would become a wholly owned subsidiary of Lesfay and own 21.6 percent of the outstanding shares. If the public offering was not effective by June 15, 1984, Lesfay would have been obliged to purchase LMX's stock for $30 million, of which Thomas' share would have been $10 million. In addition to some technical problems, the public market did not cooperate and failed to provide sufficiently high prices to go forward with the deal. Ira Hechler came up with an alternative refinancing that involved a 1984 LBO of the 1982 LBO.

Negotiations for the price to be paid in the 1984 buyout were subject to obtaining from LMX an agreement on the value of its interest in the joint venture partnership. A starting point was the determination of LMX's capital account, which consisted of 90 percent of the joint venture's earnings, less any cash distributed to LMX. It was estimated by the company that LMX's capital account at the end of 1984 would be $62.2 million, but one could only guess what its 90 percent share of earnings in 1985 and 1986 would be. None of these funds would be paid to LMX until 1987, when the excess capital account would be paid quarterly in constant blended payments of principal and interest (7 percent per year) over the next 25 years. What was the value of LMX's 10 percent of the earnings from 1987 through 2011? There was also a question of how much of these funds would go to Thomas.

Chemical Bank (a creditor shareholder of LMX) computed the present value of these earnings and interest payments due LMX to range from $78 million to $190 million based on a range of high and low earnings growth rates. Whereas this range of values due LMX was valid based on their assumptions, in reality there would be no deal unless Hechler's 1984 investors could sufficiently satisfy Hechler's 1982 investors in Lesfay. The total value of the company was a factor of how much debt its earning power could support. A deal was finally struck whereby the creditors of LMX got $30.7 million and Thomas received $15.3 million in cash, despite the fact that Thomas owned almost half of LMX's stock. Thomas officially agreed to this unequal split to minimize his potential liability to creditors of LMX, but he actually agreed because it saved the creditors ($1.06 for each $1 of claims) and he picked up a $15.3 million bundle of cash for his $275,000 investment 26 months earlier. That is a sizzling 55.8 times his investment.

The Lesfay shareholders received $96.3 million in cash, plus $36.1 million in subordinated notes. Approximately 28.4 percent of the equity investment was allocated to the subordinated lenders who invested $6 million, a discount from the face amount of $6.6 million. They got their $6.6 million debt repaid and $37.6 million of the proceeds. If the subordinated notes received as part of the purchase price were valued at two-thirds of their face value, the internal rate of return for the subordinated investors approximated 160 percent. The remaining $94.8 million of the proceeds went to the Lesfay investors whose true equity investment was only $358,000. Lesfay had retired its $10 million loan with cash distributions from the joint venture. The management group's share of the proceeds was $66.1 million, whereas Hechler's wife and Harold Geneen each got $14.4 million for their $54,335 cash investments. Their return on money initially at risk was 9.2 times, but on actual equity capital invested the return was 265 times. Hechler really does know how to leverage deals. The deal was financed this way:

Source of Funds

Bank term loans	$138,500,000
Sellers' notes	36,057,977
Subordinated notes	25,000,000
Equity capital	2,000,000
Total sources	$201,557,977

Use of Funds

Stock purchase—cash	$142,388,614
Sellers' notes	36,059,977
Repay debt	23,109,386
	$201,577,977

The lead bank in the term loan was Manufacturers Hanover, which took 50 percent of the loan and participated out 30 percent to Chemical Bank and 20 percent to Bankers Trust. Chemical Bank as a lender provided funds that allowed Chemical Bank as a creditor to recover its bad loan from the bankrupt Louis Marx & Company. The rate floated at 1 percent over prime, and the term was six years. These banks also provided a $40 million revolving credit facility for working capital and a letter of credit facility of $50 million for purchasing imported merchandise.

The structure of the 1984 buyout resembled the one of 1982. Again, a joint venture partnership was established, but this time, the partners supplying the loss carryforwards are not apt to run out of losses. The two loss partners were Goldome FSB and American Savings Bank FSB. These two New York savings banks together had NOLs exceeding $1 billion. The loss partners are allocated 90 percent of the net income from July 1, 1984 through December 31, 1988, leaving the investment partner, Lefco, with 10 percent. When the allocation of net income flip-flops in 1989, Lefco gets 85 percent and the savings banks 15 percent.

The reason the management group and the Hechler group invested so little for their percentage interest is that they are the deal makers and company runners. Odyssey Partners was offered 50.1 percent of the stock for $20.5 million. They leveraged their own interest by getting Merrill Lynch to put in $20.1 million for only 12.8 percent of the common stock. Goldome brought

Ownership of the Buyer
Investment Company Partner—Lefco

	Investment	Percentage of Equity
Merrill Lynch	$20,128,000	12.8%
John J. Pomerantz	200,000	20.0
Walter I. Leiter	66,666	6.7
Alan Golub	66,666	6.7
Odyssey Partners	373,000	37.3
Hechler family and employees	165,680	16.6
	$21,000,000	100.0%

NOL Partners—Savings Banks

	Investment	Percentage of Equity
Goldome	$3,295,000	79.5%
American Savings Bank	2,705,000	20.5
	$6,000,000	100.0%

in American Savings Bank in order to lower its ownership below 80 percent and to avoid any question that it could legally be deemed to be the employer and therefore potentially liable for the union pension funds.

In August 1986, the company went public, selling 5,000,000 shares at $18 per share. The company was a general partner to a limited partnership which, immediately prior to the effectiveness of the registration statement, exchanged common stock for the interest of the limited partners. The NOL partners, Goldome and American Savings Bank, swapped their interest for 25 percent of the common stock. The NOL partners together made an initial capital contribution of $1.0 million and invested $5.0 million in Class B subordinated debentures.

Goldome and American Savings Bank had accumulated $37.4 million in their capital account, of which all but the initial capital contribution of $1.0 million was their 90 percent allocation of the company's earnings since the 1984 buyout. The savings banks were to be allocated 90 percent of the earnings until January 1, 1989, at which point their capital accounts would have been payable to them over the following 25 years. In addition, 15 percent of the earnings over this 25-year period would accrue to the savings banks' capital accounts. Goldome and American Savings were willing to swap their partnership interests for 3,750,000 shares of stock worth $67.5 million on the public offering for an eyepopping 258 percent internal rate of return.

How can a company be sold for $54.5 million in April 1982, sold again for $178.4 million in June 1984, and go public in July 1986 at a pre-offering value of $270 million? The answer lies in the company's growing operating earnings and the increased value investors are willing to pay for these earnings. The values in the three transactions is shown as follows:

Table 5.10

	1982 Buyout	1984 Buyout	1986 Pre-IPO
Value of earnings	$54.5	$234.6	$492.8
Add free cash			3.0
Less debt		56.2	219.8
Value of equity	$54.5	$178.4	$270.0
Trailing 12 months EBIT	$19.6	$ 45.9	$ 60.4
Multiple of EBIT	2.8x	5.1x	8.2x
P/E ratio fully taxed net income	5.3x	9.1x	20.0x

EBIT rose threefold from 1982 to 1986, but the value investors were willing to pay for these earnings rose from 2.8 × to 8.2 ×, or 3.0 × higher. Thus, the value placed on earnings rose from $54.5 million in 1982 to $492.8 million in 1986 or 9 ×. This willingness on the part of investors to pay 3.0 × more for operating earnings in 1986 than in 1982 represents the value created in the refinancing transactions. The sharp rise in the stock market accounted for a substantial part of the higher valuation, but it is highly unlikely the Leslie Fay of 1982 which was selling at 5.2 × earnings when the 1982 buyout was announced would sell for 20 × earnings in 1986. In all probability, the LBOs gave management added incentive to produce the growth in earnings, and the leveraged financial structure produced a more rapidly growing bottom line. Also, the company was reborn to the equity markets, no longer tied to its low multiple past, and benefited from its new sponsorship from its lead underwriters, Merrill Lynch and Bear, Stearns.

All of the 1984 buyout investors profited handsomely. Merrill Lynch Interfunding invested $20.1 million largely in subordinated debentures and got shares worth $25.9 million on the IPO. Its internal rate of return was 57.9 percent. Odyssey Partners received stock worth $71.7 million on its $373,000 investment, or 192 times its investment in 25 months. Management did equally as well. Walter Leiter and Alan Golub saw their $66,666 investment worth $13.5 million, topping the $12.4 million that each received in the 1984 buyout.

John Pomerantz almost topped the $41.1 million he made in the 1984 buyout. His original stake of $200,000 in the 1984 buyout was worth $40.5 million in the 1986 IPO. John's share of the profit fund continued to rise. In 1985, his total remuneration was almost $3.1 million. Despite what his father may have thought, the truth is that John has done many things right. He obviously has managed Leslie Fay right, and perhaps more importantly, he took Wilmer Thomas and Ira Hechler up on their crazy proposal in 1982.

The Leslie Fay Companies, Inc. and Subsidiaries
Consolidated Balance Sheets
(In thousands)
Assets

	March 3, 1984	December 29, 1984	December 28, 1985	March 29, 1986 (Unaudited)
Current				
Cash	$ 1,953	$ 2,940	$ 4,343	$ 5,028
Accounts receivable—net of allowance of $1,085, $1,100, and $1,281 for doubtful accounts	73,413	55,035	60,177	89,931
Inventories	50,450	53,272	73,564	60,452
Prepaid expenses and other current assets	9,777	6,879	7,674	9,327
Total current assets	135,593	118,126	145,758	164,738
Property, plant and equipment, at cost less accumulated depreciation and amortization of $2,000, $4,802, and $5,504	18,533	23,703	23,017	23,384
Excess of purchase price over net assets acquired		94,969	95,000	94,753
Deferred charges		2,911	2,381	2,335
Other assets	1,298	1,501	1,393	2,284
	$155,424	$241,210	$267,549	$287,494

Liabilities and stockholders' equity (deficiency)

	March 3, 1984	December 29, 1984	December 28, 1985	March 29, 1986 (Unaudited)
Current				
Note payable—banks	$ 19,000	$ 10,500	$ 13,000	$ 29,000
Current maturities of long-term debt	6,253	13,745	22,822	24,224
Accounts payable	23,232	24,246	32,526	31,662
Accrued interest payable		7,413	6,184	6,007
Accrued compensation	8,403	6,297	12,077	7,897
Accrued expenses and other current liabilities	11,299	5,764	9,873	12,161
Total current liabilities	68,187	67,965	96,482	110,951

(cont.)

The Leslie Fay Companies, Inc. and Subsidiaries
Consolidated Balance Sheets
(continued)

	March 3, 1984	December 29, 1984	December 28, 1985	March 29, 1986 (unaudited)
Long-term debt				
Term loan—banks	19,500	122,250	100,000	93,500
Capitalized lease obligation	9,294	8,941	8,892	8,879
Other	2,287	2,069	3,670	3,276
Total long-term debt	31,081	133,260	112,562	105,655
Subordinated debt				
Class A subordinated notes		36,035	36,035	36,035
Class B subordinated notes		25,000	25,000	25,000
Total subordinated debt	6,192	61,035	61,035	61,035
Deferred credits and other noncurrent liabilities	759	8,615	8,550	8,655
Commitments and contingencies				
Stockholders' equity (deficiency)				
Common stock, $1 par value, authorized shares—50,000; outstanding shares—15,000, net of discount from par value of $12,790, $5,436, and -0-		2,210	9,564	15,000
Excess of purchase price over investors' predecessor cost of net assets acquired		(33,251)	(33,251)	(33,251)
Retained earnings		1,488	12,230	19,023
Foreign currency translation adjustment		(112)	377	426
Total stockholders' equity (deficiency)	49,205	(29,665)	(11,080)	1,198
	$155,424	$241,210	$267,549	$287,494

Summary of Consolidated Financial Data
(In thousands, except share and per share data)

	Predecessor Companies					The Company					
	Leslie Fay Inc.		The Leslie Fay Company			Historical				Pro Forma as Adjusted	
	Years Ended		Period from April 30, 1982 to December 31, 1982	Year Ended December 31, 1983	Period from January 1, 1984 to June 28, 1984	Period from June 28, 1984 to December 29, 1984	Year Ended December 28, 1985	Thirteen Weeks Ended		Year Ended December 28, 1985	Thirteen Weeks Ended March 29, 1986
	May 2, 1981	May 1, 1982						March 30, 1985	March 29, 1986		
							(Unaudited)	(Unaudited)		(Unaudited)	
Statement of Income Data											
Net sales	$236,936	$274,266	$214,763	$389,858	$202,180	$235,601	$475,399	$123,104	$164,712	$475,399	$164,712
Gross profit	73,618	91,151	75,279	136,329	64,937	76,088	162,915	42,696	56,481	162,915	56,481
Operating income	16,160	24,028	22,155	44,882	14,685	22,361	52,507	13,236	21,716	51,884	21,561
Interest expense	1,395	1,227	6,149	7,891	4,228	17,231	27,642	7,089	6,321	16,397	3,636
Amortization	12	69	114	222	101	1,461	2,984	759	732	2,455	600
Income before pro forma taxes on income and extra-ordinary item	14,753	22,732	14,813	38,927	10,356	3,669	21,881	5,388	14,663	33,032	17,325
Pro forma net income	8,214	7,148	8,027	19,686	5,430	1,572	10,859	2,820	7,097	16,417	8,385
Pro forma net income per common share						$0.10	$0.72	$0.19	$0.47	$0.82	$0.42
Weighted average common shares outstanding						15,000,000	15,000,000	15,000,000	15,000,000	20,000,000	20,000,000

LEVITZ FURNITURE CORPORATION

The Levitz Furniture buyout is the story of an unlikely LBO candidate put into play by its largest shareholder, the Pritzker Trusts, while owning only 22.5 percent of the company. The Pritzkers orchestrated the buyout and dictated the terms. Levitz is a retailer in a highly cyclical furniture business. The nation's leading furniture retailer, it had a financial scare in the 1974–75 recession and had to slim down to stay profitable during the 1980–82 recessions. These factors, however, did not discourage many from bidding for the company. The prices of the first two offers were deemed to be unfairly low by investment bankers, causing these bids to fail. In the end, the investor group switched to a tender offer; the stockholders judged it fair by tendering 95 percent of the shares. The buyout from beginning to end stretched over a year and was like a slow moving controlled auction, with Pritzker sitting in the background signaling thumbs up or down on the bidders. When he finally got a bid he liked, he gave them a big bear hug.

The Levitz family began furniture retailing in the early 1950s in Pottstown, Pennsylvania. They sought a competitive edge and developed the warehouse-showroom concept, which depended on low priced volume sales. The original warehouse-showroom was built near a rail siding, creating an atmosphere of cartons, crates, and thus low prices. Furniture retailers generally quoted 4–6 weeks normal delivery time, but in the Levitz warehouse-showroom, the goods were stocked and available for immediate pick up. The concept worked spectacularly, and Levitz increased the number of stores from two in 1964 to 55 in 1974.

Unfortunately, the 1974–75 recession hit furniture retailers hard, and Levitz found itself overstocked and losing money. Ralph Levitz and his brother Leon decided to go outside the company to obtain administrative help and hired Bob Elliott in 1974 to be the CEO. Elliott was a former regional vice-president of Montgomery Ward & Company, and experienced in operating a large store chain. Elliott discovered the company suffered from a lack of control over inventory, advertising, and purchasing. Thus, the chain was operated as a group of independently managed stores, unable to control its inventory and take advantage of its buying power. Elliott remedied this problem through centralization of control. He also abandoned the discount pricing concept and gradually moved to higher priced merchandise. He introduced gallery displays of higher priced furniture groups inside the showrooms in contrast to the low price lines on which Levitz had based its concept. Elliott slowed down the torrid expansion pace and concentrated on opening smaller stores. He focused on filling out markets with satellite stores which were showrooms for the warehouse stores up to 25 miles away. In total, from fiscal 1975 to fiscal 1984, the company opened 20 stores and closed 10. Elliott increased gross operating margins in his first five years to 44.1 percent from 40.3 percent of sales. His first five years at the helm showed sales rising from $380.5 million in fiscal 1974 to $546.6 million in fiscal 1980 and earnings rising from a small loss in 1974 to a net of $20.5 million in 1980.

Surprisingly, Bob Elliott was unable to satisfy Ralph and Leon Levitz. Their instincts were still toward discount prices, and they wanted the company to push hard for market share, probably setting off price wars. Ralph Levitz, the company's chairman, was quoted in *Business Week* as saying, "Why did the company mushroom in its formative years and why is it now creeping like a snail?" This comment was made in 1980 after four years of recovery from a deep recession and ignored rapidly rising interest rates. Bob Elliott's "snail"-paced expansion and avoidance of discount pricing undoubtedly saved the company from losing money in the 1980–82 period. However, fiscal 1980 had been a record year, and the Levitz family wanted to regain control of the company. They became confrontational with strong-willed Bob Elliott who did not intend to take orders from anyone. The Levitz brothers had sued Elliott the previous year, charging that he and the board granted excessive salaries and wasted assets. The suit was subsequently dropped.

The Pritzkers entered the picture in November 1979 by making an offer for the company at $13\frac{1}{2}$ per share. The board rejected the offer as too low. However, when the arbitrageurs dumped their stock after the deal failed, the Pritzkers were able to acquire over 20 percent of the stock in the open market and placed two directors on the board.

Jay Pritzker disagreed with the Levitz family over Elliott's leadership, and Pritzker's support enabled Elliott to survive the Levitz family attacks and the difficult economic times during the 1980–82 period. High interest rates were particularly harmful to the company because the majority of its sales are big ticket items bought on credit. Sales slipped three consecutive years from their peak of $546.6 million in fiscal 1980, to $500.7 million, $488.5 million, and $485.7 million, respectively. Elliott responded by tightly controlling inventories and cutting overhead expenses that enabled the company to remain profitable even though net income dropped from $20.5 million in fiscal 1980 to $8.8 million in fiscal 1983. These policies paid off when the economy finally recovered in fiscal 1984. Sales jumped 33 percent, and net income leaped over 3 × to $27.4 million.

After this strong performance, Jay Pritzker met with Bob Elliott and discussed the possibility of his family interests acquiring all of the company's shares. These talks led to a joint press release on June 1, 1984 stating that Dalfort Corporation, an affiliate of Hyatt Corporation (wholly owned by the Pritzker family trusts), and the parent of Braniff Inc. proposed to acquire Levitz's stock for a combination of $23 in cash and Dalfort Securities with a face value of $10.50 per share. Analysts generally valued this offer at approximately $28.50 per share and considered it too low. The stock had traded as high as $47\frac{1}{2}$ nine months earlier and earnings for the current fiscal year were estimated at $4.50 per share, putting the offer at a low P/E ratio of 6.3 ×. Four lawsuits immediately ensued, contending the price. The company was in play, however, and would remain so for the next 10 months.

On June 28, Pritzker submitted his formal offer to acquire all the company's stock. The offer was a combination of $20 cash, a 5-year equity participation certificate, plus two-tenths of a share of Dalfort convertible preferred. The board appointed a four-man ad hoc committee to evaluate the offer and make a recommendation to the board on what action to take. Little did the ad hoc committee members realize how busy they would be over the following nine months.

The ad hoc committee negotiated several changes in the offer with Pritzker, including one addition that permitted the board to consider and support any other acquisition proposal. With the latter change, the board voted to approve the offer subject to the receipt of a fairness opinion and other conditions. Whereas management's participation in the equity of the proposed purchaser was only 5 percent, Bob Elliott supported the offer out of loyalty to Jay Pritzker. The ad hoc committee retained Drexel Burnham as financial advisor, and on August 7, 1984, Drexel Burnham told the committee that it could not issue an opinion that the offer was fair. The company and Dalfort issued a joint press release announcing this development and indicated that the Prizker family interests might look favorably on proposals to buy the Pritzker Trust shares at higher prices. It is doubtful that Jay Pritzker believed from the outset that his offer would prevail, and he privately disclosed that he wanted to sell out his 22.5 percent interest at a high price, believed to be in the range of $40 per share. To accomplish this objective, he would consider participating in an LBO.

Following his open invitation to make a higher offer, Kelso attempted to structure a proposal using an ESOP. Regulations had recently been issued allowing stockholders who sell their shares to an ESOP, under certain conditions, to roll over the proceeds into other common stocks without triggering capital gains taxes. Kelso also unsuccessfully attempted to structure a deal that would provide the Pritzker Trust with the rollover privilege. Then, Morgan Stanley failed at an attempt to structure a buyout on behalf of Seamans, a discount furniture retailer. Several large furniture manufacturers and retailers gave serious consideration to making offers, but nothing materialized.

The day after the press release, Fred Alger entered the picture with a written offer to acquire all of the company's shares. Alger had closely followed the bidding since he had controlled 5.7 percent of the stock through Fred Alger Management, Inc., an investment advisory company. Alger's offer consisted of $20.00 cash and a $40.00 face amount 15-year subordinated debenture, paying no interest for five years and then paying 16 percent interest for the succeeding 10 years. This type of discount subordinated debenture had been used successfully in the Metromedia buyout earlier in the year.

The ad hoc committee negotiated some revisions in the Alger offer, including a reduction of the interest-free period on the debentures from five years to four years and the creation of a sinking fund for the debentures. The committee was concerned about the value and marketability of the debentures. In response to these concerns, Alger retained the Jeffries Group, an investment banker located in Los Angeles, to provide a standby commitment. Under this commitment, Jeffries would purchase any and all debentures offered for sale in the first 20 business days following the acquisition at a maximum of $17.00 per $40.00 face amount of the debentures. However, the $17.00 price would be reduced if interest rates rose a specified amount. Alger thus estimated the value of its offer at $37.00 per share.

The ad hoc committee had been advised that the Pritzker Trusts would sell the debentures received in the Alger offer, and the committee computed that at $17.00 a debenture, the value of the Pritzker Trusts' debentures alone was greater than 50 percent of Jeffries' net capital. Drexel Burnham viewed the offer incomplete with respect to the Jeffries commitment and advised the committee at its October 10 meeting that the offer was unfair from a financial point of view. On October 16, 1984, the board rejected the Alger offer on the recommendation of the ad hoc committee. Bob Elliott was outspokenly against the offer, pointing out that the interest on the subordinated debentures alone when payments began in 1989 exceeded pretax earnings in every year in the company's history except the current year.

At the October 10 meeting, Drexel Burnham told the committee that it had been contacted by Citicorp Venture Capital and a management group consisting of 21 members to determine whether Drexel Burnham would assist them in attempting to finance an LBO. Drexel Burnham indicated it wanted to work with Citicorp, which was not surprising because Drexel Burnham earned $100,000 for its opinion on the Dalfort offer and had the potential of earning $7.6 million in fees if the proposed deal could be financed. Drexel Burnham was an ideal partner in the deal because they were intimately familiar with the company and their high yield securities group, the leader in junk bond financing, could raise a substantial amount of mezzanine money. It was the intention of the investor group to make the highest all-cash offer to the company. In view of this, the ad hoc committee released Drexel Burnham in the best interest of the shareholders.

Another serious approach was made by Julius Trump in November, but management had committed to work with Citicorp and Drexel Burnham and no offer was ever received.

The Citicorp/Drexel Burnham investor group made a proposal of $39 per share which was approved in principle by the board on November 6, subject to a fairness opinion. Dean Witter gave its preliminary oral opinion on November 29 that the deal was fair. On December 13, the disinterested members of the board voted unanimously to approve the proposal and submit it to shareholders with the board's recommendation for approval. By the time financing commitments were obtained, interest rates generally had declined, making the deal more attractive to lenders and investors. Unfortunately, lower interest rates also resulted in a rise in the stock market generally and pushed up the prices of the companies Dean Witter considered comparable to the company. This made the $39 price look cheap, and on March 4, Dean Witter advised the board that it was unable to reaffirm its preliminary fairness opinion. Jay Pritzker then bargained his support of the investor groups' offer for a 20 percent interest in the common stock for a $3.0 million investment, and the game plan was changed to a tender offer.

The tender offer route enabled the board, which currently lacked the comfort of an expert fairness opinion, to remain neutral in its recommendation to shareholders of what action to take. The purchasing group, now consisting of Citicorp, Drexel Burnham investors, management, and the Pritzker Trusts, offered to purchase all the stock at $39, subject to obtaining at least 51 percent of the shares held by persons not affiliated with the purchasing group. The board agreed to terminate the merger agreement and remained neutral on the offer. The purchasing group, however, stated that in their opinion the offer was fair. In arriving at its opinion, the purchasing group reviewed the customary data used in forming fairness opinions, and data similar to those Drexel Burnham had reviewed in withholding its opinion on the Dalfort and Alger offers (which Dean Witter had reviewed in withholding its opinion on the Citicorp/Drexel Burnham offer). So Drexel, which in November had withheld its opinion on Alger's $37.00 offer because it was "incomplete" to the extent of the Jeffries commitment, now stated that a $39 offer was fair despite higher comparable stock prices. Perhaps the strongest point the investor group made in its opinion was that since April 1984, the company had been receptive to buyout proposals but had received no offer as high or higher. Certainly every company interested in furniture retailing, investment bankers, and LBO specialists were aware that serious inquiry would be welcomed. By this test, a fair price was the highest price any buyer was willing to pay.

Whether or not investment bankers thought the offer was fair, the stockholders loved it and tendered 95 percent of their shares. The board then recommended the merger to shareholders, and the merger closed in June, 1985.

Uses of Funds

Purchase common stock	$318.1
Existing mortgages and industrial revenue bonds	39.3
Existing obligations under capital leases	80.0
Fees and expenses	19.0
Additional working capital	1.4
	$457.8

Sources of Funds

Bank borrowings	$108.5
Senior exchangeable variable rate notes	60.0
Mortgages and industrial revenue bonds	39.3
Obligations under capital leases	80.0
Senior subordinated debentures	75.0
Subordinated debentures	45.0
Total debt	$407.8
Cumulative preferred stock	35.0
Common stock	15.0
Total equity	$ 50.0
Total sources	$457.8

The bank borrowing commitment was for $120 million maturing over seven years. The interest rate was initially set at prime plus $1\frac{1}{2}$ percent, lowered to prime plus $1\frac{1}{4}$ percent when the loan balance ranged from $70 million to $100 million, and finally dropped to prime plus 1 percent below that amount.

The bank loan's initial funding of $108.5 million represented only 23.7 percent of the total financing, a very low percentage in comparison with other large LBOs during this period. This was partly because banks cannot lend more than 50 percent to purchase stock under a Regulation Q rule, and partly because banks are uncomfortable with tender offer loans. In tender offer loans, there can be unforeseen delays in merging the purchasing company with the operating company, and the purchasing company has no assets except the operating company's stock. Until the merger takes place, the purchasing company cannot use the operating company's assets and cash flow to pay the banks' interest.

As the importance of the bank financing was diminished, the importance of Drexel Burnham's ability to structure and sell the subordinated debt to institutional investors became paramount. In the $180 million package, $60 million were senior obligations ranking *pari passu* with the bank financing. The interest rate floated at 4.25 percent over the 3-month Treasury Rate, which put the rate approximately $\frac{1}{2}$ percent above the bank loan rate of prime plus $1\frac{1}{2}$ percent. The exchangeable feature allowed the holder to exchange the notes anytime into fixed rate notes at 131 percent of the rate on long-term Treasury obligations. The notes were amortized in years 7–9. The senior subordinated debentures are unsecured and have a fixed interest rate of $15\frac{1}{4}$ percent. They are amortized in years 8–10. The $16\frac{1}{4}$ percent junior subordinated debentures are unsecured and amortized in years 11–12. Also, the company has the option to defer interest payments on these debentures of up to $16 million.

How risky is the subordinated debt placed with Drexel Burnham's investors? If one accepts Drexel Burnham's projections of cash flow, the answer is that the subordinated debt can be serviced reasonably comfortably.

The senior debt should be fully repaid in the first year and a half through a combination of strong earnings, tax savings, lower working capital, and the financing of some existing stores. The company informed all of its vendors that it would stretch its payments by one week, which generated $8.0 million in working capital. Inventories were slightly reduced, and a change in the method of handling receivables resulted in substantial tax savings. In the past, Levitz sold its receivables to GECC. Following the buyout, the company set up a credit corporation and held its receivables with funds advanced by GECC. The company could thus defer the recognition of profits and taxes on credit sales which produced tax deferrals of approximately $50 million over 18 months. As long as the block of credit sales does not shrink, the taxes due on the credit sales are permanently deferred.

Following the full repayment of the bank debt by mid-1986, the company has no schedule of repayment on the high yield debt until 1992. If one accepts Drexel Burnham's projections, which assumed a recession in 1987 and 1988 causing earnings to drop 15–35 percent, cumulative cash flow by 1992 should be quite ample to meet the high yield debt repayment schedule. Going into the repayment period 1992–97, the company should have at least $150 million in excess cash, and annual earnings from 1992 through 1997 should exceed required repayments in each year, barring a severe recession. Another source of funds is the possible sale and leaseback of owned properties. Coldwell Banker estimated a probable value of the 39 properties owned by the company of $110 million, compared to mortgages of $41.2 million on these properties. Thus, almost $69 million could be obtained by the sale and leaseback of these properties at lease payment rates more favorable than interest rates projected on the subordinated debt. The value of the company's leaseholds on 63 other properties was estimated at $166.3 million, but to convert these assets to cash would require substantially higher lease payments. Still another potential source of funds is a public offering of common stock. The company could probably go public following the projected 1987–88 recession and sell stock at 10 × projected 1989 earnings of $28 million. Net proceeds to the company of $50–70 million could be reasonably expected based on these projections. Thus, a total of $160–180 million of additional funds will probably be available to the company during the next five years in addition to projected cash flow. This figure does not include the bargain leases of $116.3 million. Since the Drexel Burnham investors' total commitment of debt, preferred, and common stock was $213.9 million, their risk would easily appear to be justified by the potential reward.

The riskiest period in all LBOs is the first two or three years when the debt is at its highest point. In Levitz's case, the highest risk will probably be the next recession, which also is likely to hit in the first two or three years. While Drexel Burnham projects the expected recession in 1987–88 will only mildly affect earnings, could the company weather the economic storm of the 1980–82 period with the new capital structure? During that period, Levitz's EBIT was $54.3 million for the two years combined. Interest of all debt is projected to total approximately $75 million for both fiscal 1987 and fiscal 1988, and the company can withhold interest on the junior subordinated debt of $14.6 million at its option. Excess depreciation and cash should enable the company to make its interest payments without resorting to the sale and leaseback of any of its stores.

The expected return for all investors is quite high if the company can meet the Citicorp/Drexel Burnham projections. A reasonable estimate of value would be to capitalize EBIT at 4.5 ×, plus free cash, less outstanding debt. The multiple of earnings would be comparable to 8.7 × fully taxed earnings. This valuation formula would put the value of the company in 10 years at $475 million. Assuming all of the stock was sold for this amount in the tenth year, the following table shows the return for each investor group.

The Drexel Burnham institutional investors will see an excellent return on their total investment if these projections are reached. The total internal rate of return of 19 percent compounded over 10 years is exceptionally good. Most mezzanine internal rates of return are computed over five years and are tar-

Return on Investment
(000 omitted)

| Investor | Investment | | Cumulative Expected 10-Year Return | | | | | 10-Year Return | |
	Amount	Type	Dividend	Interest	Principal	Equity	Total	IRR	Times Investment
Drexel Burnham Investors	$ 7,500	Common	$59,151			$237,500			
	28,167	Preferred			$ 28,167				
	178,200[1]	Debt		$247,000	180,000				
Total	$213,867		$59,151	$247,000	$208,167	$237,500	$751,818	19.0%	3.5x
Citicorp Investors	$2,250	Common				71,250			
	4,833	Preferred	7,250		4,833				
Total	$7,083		$7,250		$4,833	$71,250	$83,333	31.4%	11.8x
Management	$2,250	Common				$71,250			
	2,000	Preferred	3,000		2,000				
Total	$4,250		$3,000		$2,000	$71,250	$76,250	35.8%	17.9x
Pritzker Trusts	$3,000	Common		$3,500[2]		$95,000	$98,500	60.7%	32.8x

[1]Net of 1% commitment fee.
[2]Consulting fees.

geted in the 25 percent range for an investment similar to Levitz. This computation implicitly assumes that all cash flows are reinvested at the 25 percent rate, which is unlikely to be the case. The internal rate of return of 19 percent over 10 years for the Drexel Burnham investors also assumes a reinvestment of cash flows at the 19 percent rate, but this reinvestment rate is closer to the rates available in other reinvestment opportunities.

Citicorp investors stand to make 11.8 × their $7.1 million investment for an internal rate of return of 31.4 percent over 10 years. Management tops this with an expected return of 17.9 × their investment of $4.3 million. Bob Elliott received 4 percent of the company for an investment of $1.1 million, which should return him $20 million over a 10-year period. The best return is likely for the Pritzker Trusts, who started the whole saga with their initial buyout proposal. Jay Pritzker forced his participation in the deal in return for his support. Citicorp and Drexel Burnham reluctantly agreed that if Pritzker opposed the deal, the tender offer could fail. Thus, Pritzker struck a deal whereby the Pritzker Trusts invested only a straight common stock, not in any of the unwanted preferred stock. In addition, a Pritzker affiliate, the Hyatt Corporation, will be paid a fee of $3.5 million for "financial services" over three years. The demand to be paid a $3.5 million fee over the first three years, when cash is most needed to service debt, is perhaps indicative of Pritzker's priorities. The Pritzkers' expected 10-year return on the $3.0 million investment is 32.8 ×, or $98.5 million. They were able to cash in their shares at $39 on the deal for a total of $71.5 million. There is no question that Jay Pritzker knows how to play the corporate takeover game. He suggested they play a friendly game, and he dealt the cards. Whereas he did not win the bid, he played the last trump card and ended up the biggest winner of all.

RELIABLE STORES, INC.

The Reliable Stores' LBO is an example of the Oppenheimer technique of LBOs developed during a period when effective capital gains taxes were approximately 49 percent. The technique involved the cash purchase of all the operating assets from a company, which then became an investment company. Shareholders could remain at their option and share in ownership of income from a portfolio of tax-free securities. Unlike the conventional LBO structure today, management did not share in stock ownership but rather a generous profit fund based on earnings. The outstanding performance of Reliable, particularly during periods of recession and high interest rates, is proof that the profit fund provided strong incentives for management. It enabled the top five executives to earn in 1985 an average over six times their prebuyout compensation seven years earlier. Reliable's new owners sought various ways to refinance the original buyout. They settled on a sale of half their stock to the company's ESOP and took advantage of regulations enabling them to defer capital gains taxes.

If experience is the best teacher, Reliable Stores' management is the most learned in the industry. In 1985, the top five members of the management team

Levitz Furniture Corporation Selected Financial Data

	Nine Months-Ended October 31 (Unaudited)		Year Ended January 31				
	1984	1983	1984	1983	1982	1981	1980
	(In thousands, except per share data)						
Net sales	$ 551,661	$ 450,383	$ 644,435	$ 485,721	$ 488,544	$ 500,752	$ 546,580
Gross profit	249,249	198,743	286,058	214,481	219,578	220,701	240,814
Gross profit percentage	45.18%	44.13%	44.39%	44.16%	44.95%	44.07%	44.06
Income before income taxes	$ 44,076	$ 29,979	$ 51,419	$ 16,088	$ 15,300	$ 24,601	$ 38,505
Net income	22,369	15,832	27,409	8,765	8,873	13,458	20,527
Earnings per share	$ 2.74	1.94	3.37	1.07	1.05	1.58	2.42
Return on ending shareholders' equity	12.85%	10.86%	17.57%	6.58%	6.82%	10.37%	17.03%
Working capital	$ 61,397	$ 51,772	$ 47,825	$ 49,935	$ 55,864	$ 62,641	$ 60,912
Property under capital leases, net	64,951	75,718	67,130	78,609	86,447	89,912	94,156
Capital lease obligations	83,609	96,171	85,311	98,938	107,647	109,896	112,626
Debt other than capital leases	41,650	27,549	42,972	26,547	35,789	24,710	23,045
Shareholders' equity	174,047	145,843	155,960	133,167	130,608	129,767	120,547
Average common shares outstanding	8,152,000	8,143,000	8,143,872	8,154,972	8,443,934	8,514,682	8,496,560
Total assets	$ 409,758	$ 366,086	$ 377,852	$ 318,560	$ 315,870	$ 319,296	$ 313,581
Cash dividends per share	$ 0.59	$ 0.41	$ 0.59	$ 0.50	$ 0.50	$ 0.50	$ 0.45
Book value per share	$ 21.34	$ 17.90	$ 19.14	$ 16.37	$ 15.70	$ 15.23	$ 14.16
Ratio of earnings to fixed charges	6.11	4.14	5.03	2.16	2.10	2.82	3.82

had worked for the company an amazing 213 years, or more than 42 years per man. Seven years after the company's 1978 LBO, the company's operating earnings were up threefold over pre-LBO levels.

The buyout process began for Reliable Stores, Inc. in June 1976 when an anonymous letter arrived. It outlined the structure of a proposed buyout of Reliable sponsored by Oppenheimer and Company. Reliable management knew of Oppenheimer and thought the proposal contained enough merit to consult the directors about it.

The proposal suggested a price substantially higher than the current market price. Reliable directors felt responsible to shareholders to follow up on the proposal, but the author of the letter never contacted Reliable after that, despite promises that he would.

In the spring of 1977, Frank C. Brown and Company wrote a practically identical letter outlining a proposal that eventually led to a buyout of Reliable Stores by Oprel Corporation, a company newly formed by Oppenheimer and Company. This finder was paid $350,000 for the introduction.

Reliable began in 1895 when Aaron Straus bought his first furniture store in Baltimore, Maryland, establishing a growth policy of buying existing stores that had persisted. By the 1920s, Straus presided over a national chain of stores, a growth that paralleled the Phillip Levy chain.

Levy overexpanded, however, and went bankrupt in 1924. Straus bought the Levy chain from the receivers, and after closing some stores, restored it to profitability. The company then began buying only profitable stores with established names.

Straus entered the jewelry business in 1934 by buying the Castleberg's stores in Baltimore. Straus did not plan to go specifically into jewelry, but he was an expert in the high ticket retail business and credit sales. The company then acquired Shaw's, a jewelry chain in Texas.

The company went public in 1934 and was listed on the American Stock Exchange, moving to the NYSE in 1936. It paid dividends every year since 1934 until its acquisition in 1978.

Reliable continues to operate as an amalgamation of independent stores. Many years ago, Reliable's stores tried mass merchandising, but the company found that merely decreasing the price does not necessarily increase volume. Reliable also tried specialized colonial furniture stores of the Ethan Allen motif, but found that full-service conventional furniture operations worked better for their stores.

Reliable's jewelry stores operate more effectively as a chain, and in this category, the company has opened completely new stores in regional malls where they can benefit from traffic. The jewelry division of the company operates from a more pyramidal structure. One person heads jewelry and has several regional supervisors reporting to him.

At the time of the Oprel offer, Reliable was operating 147 stores and leasing departments in two other stores. Furniture and appliance stores generated 78 percent of sales volume in 1977, with the jewelry stores accounting for the remaining 22 percent.

Reliable operated stores in 67 cities. Home furnishing sales included furniture, appliances, carpets, draperies, lamps, and fixtures. Jewelry sales included diamonds, watches, rings, charms, necklaces, and costume jewelry. After the LBO on February 1, 1978, the company concentrated on furniture and deemphasized jewelry stores. The number of furniture stores rose from 64 to 101 by 1985, and jewelry stores declined from 89 to 73 over this 7-year period.

The Aaron Straus and Lillie Straus Foundation was Reliable's principal shareholder, with 26.8 percent at the time of the buyout. The company's four top executives were trustees of the Foundation, which when added to their own stock ownership gave them effective control of the company.

The first buyout offer suggested a price of $14 per share. Management successfully negotiated that to $16\frac{3}{4}$ per share, arguing that its inventories and company-owned stores and real estate not used in operations were undervalued. The buyout price of $16\frac{3}{4}$ consisted of $16.58 per share cash purchase price plus $0.17 per share dividend. This compared to the high–low price range of the stock on the NYSE of $9\frac{1}{8}$–$5\frac{1}{4}$ in 1976 and $11–8\frac{1}{8}$ in 1977. Immediately before the announcement that an agreement of sale had been signed, the price was $13\frac{7}{8}$.

The offer was to purchase Reliable's assets and keep the old corporation in existence as an investment company. At that time, effective capital gains tax approached 49 percent, and the two top executives were well advanced in age. Meyer Barnett, president, was 82 and had worked for Reliable or its predecessors for 62 years. Lewis Hamburger, then chairman, was 83 and had joined the company in 1921. Barnett and Hamburger each owned approximately $500,000 of stock, of which taxes would claim almost half. They could minimize the aftertax residual of their estates by paying capital gains tax first on the sale, then estate taxes on the aftertax proceeds.

All shareholders therefore were offered a chance to tender their shares for $16.58 or remain as shareholders in the old company, which became RES Investment Company, a closed-end management investment company with assets of about $10 million. Approximately one-third of the shares were not tendered for cash and remained in the investment company. All of the cash proceeds from the sale remaining in the investment company were invested in a diversified list of tax-free bonds, and all of the income was distributed to the shareholders free of federal taxes.

The RES Investment Company steadily declined in assets and in number of shareholders largely due to shareholders' tendering their stock to the company, which is allowed once a year at the discretion of the board. RES Investment Company reorganized in 1984 to free itself from certain contingent liabilities, mostly relating to real estate taxes. In 1986, it began negotiating a merger with a mutual fund, a tactic that became popular in the 1970s. This merger enabled shareholders to sell their company's assets for cash without triggering capital gains taxes and to end up with mutual fund shares that were marketable. The IRS approved two deals with letter rulings, then reversed itself and said the transactions did not meet the conditions for "continuity of business'' necessary in a tax-free reorganization. The RES Investment Company remained an investment company for over five years in order to meet the conditions necessary for a tax-free exchange.

To finance the LBO, Oprel Corporation invested $10 million, all but approximately $2.3 million of which was borrowed. Another $11.5 million was obtained by the sale and leaseback of real estate. The remaining $8.5 million of the $29.4 million purchase price came from the sale of accounts receivables. Since the asset sale was approximately $2.9 million below book value, the company was able to obtain a tax refund of approximately $1.4 million.

The largest single shareholder in Reliable was Odyssey Partners, with 54.8 percent of the common stock. Odyssey, an affiliate of Oppenheimer and Company, Inc. was represented on Reliable's board by Leon Levy, chairman of the board of Oppenheimer Management Corporation; Jack Nash, CEO of Oppenheimer and Company; and John Bretl, vice-president of Oppenheimer and Company. The original nine-man board included four from management and five representing the outside investors.

The next single largest stockholder was Ira Hechler with 20 percent. At the time of the buyout, Hechler was a consultant to Oppenheimer and its director for special acquisitions. Hechler is known for his innovative financial structuring, which will be demonstrated again in the refinancing of Reliable. Hechler structured the Leslie Fay buyout by using a joint venture partnership with a company that had sizable tax losses to shelter earnings in the initial years. This structure was not needed in the Reliable deal because the company sold its receivables and elected for income tax purposes to record income on the installment method, thereby accounting for sales only when cash is collected from customers. This had the effect of delaying the reporting of substantial income in the first year, which resulted in significant tax losses. The company thus provided for taxes for reporting purposes, but all taxes were deferred by carrying forward the large first-year losses.

Oppenheimer's buyout formula differs from conventional methods in that management is not offered any stock in the new company. Management does receive long-term contracts and incentive bonuses based on the businesses' future earnings. In the management agreement of the Reliable deal, the top eight management people formed a partnership that would manage the company for 15 years. The partners received annual salaries and participation in a profit fund. The fund amounts, in effect, to 15 percent of pretax earnings after the base year's earnings are exceeded. As a result of this arrangement, the top four executives each earned over $500,000 in 1985 compared to an average of $81,600 in 1977, the year prior to the buyout.

The profit fund's base year pretax earnings are $5.37 million, the actual pretax income in fiscal 1977. In 1985, earnings before profit fund contributions and taxes were in excess of $27 million, demonstrating the powerful incentive the profit fund provided. For all the positive results produced by the profit fund, there is one minor negative. The company must keep three sets of books because the profit fund calculation is based on prebuyout accounting.

Meyer Barnett retired as chairman in 1985 at age 89 (outlasting Lewis Hamburger, former chairman, who retired in 1980 at 85), and as a consultant retained a 6 percent interest in the profit fund. Three other top executives will become consultants at age 65 and receive 50 percent of their salaries when they retire.

Hamburger and Barnett headed the management team at the time of the buyout. Arthur Korn, then 68, was executive vice-president. The youngsters were Al Coplan, then 53, vice-president and treasurer; and Meyer Barnett's son Dick, then 44, vice-president, furniture division. Coplan, who had been with the company 27 years at the time of the buyout, was made president and CEO in 1980, and then appointed chairman and CEO in 1985. His financial background undoubtedly qualified him to guide the company through a period of $21\frac{1}{2}$ percent prime rate and credit controls. The company was heavily burdened with long-term debt and dependent on floating rate debt to finance its important credit sales.

The company's cash flow from operations remained a healthy $2.9 million in fiscal 1981, despite the high floating interest rate on its debt and the depressing impact of high interest charges on high ticket, easily postponable furniture and jewelry sales. Operating income dropped only $240,000 in the January 1981 year, which spanned the period of highest interest rates and the resulting recession. The company also mastered the 1982 recession, showing an operating profit gain of 5 percent on a sales increase of 18 percent.

It is clear that a company with a long history, led by a competent management group long on experience, can survive the worst of times and prosper in the best with the proper incentives. The profit pool provided the incentives, enabling the top five management people to share in the fivefold increase in operating earnings over fiscal 1977 by increasing their pre-LBO compensation over sixfold. Despite the executives' average age of 70, they produced record results in 1985 by a wide margin.

The following table demonstrates the profit improvement from the last 12-month period before the buyout to results in 1985.

	12 Months Ended (000 omitted)		
	Oct. 31, 1977	Jan. 31, 1985	Percent Change
Net sales	$82,299	$182,473	121.7%
Cost of goods sold	48,021	96,632	101.2
Selling, general and administrative expenses	25,485	63,079	147.5
EBIT	8,793	22,762	158.9
Interest expense, net	865	7,365	751.4
Earnings before taxes	7,928	15,726	98.4
Taxes	3,898	7,470	91.6
Net income	4,030	8,256	104.9

This substantial increase in sales and earnings was achieved despite a higher interest rate environment and only a 14 percent increase in the number of stores.

In August 1983, the company filed a prospectus with the SEC to sell 2 million shares at a price estimated between $13–15 per share. Seven hundred thousand of these shares were to be new ones sold by Reliable to raise equity funds, and 1.3 million shares were to be offered by selling shareholders. These 48 shareholders were to sell 21 percent of their shares each. The estimated price range put the value of the company between $78 million and $90 million. The trailing 12-month earnings per share was $1.05, which raised the P/E ratio from 12.4 × to 15.3 ×. The price for furniture stocks peaked in June 1983, and by the time the deal was filed, had dropped 10–15 percent. As marketing of the stock proceeded, it became clear that the stock could not be sold at the $13–15 level. When it appeared the deal could only be sold at $10 per share, the offering was withdrawn.

Reenter Ira Hechler.

Hechler had been attempting to devise a variation of his LBO structure of joint venturing with an NOL company to shelter taxes. This method carries a small risk in the area of allocation of gains and losses between the two joint venture partners and creates an excess capital account for the NOL partner that would burden earnings for some 25 years in the future. Typically, the NOL company would expect to negotiate a settlement of their interests after a few years. Since earnings cannot be predicted precisely over five years, the amount of excess capital accounts cannot be accurately determined, thus adding to the inability of the other equity investors to reasonably estimate their possible returns.

An alternative to the loss company partnership structure would be to have the loss company actually acquire at least 80 percent of both the voting stock and of the initial year's value of the stock. Both Goldome and Empire Savings Bank in New York became active in pursuing Hechler-formatted deals, as they both had huge tax losses. Goldome's alone exceeded $1 billion.

Hechler structured a refinancing proposal for Reliable with Empire Savings Bank. The value of the proposal was $50 million, with the banks, led by Manufacturers Hanover, committing to put up $40 million. Empire would purchase all of a $10 million issue of voting preferred and 50.1 percent of a $1 million common stock issue, thus having 95 percent of both the vote and the equity dollars invested. Empire could have consolidated Reliable's earnings for tax purposes, which would have completely sheltered Reliable's earnings from taxes for the foreseeable future.

The old stockholders who were sellers would purchase 42.9 percent of the new stock, and the remaining 7 percent would be bought by management. Although management still had nine years left in the profit pool, its members persuaded the old shareholders to let them participate in the new stock. The original stockholders made a $10 million investment in the buyout of which approximately $7.7 million was borrowed. Thus, they would have netted $42.3

million on an equity investment of $2.3 million and would have acquired a 42.9 percent stake in Reliable for an investment of $429,000.

The Hechler refinancing proposal, however, was dropped in 1984 due to a change in an IRS ruling. Whereas earnings were increasing by 46 percent in fiscal 1984, a period of strong economic growth, there was still a need to shelter earnings from taxes to give additional comfort to the lenders. EBIT reached $18.4 million in fiscal 1984, but interest on existing debt amounted to $5.6 million. The addition of $50 million in acquisition debt on top of the existing debt of $67.8 million would have dropped pretax earnings in fiscal 1984 to around $6.0 million. If full taxes were paid, the cash flow would have been insufficient to repay the acquisition debt over a 10-year period. Earnings in fiscal 1985 increased 23.6 percent over fiscal 1984, and EBIT amounted to $22.8 million compared to only $12.6 million two years earlier. On these strong earnings, a new plan was developed whereby the old shareholders would sell 50.1 percent of their stock to an ESOP established in January 1985 for this purpose. The sale price was $40 million, which put a value on the company of $80 million. This was a reasonable 3.5 × fiscal 1985 EBIT. The purchase price was payable $30 million in cash and $10 million in 11.7 percent subordinated notes.

The ESOP borrowed the $30 million cash portion of the purchase, and the loan was guaranteed by the company. The initial ESOP contribution was $7.0 million, which was used to pay interest and principal on the $30 million bank loan. At this rate of contribution, the ESOP loan would be fully repaid in seven years out of pretax earnings. All contributions to the ESOP are tax-deductible and accrue to the benefit of the 2000 employees who participate. All full-time employees participate, except union members for whom the company is required to make contributions to union-sponsored pension plans.

The ESOP purchase of 50.1 percent of the shareholders' stock allowed the company to use "push down" accounting, which stepped up the basis on half of the assets to the selling price and resulted in a positive net worth. The ESOP purchase also enabled the sellers to take advantage of the rollover provisions allowed in the 1984 tax law. When an ESOP purchases at least 30 percent of the stock in a closely held company, the sellers can reinvest those funds in qualified securities and not trigger capital gains taxes. The cost basis on its old stock becomes the cost basis on its new stock. Thus, the selling stockholders received $30 million cash to be invested within a year in a new stock portfolio and $10 million in subordinated notes. They also retained stock in Reliable worth $40 million. This $80 million compares with approximately $75 million that the shareholders would have received if the Hechler proposal had succeeded. Hechler's proposed sale of all the stock for $50 million would have been taxable and would have netted stockholders around $41 million after taxes. Their 42.9 percent continued ownership of Reliable would be worth $34 million net of the cost of investment.

The $80 million value represents an 8 × gain on the initial $10 million investment but 31.4 × the true equity investment of $2.3 million. This produced an excellent internal rate of return of 63.6 percent annually over seven years.

The LBO of Reliable proved beneficial for all participants. The public stockholders received a reasonable premium for their stock; the investors made an excellent return on their investment, and management profited handsomely by the profit fund arrangement. The investors did find it somewhat difficult to cash in their investment. The potential to sell out to another company was hindered by the presence of the profit fund and the low book value, compared to a reasonable price based on earnings. The company attempted to go public in 1983, but the window of opportunity closed before their price objectives could be realized. They then attempted to do a second LBO using the structure of pairing an investment company with a loss partner. When this proposal failed, the company devised a purchase by the ESOP of half of the investors' stock. After some aborted attempts, the investors finally sold half their stock to the ESOP at a price providing them with an excellent return. The prospects for future enhancement of the value of the stock are good as the excellent management team has seven years remaining on their profit fund arrangement and, as the highest paid employees, will be the biggest beneficiaries of the stock held in the ESOP.

Reliable Stores Consolidated Balance Sheet
(000 omitted)

	January 31, 1977	January 31, 1977
Assets		
Cash	$ 957	$ 1,540
Short-term investments		
Accounts receivables	28,133	101,490
Inventories	16,248	36,580
Prepaids	385	880
Receivable, pension plan		9,006
Current assets	45,723	149,497
Net property and equipment	10,794	15,019
Other assets	268	937
Total assets	$56,785	$165,453
Liabilities		
Bank credit line		$ 5,267
Short-term borrowings	$ 2,340	52,000
Accounts payable	4,223	18,870
Current maturities, long-term debt	924	2,841
Deferred taxes		22,508
Accruals	8,601	18,514
Current liabilities	16,088	120,050
Long-term debt	8,722	21,465
Pension reserves	762	
Total liabilities	25,572	141,515
Common stock	4,888	58
Paid in capital	309	484
Retained earnings	27,602	23,396
Total equity	32,799	23,938
Less treasury stock	1,586	
Total liabilities and equity	$56,785	$165,453

Reliable Stores
Operating Expenses
(000 omitted)

Fiscal Years Ended January 31

	1977[1]	1979	1980	1981	1982	1983	1984	1985
Net sales	$74,280	$90,897	$96,255	$96,064	$109,191	$126,129	$157,844	$182,473
Operating expenses	67,982	84,027	87,951	88,000	97,126	113,490	139,415	159,711
EBIT	6,298	6,870	8,304	8,064	12,065	12,639	18,429	22,762
Interest expense	919	3,626	6,225	6,577	6,849	6,679	5,625	7,365
Disposal gains		405		930		753	802	
Taxes	2,628	1,473	808	1,072	2,279	2,334	6,397	7,470
Net income	2,751	2,176	1,271	1,345	2,937	4,379	7,209	8,256

[1]1977 is the only pre-merger year given in the table.

Appendix. Financial Analysis of Pannill Knitting Buyout

Pannill Knitting Company, Inc.
Analysis of a Leveraged Buyout
Case 1
Data of Analysis: 3/5/85

Acquisition Funding Analysis ($000)	
Sources	
Cash on hand	$14,395
Revolving credit line	47,000
Term loan	108,000
Subordinated debt	50,000
Preferred stock	10,000
Common stock	14,570
Total sources	$243,965
Uses	
Acquisition of stock	$228,191
Repayment of existing debt	974
Estimated transaction costs	2,600
Estimated recapture taxes	12,200
Total uses	$243,965

Pannill Knitting Company, Inc.
Proforma Consolidated Capitalization
($000)

	Amount	(%)
Revolving credit line	$47,000	20.47
Term loan	108,000	47.04
Total senior bank debt	155,000	67.52
Subordinated debt	50,000	21.78
Total debt	205,000	89.30
Preferred stock	10,000	4.36
Common stock	14,570	6.35
Total equity	24,570	10.70
Total capitalization	229,570	100.00

Pannill Knitting Company, Inc.
Balance Sheet Adjustments
($000)

Assets	Actual as of 3/3/84	Step-Up (see allocation of purchase price premium)	Other Adjustments	Opening Balance Sheet
Cash	$27,129	$0	($14,395)	$12,734
Accounts receivable	29,314	0		29,314
Inventories	21,288	$30,233		51,521
Other	0	0		0
Current assets	77,731			93,569
Land	2,488	4,498		6,986
Buildings	17,400	32,025		49,425
Machinery & equipment	6,400	20,146		26,546
Furniture & fixtures	381	667		1,048
Vehicles	100	424		524
Leasehold improvements	0	0		0
Total PP&E	26,769			84,529
Less: accumulated depreciation	0		0	0
Total PP&E, net	26,769			84,529
Customer lists	0	17,465		17,465
Sales backlog	0	5,065		5,065
Software	0	873		873
Transaction costs	0	2,600		2,600
Goodwill	0	41,915		41,915
Other	598	0	5,000	5,598
Total assets	$105,098			$251,614

Pannill Knitting Company, Inc.
Balance Sheet Adjustments (*continued*)
($000)

Liabilities and Stockholders' Equity	Actual as of 3/3/84	Adjustments	Other Adjustments	Opening Balance Sheet
Payables & accruals (incl. other)	$17,044	$0		$17,044
Outstanding short-term debt	179	(179)		0
Current portion of debt:				
Revolving credit line	0	47,000		47,000
Term loan	0	5,000		5,000
Current liabilities	17,223			69,044
Outstanding long-term debt	795	(795)		0
Term loan	0	103,000		103,000
Subordinated debt	0	55,000		55,000
Total long-term debt	795			158,000
Other long-term liabilities	0	0		0
Total liabilities	18,018			227,044
				0
Preferred stock	0	0	10,000	10,000
Common stock	7,000	(7,000)	14,570	14,570
Retained earnings	80,080	(80,080)		0
Total stockholders' equity	87,080			24,570
Total liabilities and stockholders' equity	$105,098			$251,614

Pannill Knitting Company, Inc.
Summary of Buyout Indebtedness
($000)

Assumed average prime rate   12.50%
Average bank borrowing rate:
Revolving credit line   prime +   1.50%
Term loan   prime +   1.50%

A.) Revolving credit agreement

Amount	$47,000
Interest rate	14.00%
Term (years)	5
-interest only	5
-principal and interest	0
Principal payments made	at maturity
Principal payments begin	at maturity
Date loan closed	4/20/84
Amortization schedule:	

Year	
1	$0
2	0
3	0
4	0
5	47,000
6	0
7	0
8	0
9	0
10	0
11	0
12	0

B.) Bank term loan

Amount	$108,000
Interest rate	14.00%
Term (years)	10
-interest only	0
-principal and interest	10
Principal payments made	quarterly
Principal payments begin	7/31/84
Date loan closed	4/20/84
Amortization schedule:	

Year	
1	$5,000
2	7,500
3	11,000
4	11,000
5	11,000
6	11,000
7	11,000

	Year	8	$13,500
		9	13,500
		10	13,500
		11	0
		12	0

C.) Subordinated debt

Face amount	$55,000
Net amount	50,000
Interest rate: years 1–3	12.00%
years 4–12	15.00%
Term (years)	12
-interest only	6
-principal and interest	6
Principal payments made	quarterly
Principal payments begin	7/31/90
Date loan closed	4/20/84

Amortization schedule:

	Year	1	$0
		2	0
		3	0
		4	0
		5	0
		6	0
		7	6,000
		8	6,000
		9	6,000
		10	6,000
		11	6,000
		12	25,000

Pannill Knitting Company, Inc.
Stockholders' Equity
($000)

A.) Preferred stock

Liquidation value	$10,000
Number of shares issued	100,000
Liquidation value per share	$100.00
Net amount	10,000
Dividend rate: years 1–3	12.00%
years 4–12	15.00%
Term (years)	12
—dividends only	6
—redemptions and dividends	6
Dividend payments made	quarterly
Redemption payments begin	7/31/90
Date preferred stock issued	4/20/84

Redemption schedule:

Year	
1	$0
2	0
3	0
4	0
5	0
6	0
7	1,000
8	1,000
9	1,000
10	1,000
11	1,000
12	5,000

B.) Common stock

Amount	$14,570
Number of shares issued	971,333
Issue price per share	$15.00
Dividend rate	nil
Dividend payments made	n.a.
Date stock issued	4/20/84

Pannill Knitting Company, Inc.
Other Assumptions for Financial Model
(All dollar figures in 000, except per share data)
(continued)

(8) Transaction costs

Legal	$750
Accounting	350
Investment banking fees	200
Bank fees and miscellaneous	1,300
	$2,600

For projection purposes, transaction costs will be amortized over a five-year period on a straight-line basis and will not be allocated to the purchased assets.

(9) Projected interest income

Interest will be calculated on accumulated cash after repayment of debt.

Interest rate	9.00%

(10) Goodwill

Non-amortizable for tax purposes, but amortizable over 15 years for financial reporting purposes.

	Appraised	Tax Allocation
Goodwill	$24,000	$41,915

Pannill Knitting Company, Inc.
Securities Ownership
($000)

	Sub-ordinated Debt	Preferred Stock	Common Stock	Total Amount Invested	Initial Common Stock Ownership Interest
Mezzanine investors	$50,000	$10,000	$4,500	$64,500	30.00%
Butler Capital	0	0	3,150	3,150	21.00
Management and other employees	0	0	7,350	7,350	49.00
Total	$50,000	$10,000	$15,000	$75,000	100.00

Pannill Knitting Company, Inc.
Other Assumptions for Financial Model
(All dollar figures in 000, except per share data)

(1) Purchase price of stock

Shares outstanding (000)	438,829
Price per share	$520.00
Total price	$228,191
Multiple of EBIT	5.02

The buyout is assumed to take place on 4/20/84 which is assumed to be the beginning of the first fiscal year. Unless otherwise noted, all financial statement data is assumed to be as of 3/3/84.

(2) Income taxes

Combined federal and state rate: 48.00%

(3) Excess inventory valuation

The excess inventory valuation over FIFO costs is assumed to be realized in the first year of operations.

Allocated value in buyout	$51,521	Tax
FIFO inventory	27,691	(LIFO of $21,288 plus LIFO reserve of $6,403)
Excess inventory valuation	$23,830	

(4) Projected sales

Base period sales: $172,800

Years:	1	2	3	4	5	6	7	8-12
Inflation factor	5.0%	5.0%	5.0%	5.0%	5.0%	5.0%	5.0%	5.0%
Unit sales increase	3.0%	3.0%	3.0%	3.0%	3.0%	3.0%	3.0%	3.0%
Total rate of increase	8.0%	8.0%	8.0%	8.0%	8.0%	8.0%	8.0%	8.0%

(5) Projected costs of operations
(excluding depreciation)

Years:	1	2	3	4	5	6	7	8-12
% of sales	74.30%	75.30%	74.30%	77.30%	78.40%	78.30%	78.30%	78.30%

(6) Projected working capital

Target minimum cash balance	$12,734
Rate of increase in working capital based on each year's sales increase	20.0%

(7) Relationship of inventory, receivables, and payables

For pro forma balance sheet purposes, inventory and receivables are assumed to maintain the same mathematical relationship to sales as calculated from the financial statements as of 3/3/84. Payables are calculated as a plug for working capital.

	Inventory	Receivables
Balance	$27,691	$29,314
1984 sales	$160,052	$160,052
Ratio	16.5%	17.5%

(cont.)

(11) Depreciation of Purchased Assets

Assumed beginning date on which purchased assets are placed in service: 4/20/84

Description	Method	Period	Cost	1	2	3	4	5
Buildings	straight-line	18	$49,425	$2,746	$2,746	$2,746	$2,746	$2,746
Machinery & equipment	ACRS	5	26,546	3,982	5,840	5,575	5,575	5,575
Furniture & fixtures	straight-line	5	1,048	210	210	210	210	210
Vehicles	ACRS	3	524	131	199	194	0	0
Leasehold improvements	straight-line	1	0	0	0	0	0	0
Total			$77,543	$7,068	$8,995	$8,724	$8,530	$8,530

Description	6	7	8	9	10	11	12	Total
Buildings	$2,746	$2,746	$2,746	$2,746	$2,746	$2,746	$2,746	$32,950
Machinery & equipment	0	0	0	0	0	0	0	$26,546
Furniture & fixtures	210	210	210	210	210	210	210	$2,515
Vehicles	0	0	0	0	0	0	0	$524
Leasehold improvements	0	0	0	0	0	0	0	$0
Total	$2,955	$2,955	$2,955	$2,955	$2,955	$2,955	$2,955	$62,535

(cont.)

Pannill Knitting Company, Inc.
Other Assumptions for Financial Model
(All dollar figures in 000, except per share data)
(continued)

(12) Capital additions

Machinery and Equipment:
Investment tax credit based on a rate of 10.00%

Year	Additions	Depreciation: 1	2	3	4	5	6	7
1	$4,000	$600	$880	$840	$840	$840	$0	$0
2	4,240	0	636	933	890	890	890	0
3	4,494	0	0	674	989	944	944	944
4	4,764	0	0	0	715	1,048	1,000	1,000
5	5,050	0	0	0	0	758	1,111	1,061
6	5,353	0	0	0	0	0	803	1,178
7	5,674	0	0	0	0	0	0	851
8	6,015	0	0	0	0	0	0	0
9	6,375	0	0	0	0	0	0	0
10	6,758	0	0	0	0	0	0	0
11	7,163	0	0	0	0	0	0	0
12	7,593	0	0	0	0	0	0	0
Total	$67,479	$600	$1,516	$2,447	$3,434	$4,480	$4,749	$5,033

Year   *Depreciation:*

Year	8	9	10	11	12	Total	ITC
1	$0	$0	$0	$0	$0	$4,000	$400
2	0	0	0	0	0	4,240	424
3	0	0	0	0	0	4,494	449
4	1,000	0	0	0	0	4,764	476
5	1,061	1,061	0	0	0	5,050	505
6	1,124	1,124	1,124	0	0	5,353	535
7	1,248	1,192	1,192	1,192	0	5,674	567
8	902	1,323	1,263	1,263	1,263	6,015	602
9	0	956	1,403	1,339	1,339	5,036	638
10	0	0	1,014	1,487	1,419	3,920	676
11	0	0	0	1,074	1,576	2,650	716
12	0	0	0	0	1,139	1,139	759
	$5,336	$5,656	$5,995	$6,355	$6,736	$52,335	$6,748

(cont.)

Pannill Knitting Company, Inc.
Other Assumptions for Financial Model
(All dollar figures in 000, except per share data)
(continued)

Buildings:

Buildings are depreciated under ACRS- straightline over (years): 18
Placed in service mid-year.

Year	Additions	Depreciation: 1	2	3	4	5	6	7
1	$3,000	83	167	167	167	167	167	167
2	3,000	0	83	167	167	167	167	167
3	0	0	0	0	0	0	0	0
4	0	0	0	0	0	0	0	0
5	0	0	0	0	0	0	0	0
6	0	0	0	0	0	0	0	0
7	0	0	0	0	0	0	0	0
8	0	0	0	0	0	0	0	0
9	0	0	0	0	0	0	0	0
10	0	0	0	0	0	0	0	0
11	0	0	0	0	0	0	0	0
12	0	0	0	0	0	0	0	0
Total	$6,000	$83	$250	$333	$333	$333	$333	$333
Tot. Depr.-Add.		$683	$1,766	$2,780	$3,767	$4,813	$5,082	$5,367

Depreciation:

Year	8	9	10	11	12	Total
1	$167	$167	$167	$167	$167	$1,917
2	167	167	167	167	167	1,750
3	0	0	0	0	0	0
4	0	0	0	0	0	0
5	0	0	0	0	0	0
6	0	0	0	0	0	0
7	0	0	0	0	0	0
8	0	0	0	0	0	0
9	0	0	0	0	0	0
10	0	0	0	0	0	0
11	0	0	0	0	0	0
12	0	0	0	0	0	0
Total	$333	$333	$333	$333	$333	$3,667
Tot. Depr.-Add.	$5,669	$5,989	$6,328	$6,688	$7,069	$56,002

Significant portions of building additions may also qualify for investment tax credits and five-year ACRS treatment as "Other Intangible Property."

(cont.)

Pannill Knitting Company, Inc.
Other Assumptions for Financial Model
(All dollar figures in 000, except per share data)
(continued)

(13) Allocation of Purchase Price

($000)

Calculation of Purchase Price

Common stock	$228,191
Existing debt repaid	974
Liabilities assumed	17,044
Recapture taxes-LIFO, ITC, etc.	12,200
Total purchase price to be allocated	258,409
Transaction costs	2,600
Total purchase price	$261,009

Allocation of Purchase Price

	3/3/84 Balance Sheet	Appraised Value	Allocation of Excess Purchase Price	Depreciation/ Amortization Period
Cash	$27,129	$27,129	$27,129	1
Accounts receivable	29,314	29,314	29,314	1
Inventories	21,288	29,500	51,521	1
Land	2,488	4,000	6,986	1
Buildings	17,400	28,300	49,425	18
Machinery & equipment	6,400	15,200	26,546	5

Furniture & fixtures	381	600	1,048	5
Vehicles	100	300	524	3
Leasehold improvements	0	0	0	1
Goodwill	0	24,000	41,915	1
Customer lists	0	10,000	17,465	5
Sales backlog	0	2,900	5,065	1
Software	0	500	873	5
Other assets	598	598	598	0
Total	$105,098	$172,341	$258,409	

(14) Amortization Schedule for Intangible Assets (excludes Goodwill)

	Amort. Period	Years: 1	2	3	4	5	6	7
Customer lists	5	3,493	3,493	3,493	3,493	3,493	0	0
Sales backlog	1	5,065	0	0	0	0	0	0
Software	5	175	175	175	175	175	0	0
Transaction costs	5	520	520	520	520	520	0	0
Total annual amortization expense		$9,252	$4,188	$4,188	$4,188	$4,188	$0	$0

(cont.)

Pannill Knitting Company, Inc.
Other Assumptions for Financial Model
(All dollar figures in 000, except per share data)
(continued)

(15) Calculation of Annual Interest Expense

Years:

	1	2	3	4	5	6	7
Revolving credit line	$6,580	$6,173	$6,039	$5,696	$5,227	$4,373	$4,329
Term loan	15,120	14,420	13,370	11,830	10,290	8,750	7,210
Mortgage	0	0	0	0	0	0	0
Subordinated debt	6,600	6,600	6,600	8,250	8,250	8,250	8,250
Total annual interest expense	$28,300	$27,193	$26,009	$25,776	$23,767	$21,373	$19,789

Years:

	8	9	10	11	12
Revolving credit line	$4,892	$5,369	$5,355	$4,791	$1,636
Term loan	5,670	3,780	1,890	0	0
Mortgage	0	0	0	0	0
Subordinated debt	7,350	6,450	5,550	4,650	3,750
Total annual interest expense	$17,912	$15,599	$12,795	$9,441	$5,386

Pannill Knitting Company, Inc.
Projected Mezzanine Investors'
Five-Year Rate of Return
($000)

	Multiple of Net Income		
	8	9	10
Projected net income in year 6[1]	$11,098	$11,098	$11,098
Aggregate market value of common stock	$88,782	$99,880	$110,978

Proforma Cash Flows for Years

	0	1	2	3	4	5	*Multiple of Net Income*		
							8	9	10
Initial investment	($64,500)								
Interest and dividend income		7800	7800	7800	9450	36,085			
Capital repayment[2]						65,000			
Share of proceeds from sale of equity							26,635	29,964	33,293
Internal rate of return on investment[3]							18.19%	18.75%	19.30%

[1]On a financial reporting basis.
[2]Assumes mezzanine debt and preferred stock repaid at face value.
[3]Compounded quarterly.

Pannill Knitting Company, Inc.
Leveraged Buyout
Projected Income Statements
(Consolidated tax basis)
($000)

				Years			
	1	2	3	4	5	6	7
Sales	$172,800	$186,624	$201,554	$217,678	$235,092	$253,900	$274,212
Interest income	1,146	1,146	1,146	1,146	1,146	1,146	1,146
Operating costs	125,134	139,382	152,640	167,119	182,932	197,657	231,562
Earnings before interest and taxes	44,410	46,096	47,768	49,413	51,014	55,097	59,504
Adjustments:							
Interest expense	28,300	27,193	26,009	25,776	23,767	21,373	19,789
Depreciation—purchased assets	7,068	8,995	8,724	8,530	8,530	2,955	2,955
Depreciation—capital additions	683	1,766	2,780	3,767	4,813	5,082	5,367
Excess inventory valuation	23,830	0	0	0	0	0	0
Amortization—intangible assets	9,252	4,188	4,188	4,188	4,188	0	0
Adjusted taxable income	(24,724)	3,955	6,067	7,152	9,717	25,687	31,393
Net operating loss generated	24,724	0	0	0	0	0	0
NOL carrryover (prior years)	0	24,724	20,915	15,005	8,418	0	0
NOL utilized	0	3,809	5,910	6,587	8,418	0	0
NOL available for future years	24,724	20,915	15,005	8,418	0	0	0
Taxable income before taxes	(24,724)	146	157	565	1,299	25,687	31,393
Income taxes	0	70	75	271	623	12,330	15,069
Investment tax credit generated	400	424	449	476	505	535	567
ITC carryover (prior years)	0	400	0	0	1	(0)	0
ITC utilized	0	824	449	476	506	535	568
ITC available for future years	400	0	0	1	(0)	0	(0)
Total income taxes	0	(754)	(374)	(205)	117	11,795	14,501
Book net income	($24,724)	$4,709	$6,441	$7,357	$9,599	$13,892	$16,892

		Years			
	8	9	10	11	12
Sales	$296,149	$319,841	$345,428	$373,062	$402,907
Interest income	1,146	1,146	1,146	1,146	1,146
Operating costs	229,305	247,502	266,878	292,108	315,476
Earnings before interest and taxes	64,264	69,406	74,958	82,101	88,577
Adjustments:					
Interest expense	17,912	15,599	12,795	9,441	5,386
Depreciation—purchased assets	2,955	2,955	2,955	2,955	2,955
Depreciation—capital additions	5,669	5,989	6,328	6,688	7,069
Excess inventory valuation	0	0	0	0	0
Amortization—intangible assets	0	0	0	0	0
Adjusted taxable income	37,728	44,862	52,879	63,016	73,167
Net operating loss generated	0	0	0	0	0
NOL carryover (prior years)	0	0	0	0	0
NOL utilized	0	0	0	0	0
NOL available for future years	0	0	0	0	0
Taxable income before taxes	37,728	44,862	52,879	63,016	73,167
Income taxes	18,109	21,534	25,382	30,248	35,120
Investment tax credit generated	602	638	676	716	759
ITC carryover (prior years)	(0)	0	(0)	0	(0)
ITC utilized	601	638	675	717	759
ITC available for future years	0	(0)	0	(0)	(0)
Total income taxes	17,508	20,896	24,707	29,531	34,361
Book net income	$20,219	$23,966	$28,172	$33,485	$38,806

Pannill Knitting Company, Inc.
Leveraged Buyout
Projected Cash Flow Statements
($000)

				Years			
	1	2	3	4	5	6	7
Book net income	($24,724)	$4,709	$6,441	$7,357	$9,599	$13,892	$16,892
Adjustments:							
Add:							
Depreciation	7,752	10,761	11,504	12,297	13,343	8,037	8,322
Excess inventory valuation	23,830	0	0	0	0	0	0
Amortization	9,252	4,188	4,188	4,188	4,188	0	0
Subtract:							
Increase in working capital	0	2,765	2,986	3,225	3,483	3,762	4,062
Capital expenditures	7,000	7,240	4,494	4,764	5,050	5,353	5,674
Scheduled payments:							
Term loan	5,000	7,500	11,000	11,000	11,000	11,000	11,000
Subordinated debt	0	0	0	0	0	0	6,000
Redemption of preferred stock	0	0	0	0	0	0	1,000
Preferred stock dividends	1,200	1,200	1,200	1,500	1,500	1,500	1,500
Net cash flow	2,910	952	2,452	3,353	6,097	315	(4,022)
Opening cash balance	12,734	12,734	12,734	12,734	12,734	12,734	12,734
Total cash	15,644	13,686	15,186	16,087	18,831	13,049	8,712
less: Minimum cash balance	(12,734)	(12,734)	(12,734)	(12,734)	(12,734)	(12,734)	(12,734)
Available for prepayment of debt	2,910	952	2,452	3,353	6,097	315	(4,022)
Prepayment of:							
Revolving credit line	2,910	952	2,452	3,353	6,097	315	(4,022)
Term loan							
Subordinated debt							
Excess cash	0	0	0	0	0	0	0
add: Minimum cash balance	12,734	12,734	12,734	12,734	12,734	12,734	12,734
Ending cash	$12,734	$12,734	$12,734	$12,734	$12,734	$12,734	$12,734

Years

	8	9	10	11	12
Book net income	$20,219	$23,966	$28,172	$33,485	$38,806
Adjustments:					
Add:					
Depreciation	8,624	8,944	9,284	9,643	10,025
Excess inventory valuation	0	0	0	0	0
Amortization	0	0	0	0	0
Subtract:					
Increase in working capital	4,387	4,738	5,117	5,527	5,969
Capital expenditures	6,015	6,375	6,758	7,163	7,593
Scheduled payments:					
Term loan	13,500	13,500	13,500	0	0
Subordinated debt	6,000	6,000	6,000	6,000	25,000
Redemption of preferred stock	1,000	1,000	1,000	1,000	5,000
Preferred stock dividends	1,350	1,200	1,050	900	750
Net cash flow	(3,409)	98	4,030	22,539	4,518
Opening cash balance	12,734	12,734	12,734	12,734	12,734
Total cash	9,325	12,832	16,764	35,273	17,252
less: Minimum cash balance	(12,734)	(12,734)	(12,734)	(12,734)	(12,734)
Available for prepayment of debt	(3,409)	98	4,030	22,539	4,518
Prepayment of:					
Revolving credit line	(3,409)	98	4,030	22,539	4,518
Term loan					
Subordinated debt					
Excess cash	0	0	0	0	0
add: Minimum cash balance	12,734	12,734	12,734	12,734	12,734
Ending cash	$12,734	$12,734	$12,734	$12,734	$12,734

Pannill Knitting Company, Inc.
Leveraged Buyout
Projected Balance Sheets
(consolidated tax basis)
($000)

				End of Years			
Assets	1	2	3	4	5	6	7
Cash	$12,734	$12,734	$12,734	$12,734	$12,734	$12,734	$12,734
Accounts Receivable	29,376	31,726	34,264	37,005	39,966	43,163	46,616
Inventory	27,648	29,860	32,249	34,828	37,615	40,624	43,874
Other	0	0	0	0	0	0	0
Current assets	69,758	74,320	79,247	84,568	90,314	96,521	103,224
Land	6,986	6,986	6,986	6,986	6,986	6,986	6,986
Buildings	52,425	55,425	55,425	55,425	55,425	55,425	55,425
Machinery & equipment	30,546	34,786	39,280	44,044	49,094	54,447	60,121
Furniture & fixtures	1,048	1,048	1,048	1,048	1,048	1,048	1,048
Vehicles	524	524	524	524	524	524	524
Leasehold improvements	0	0	0	0	0	0	0
Total PP&E	91,529	98,769	103,263	108,027	113,077	118,430	124,104
less: accumulated depreciation	7,752	18,512	30,017	42,314	55,657	63,694	72,016
Total PP&E, net	83,777	80,257	73,247	65,713	57,420	54,736	52,088
Intangible assets (excludes goodwill)	16,750	12,563	8,375	4,188	0	0	0
Goodwill	41,915	41,915	41,915	41,915	41,915	41,915	41,915
Other	5,598	5,598	5,598	5,598	5,598	5,598	5,598
Total assets	$217,799	$214,653	$208,382	$201,982	$195,248	$198,770	$202,825

			End of Years		
Assets	8	9	10	11	12
Cash	$12,734	$12,734	$12,734	$12,734	$12,734
Accounts Receivable	50,345	54,373	58,723	63,421	68,494
Inventory	47,384	51,175	55,268	59,690	64,465
Other	0	0	0	0	0
Current assets	110,463	118,282	126,725	135,845	145,693
Land	6,986	6,986	6,986	6,986	6,986
Buildings	55,425	55,425	55,425	55,425	55,425
Machinery & equipment	66,136	72,511	79,269	86,432	94,025
Furniture & fixtures	1,048	1,048	1,048	1,048	1,048
Vehicles	524	524	524	524	524
Leasehold improvements	0	0	0	0	0
Total PP&E	130,119	136,494	143,252	150,415	158,008
less: accumulated depreciation	80,641	89,585	98,869	108,512	118,537
Total PP&E, net	49,478	46,909	44,383	41,903	39,471
Intangible assets (excludes goodwill)	0	0	0	0	0
Goodwill	41,915	41,915	41,915	41,915	41,915
Other	5,598	5,598	5,598	5,598	5,598
Total assets	$207,455	$212,704	$218,622	$225,261	$232,678

(cont.)

Pannill Knitting Company, Inc.
Leveraged Buyout
Projected Balance Sheets
($000) (consolidated tax basis) (continued)

	End of Years						
Liabilities and Stockholders' Equity	1	2	3	4	5	6	7
Payables and accruals	$17,063	$18,860	$20,801	$22,897	$25,161	$27,606	$30,247
Current portion of debt:							
Revolving credit line	40,090	43,138	40,685	37,332	31,235	30,920	34,942
Term loan	7,500	11,000	11,000	11,000	11,000	11,000	13,500
Subordinated debt	0	0	0	0	0	6,000	6,000
Current liabilities	68,653	72,998	72,486	71,229	67,396	75,526	84,688
Term loan	95,500	84,500	73,500	62,500	51,500	40,500	27,000
Subordinated debt	55,000	55,000	55,000	55,000	55,000	49,000	43,000
Total long-term debt	150,500	139,500	128,500	117,500	106,500	89,500	70,000
Other liabilities	0	0	0	0	0	0	0
Total liabilities	219,153	212,498	200,986	188,729	173,896	165,026	154,688
Preferred stock	10,000	10,000	10,000	10,000	10,000	10,000	9,000
Common stock	14,570	14,570	14,570	14,570	14,570	14,570	14,570
Retained Earnings	(25,924)	(22,415)	(17,174)	(11,317)	(3,218)	9,174	24,566
Total stockholders' equity	(1,354)	2,155	7,396	13,253	21,352	33,744	48,136
Total liabilities and stockholders' equity	$217,799	$214,653	$208,382	$201,982	$195,248	$198,770	$202,825

| | | End of Years | | | |
Liabilities and Stockholders' Equity	8	9	10	11	12
Payables and accruals	$33,098	$36,178	$39,505	$43,097	$46,977
Current portion of debt:					
Revolving credit line	38,350	38,253	34,223	11,684	7,165
Term loan	13,500	13,500	0	0	0
Subordinated debt	6,000	6,000	6,000	25,000	0
Current liabilities	90,949	93,931	79,727	79,781	54,142
Term loan	13,500	0	0	0	0
Subordinated debt	37,000	31,000	25,000	0	0
Total long-term debt	50,500	31,000	25,500	0	0
Other liabilities	0	0	0	0	0
Total liabilities	141,449	124,931	104,727	79,781	54,142
Preferred stock	8,000	7,000	6,000	5,000	0
Common stock	14,570	14,570	14,570	14,570	14,570
Retained Earnings	43,436	66,202	93,324	125,910	163,965
Total stockholders' equity	66,006	87,772	113,894	145,480	178,535
Total liabilities and stockholders' equity	$207,455	$212,704	$218,622	$225,261	$232,678

Glossary

Arbitrageur A speculator who simultaneously buys and sells like securities or commodities to take advantage of price differences.

Asset-Based Financing Borrowings collateralized by assets, usually accounts receivable or inventory.

Bonds—Convertible Bonds which give the holder the option to convert the bond into the common stock of the issuing company.

Bonds—Term Bonds which have fixed dates of maturity.

Book Value Net worth, or assets less liabilities recorded on a company's balance sheet.

Break-up Value The value of assets if sold individually, usually in liquidation.

Call Option An option to purchase a specified number of shares of a stock at a stated price by a certain date.

Capital Account An equity account, usually in a partnership, which is the sum of the partners capital contributions plus share of net income less any distributions to that partner.

Capital Structure Long-term debt plus equity as recorded on a company's balance sheet.

Capitalization Rate The rate used as a multiple of a company's earnings to determine the value of the company.

Carryback or Carryforward Net operating losses (NOLs) can be carried back or used to recover taxes paid over the prior three years or carried forward or used to offset future tax liabilities on net operating income.

Cash Flow The result of all sources of cash less all uses of cash.

Cash Tender Offer A cash offer to purchase stock at a certain price by a certain date.

Closely-held Company A company with a small number of stockholders owning stock not actively traded.

Covenants Limitations placed on corporate debt. Affirmative covenants require the company to maintain positive positions whereas negative covenants prohibit the company from certain actions.

Debenture   A note, usually long-term, secured by the general credit of the issuer rather than by specified assets.

Debt-to-equity Ratio   Total long-term debt divided by net worth or stockholders' equity.

Discounted Cash Flow   The discounting of future cash flows to their present value.

Employee Stock Ownership Plans (ESOPs)   A stock bonus plan which is qualified by the Labor Department and under which the employer makes pre-tax contributions primarily for the purchase of the employers' common or preferred stock for the benefit of the employees.

Evergreen Loan   A loan commonly collateralized by working capital assets which has no fixed repayment date.

Exit P/E Ratio   The ratio of price times earnings which is assumed when LBO investors sell their common stock.

Fair Market Value   A value usually determined by appraisal which an informed buyer would offer and an informed seller would accept.

Fairness Opinion   An opinion usually given by an investment banker as to the fairness of a proposed transaction from a financial point of view.

Founders' Stock   Stock purchased by the founders of a company usually at a lower price than paid by other investors.

Going Public or Private   Going public is making a registered initial offering of stock to the public. Going private is the purchase of substantially all of the stock from the public usually in a merger or tender.

Golden Parachute   Provisions in an employment contract which provide for very large payments to an executive who loses his job due to a takeover of the company.

Goodwill   An intangible asset usually created by the purchase of assets at a price higher than fair market value. Also, a value which is intangible such as a company's name or reputation.

Gross Margin   The amount by which sales exceed the cost of goods sold and before any deduction of sales, general and administrative expenses.

Installment Sale   A sale of common stock or other assets for cash and notes made in more than one payment. Under certain conditions, capital gains taxes are triggered only as installment notes are repaid.

Intangible Assets   An asset which has no material or physical value. A company's name or goodwill are intangible assets.

Internal Rate of Return (IRR)   The IRR is the rate at which the cash received by investors must be discounted in order for the discounted total of such amounts to be equal to the investor's original investment.

Investment Company   A regulated company which makes investments of its shareholders' capital. A mutual fund type company which is not taxed at the corporate level but is able to "pass through" to its shareholders the character of the income it distributes and avoid double taxation.

Investment Tax Credit (ITC)   Tax credits based on a percentage of investments in certain equipment, usually with a useful life of 3–5 years.

Junk Bonds   Below investment grade bonds offering a high yield to the investor in return for accepting high risk.

Mezzanine Financing   The investment which bridges the gap between senior debt financing and equity, usually in the form of subordinated debt or preferred stock with some equity participation.

Net Operating Losses (NOLs)   Losses which can be carried forward to shelter future taxable income.

Pari Passu   Equal position. In debt covenants, debt which ranks pari passu with other debt will share in assets equally upon liquidation.

Preferred Stock   A class of stock or equity which has priority over common stock but ranks below debt in earnings and upon liquidation.

Present Value   The current value of a future payment or payments, discounting such payments to compensate for uncertainty and possibly the inadequacy of current income on such payments.

Price/Earnings (P/E) Ratio   The price of a common stock divided by its earnings per share.

Put Option   An option to sell a specified number of shares of stock at a stated price by a certain date.

Recapitalization Merger   A merger which for accounting purposes is not treated as a purchase but rather as an untaxed reorganization in which assets cannot be appraised at their fair market value; taxes paid over the prior three years are available for refund.

Recapture   The adding back to taxable income items which were sheltered from taxes by depreciation or which generated tax credits, such as with ITCs.

Revolving Loan   A loan on which payments are continuously made as merchandise is sold or receivables are collected. Revolving loans are usually renewable or "evergreen" as new collateral is generated.

Right of First Refusal   A privilege to purchase assets offered, usually stock, before such stock is offered to others.

Sale and Leaseback   The sale of property to an investor who leases it back to the seller, thus providing capital to the seller.

Sellers' Notes   A note given to the seller as part of the purchase price.

Schedule 13-D   An investor who acquires 5 percent or more ownership of a company reporting to the SEC must disclose his ownership percentage and purpose within ten days of purchase by filing Schedule 13-D with the SEC.

Section 338 Election   Under the provisions of the IRS code section 338, an acquiror of all the stock of a company can elect to treat the acquisition as an asset purchase.

Senior Debt   Secured or unsecured debt which has the highest preference in liquidation.

Sinking Fund   A fund set up in a bond debenture into which cash is deposited to retire certain amounts of debt by certain dates.

Strip Financing   The sharing of a portion of each type of debt or equity security by investors is a vertical strip financing, in contrast to a horizontal strip where each investor invests in only one type of security such as senior debt or preferred stock.

Subordinated Debt   An unsecured debt which ranks below senior debt but above preferred and common stock in liquidation.

Tangible Assets   Assets which have a material or physical value.

Tax Loss Carryforward   NOLs which can be used to shelter future net operating income from tax liability.

Term Bonds   Bonds which have fixed dates of maturity.

Warrant   A security which entitles the holder to purchase common stock at a stated price by a certain date.

White Knight   An investor who is invited to save the company from an unfriendly takeover attempt.

Index